SOCIAL ANXIETY DISORDER: RESEARCH AND PRACTICE

Mark H. Pollack, M.D., Naomi M. Simon, M.D., Michael W. Otto, Ph.D.

Center for Anxiety and Traumatic Stress Related Disorders

Massachusetts General Hospital, Boston, MA

Professional Publishing Group. Ltd.
New York, NY

SOCIAL ANXIETY DISORDER: RESEARCH AND PRACTICE

Mark H. Pollack, M.D., Naomi M. Simon, M.D., Michael W. Otto, Ph.D.

Sponsored by Wyeth Pharmaceuticals

Wyeth®

ISBN 0-9713017-3-5

Professional Publishing Group, Ltd.
42 West 24th Street, New York, NY 10010

Printed in the U.S.A.

Table of Contents

Preface

We are pleased to present you with **Social Anxiety Disorder: Research and Practice**, a comprehensive review of this common, distressing, and disabling illness and its treatment. Sponsored through an unrestricted educational grant from Wyeth Pharmaceuticals, we hope this textbook will be a useful educational tool that will add to your understanding of social anxiety disorder and assist you in treating your patients affected by this condition.

Many experts in the study of social anxiety disorder contributed to the creation of this book, and we would like to thank them for their hard work and dedication. The comments and suggestions of Dr. Michael Wolf of Professional Publishing Group, and his expert management of the publishing process, are also greatly appreciated. We would also like to acknowledge our colleagues and staff at the Massachusetts General Hospital, whose tireless dedication to their patients and commitment to excellence in research and teaching remain an ongoing source of inspiration to us.

Mark H. Pollack, M.D.
Naomi S. Simon, M.D.
Michael W. Otto, Ph.D.
Editors

Contributors

Umberto Albert, M.D.
Psychiatrist
Department of Neurosciences
University of Turin, Italy

Filippo Bogetto, M.D.
Professor of Psychiatry
Department of Neurosciences
University of Turin, Italy

Lynette Dufton, B.A.
Research Coordinator
Pediatric Psychopharmacology Unit
Massachusetts General Hospital
Boston, Massachusetts

Francisco J. Farach, B.A.
Research Coordinator
Center for Anxiety and
Traumatic Stress Related Disorders
Massachusetts General Hospital
Boston, Massachusetts

Jack. M. Gorman, M.D.
Interim Chairman and
Professor of Psychiatry
Department of Psychiatry
Mount Sinai School of Medicine
New York, New York

Aude Henin, Ph.D.
Assistant in Psychology
Massachusetts General Hospital
and
Instructor in Psychology in Psychiatry
Harvard Medical School
Boston, Massachusetts

Dina R. Hirshfeld-Becker, Ph.D.
Director of Anxiety Research
Pediatric Psychopharmacology Unit
Massachusetts General Hospital
and
Assistant Professor of Psychology
in Psychiatry
Harvard Medical School
Boston, Massachusetts

Elizabeth A. Hoge, M.D.
Clinical Fellow in Psychiatry
Massachusetts General Hospital
Harvard Medical School
Boston, Massachusetts

Justine M. Kent, M.D.
Assistant Professor of Clinical
Psychiatry
Department of Psychiatry
Columbia University College of
Physicians & Surgeons
New York, New York

Nicole B. Korbly, B.A.
Research Assistant
Center for Anxiety and
Traumatic Stress Related Disorders
Massachusetts General Hospital
Boston, Massachusetts

Giuseppe Maina, M.D.
Associate Professor of Psychiatry
Department of Neurosciences
University of Turin, Italy

Sanjay J. Mathew, M.D.
Fellow
Department of Psychiatry
Columbia University College of
Physicians & Surgeons
New York, New York

Despina C. Nicolaou, M.S.
Research Coordinator
Center for Anxiety and
Traumatic Stress Related Disorders
Massachusetts General Hospital
Boston, Massachusetts

Michael W. Otto, Ph.D.
Director,
Cognitive-Behavior Therapy Program
Massachusetts General Hospital
and
Associate Professor of Psychology
in Psychiatry
Harvard Medical School
Boston, Massachusetts

Mark H. Pollack, M.D.
Director, Center for Anxiety and
Traumatic Stress Related Disorders
Massachusetts General Hospital
and
Associate Professor of Psychiatry
Harvard Medical School
Boston, Massachusetts

Stephanie R. Racette, M.A.
Research Coordinator
Psychiatric Genetics Program
in Mood and Anxiety Disorders
Outpatient Division
Massachusetts General Hospital
Boston, Massachusetts

Adam S. Radomsky, Ph.D.
Assistant Professor and Director
Fear and Anxiety Disorders Laboratory
Department of Psychology
Concordia University
Montreal, Quebec

Nadine Recker Rayburn, M.A.
Clinical Fellow in Psychology
Department of Psychiatry
Massachusetts General Hospital
Harvard Medical School
Boston, Massachusetts

Steven A. Safren, Ph.D.
Associate Director,
Cognitive-Behavior Therapy Program
Massachusetts General Hospital
and
Assistant Professor of Psychology in
Psychiatry
Harvard Medical School
Boston, Massachusetts

**Jitender Sareen
B.Sc., M.D., FRCPC**
Assistant Professor of Psychiatry
Department of Psychiatry
University of Manitoba
Winnipeg, Manitoba

Naomi M Simon, M.D.
Associate Director
Center for Anxiety and Traumatic Stress
Related Disorders
Massachusetts General Hospital
and
Instructor in Psychiatry
Harvard Medical School
Boston, Massachusetts

Jordan W. Smoller, M.D., Sc.D.
Director,
Psychiatric Genetics Program in
Mood and Anxiety Disorders
Outpatient Division
Department of Psychiatry
Massachusetts General Hospital
and
Assistant Professor of Psychiatry
Harvard Medical School
Boston, Massachusetts

Murray B. Stein, M.D.
Professor of Psychiatry In-Residence
University of California, San Diego
and
Director,
Anxiety & Traumatic Stress Clinics
Veterans Affairs San Diego
Healthcare System
San Diego, California

Chapter 1
Social Anxiety Disorder:
Phenomenology, Epidemiology and Comorbidity

Nicole B. Korbly, M.D. and Naomi M. Simon, M.D.

Phenomenology

The fundamental characteristic of Social Anxiety Disorder (SAD; alternatively called Social Phobia) is a fear of embarrassment or humiliation in situations that involve performance, evaluation, or potential scrutiny by others. The disorder was first described in the Diagnostic and Statistical Manual of Mental Disorders 3rd edition (DSM-III; American Psychiatric Association, 1980); however, it was initially limited to anxiety in performance situations. Subsequently, the DSM-III-Revised (APA, 1987) expanded the diagnostic criteria of the disorder to include a wider variety of social situations. Currently, the DSM-IV defines SAD as an excessive and persistent anxiety or discomfort that occurs in anticipation of or upon exposure to one or more social or performance situations (APA, 1994). This fear of social or performance situations persists despite the awareness of the individual that the fear is unreasonable or excessive. Exposure to feared situations results in acute anxiety, frequently with associated physical symptoms of anxiety including sweating, shaking, blushing, palpitations, nausea, and diarrhea. As a result, the feared social or performance situations are either avoided, or endured with significant distress. Patients frequently report significant anticipatory anxiety prior to a feared social and performance situation, and may report panic attacks upon exposure to such situations. A key feature of the disorder is the ensuing loss of social and occupational functioning that results, particularly when there is significant avoidance. Patients frequently report, for example, that they never completed college, refused work promotions, or altered their career choices to limit exposure to social interaction and performance situations. Commonly feared and/or avoided situations include meeting new people, attending parties or social gatherings, participating in group meetings, being the center of attention, interacting with authority figures, confrontation, public speaking, and eating or drinking in public.

Social Anxiety Disorder has two distinct subtypes, generalized and non-generalized SAD. The non-generalized subtype, commonly referred to as performance type, is generally limited to public speaking or other performance situations. The non-generalized subtype of SAD is usually less disabling, although it may result in underachievement at work or school (Stein et al, 1996). In contrast, the generalized subtype of SAD is associated with greater impairment because the anxiety is pervasive and occurs in numerous, or sometimes nearly all social and performance situations. Individuals with generalized SAD often fear and avoid social situations that are interactional (eg, social gatherings and meeting new people), in addition to performance situations (eg, public speaking). Thus, SAD is a disabling disorder that has the potential to severely impair social, educational, or occupational functioning.

Epidemiology

Prevalence of SAD in the General Population

Numerous epidemiologic studies suggest that SAD is a relatively common psychiatric disorder in the community. Although the exact prevalence rate has been disputed, the range of lifetime prevalence rates in Western countries appears to be between 7% and 13% (for a review, see Furmark, 2002). Established prevalence rates in the United States are primarily based on two large-scale epidemiologic studies of psychiatric disorders in the general population. The Epidemiologic Catchment Area study (ECA) assessed more than 13,000 adults in four communities using DSM-III diagnostic criteria and found a 2.8% prevalence of lifetime disorder and a 1.5% prevalence of SAD in the past 6-months (Schneier et al, 1992). The National Comorbidity Survey (NCS) assessed DSM-III-R psychiatric disorders from over 8,000 people and is generally believed to be more sensitive to detecting lifetime disorders; the NCS found a 13.3% prevalence of lifetime SAD and a 7.9% prevalence of SAD in the past 12-months (Kessler et al, 1994). The generalized subtype occurred in two-thirds of those diagnosed with SAD, with the non-generalized subtype present in one-third (Kessler et al, 1998). These prevalence rates make SAD the third most common mental health disorder, behind major depression and alcohol dependence (Kessler et al, 1994).

Estimations of prevalence rates are limited by the variability in rates reported, which have varied significantly between studies. This is particularly true for epidemiologic studies conducted in different countries. Discrepancies in prevalence rates may be explained by differences in the following: diagnostic criteria (ie, DSM-III, DSM-III-R, or DSM-IV), diagnostic threshold (ie, required level of impairment, interference, or distress necessary to meet diagnostic criteria), assessment method (eg, self-report surveys vs. interviews), and prevalence period selected (eg., past 6 vs. 12 months) (Furmark, 2002). Narrow and colleagues attempted to resolve these discrepancies in methodological variables by applying a clinical significance criterion (defined as causing impairment or requiring treatment) to the ECA and NCS studies; when the data from both studies were reanalyzed, the prevalence rate of SAD in the past 12 months was 3.7% (Narrow et al, 2002).

Course of Illness
Social Anxiety Disorder characteristically has an early age of onset and long duration of illness, and frequently has a chronic course. Numerous studies have demonstrated that SAD tends to have onset in adolescence, usually around 16 years of age [with a mean of 15.5 years in the ECA data (Schneier et al, 1992), and 16 years in the NCS study (Magee et al, 1996)]. Rarely does SAD onset occur after the age of 25 (Schneier et al, 1992). Although the average age of onset of SAD appears to be in early to late adolescence, patients commonly report the presence of SAD symptoms since early childhood. Many patients report being shy as young children, and then becoming aware of their anxiety symptoms when starting formal schooling. Biologically based temperamental factors during childhood, such as behavioral inhibition, may predispose certain children to the development of the disorder (Biederman et al, 2001).

The course of SAD is typically chronic with a mean duration of illness of around 25 years and low rates of recovery (DeWit et al, 1999; Davidson et al, 1993); for many, SAD is a lifelong illness (Yonkers et al, 2001). Occasionally, SAD symptoms may lessen in severity during adulthood (Scheiner et al, 1992), perhaps in part because some older adults with the disorder develop an avoidant lifestyle within which they are less concerned with social evaluation. For example, patients may choose an occupation in which presentations to groups and interaction with new people is not required.

Demographics
Epidemiologic studies indicate that more women experience SAD than men. Both the ECA and NCS report a male to female gender ratio around 2 to 3 (Schneier et al, 1992; Magee et al, 1996). In the NCS, men had an 11.1% prevalence of lifetime SAD versus a lifetime prevalence of 15.5% in women

(Kessler et al, 1994). Although women are more often affected by the disorder, men are more likely to seek treatment; it has been hypothesized that this discrepancy may be due to social expectations, gender roles, or differing levels of distress, with symptoms causing more impairment for men than women (Weinstock, 1999). Gender, however, does not appear to influence age of onset, duration of illness (Bourdon et al, 1988; Schneier et al, 1992), nor comorbidity (Kessler et al, 1999). In addition, remission rates do not appear to be affected by gender; however, findings from one longitudinal study indicate that women with history of suicide attempts and comorbid disorders such as agoraphobia may have a more chronic course of illness (Yonkers et al, 2001). In this study, rates of unipolar depression comorbid with SAD did not vary by gender, in contrast to the well-documented higher rates of unipolar depression in general for women; this was interpreted as demonstrating that the greater risk for depression associated with SAD in general overwhelmed any gender differences in depression prevalence (Yonkers et al, 2001). An alternate explanation, as previously suggested by Breslau and colleagues, may be that the gender difference reported for depression is explained by the gender difference in anxiety disorder prevalence (Breslau et al, 1995).

The majority of individuals with SAD tend to be single or unmarried (Magee et al, 1996; Davidson et al, 1993). Social anxiety disorder has also been associated with increased difficulties in school and lower educational achievement (Magee et al, 1996; Schneier et al, 1992; Davidson et al, 1993). Thus, SAD may result in movement towards lower socioeconomic status (Magee et al, 1996), and has been associated with elevated rates of financial dependency (Schneier et al, 1992) and more unstable employment (Davidson et al, 1992). Family history of psychiatric illness and family disruption (ie, separation or divorce of parents) both occur more frequently in individuals with SAD (Davidson et al, 1993). Results from a retrospective study of an epidemiological sample found an association of SAD with certain childhood risk factors (eg, absence of close relationship with an adult, parental marital conflict, frequent moves in childhood) (Chartier et al, 2001). Prospective naturalistic studies are needed to better elucidate potential risk factors for SAD. There appear to be no significant differences in race or ethnicity in SAD within the general population of the United States (Magee et al, 1996), although prevalence rates may be influenced by cultural differences, particularly between countries. For example, Asian communities report the lowest lifetime prevalence rates of SAD at under 1.0% (Furmark, 2002).

Comorbidity

There is a high rate of comorbid psychiatric illness associated with Social Anxiety Disorder. In the NCS, 81% of people with SAD reported at least one other lifetime DSM-III-R psychiatric diagnosis; 19% reported one other disorder, 14% reported 2 other disorders, and 48% reported 3 other disorders (Magee et al, 1996). A second anxiety disorder was present in 57% of people with SAD, while 41% had a comorbid affective disorder, and 40% had comorbid substance use disorders (Magee et al, 1996). In line with the overall greater severity of illness associated with generalized SAD (Kessler et al, 1998), individuals with the generalized subtype of SAD are more likely to suffer from comorbid mood and anxiety disorders than individuals with the nongeneralized subtype (Wittchen et al, 1999; Stein & Chavira, 1998). The presence of an anxiety disorder in early adolescence, including SAD, predicts clinically significant depressive and anxiety disorders in early adulthood (Pine et al, 1998), and the presence of SAD has been linked to greater severity and persistence of mood disorders (Merikangas & Angst, 1995; Alpert et al, 1997). The onset of SAD appears to frequently precede the onset of other comorbid disorders (Magee et al, 1996; Schneier et al, 1992). In particular, individuals with SAD are at increased risk for later development of major depression (MDD). In the NCS, secondary MDD was present in 37% of those with SAD (Kessler et al, 1996); further, the lifetime rates of comorbid MDD have been reported near 60% in clinical samples (Merikangas & Angst, 1995). SAD onset typically occurs many years prior to the onset of depression (Kessler et al, 1999), and may be a risk factor for subsequent major depression (Stein et al, 2001). In a primary care sample, 70% of patients with early onset SAD (defined as younger than age 15) were found to have comorbid MDD (Lecrubier & Weiller, 1997). Further, one prospective, longitudinal study found that persons with the combination of SAD and depression in adolescence or early adulthood are at the greatest risk for subsequent depression, and are also at risk to experience a more difficult course of illness (Stein et al, 2001). Individuals with SAD are also at increased risk of suicidal ideation (Schneier et al, 1992) and have an increased rate of suicide attempts (Davidson et al, 1993) compared to the general population; however, the presence of SAD may not increase risk of suicide attempts during MDD episodes beyond that associated with MDD alone (Kessler at al., 1999).

In addition, emerging evidence suggests the fallacy of clinical lore supporting the notion that SAD and bipolar disorder are incongruent. Perugi and colleagues, in particular, have reported an association between bipolar II disorder and SAD in primary anxiety disordered samples, and have proposed that SAD may be the opposite end from hypomania in a spectrum of bipolar illness including "constraint vs hypomanic disinhibition" (Perugi et al, 1999; Perugi , Akiskal et al, 2001; Perugi, Frare et al , 2001). Although limited by the study's retrospective nature, this group has reported that SAD symptoms resolve in the context of hypomanic episodes (Perugi , Akiskal et al, 2001). Himmelhoch reported that 14 of 32 SAD patients had induction of hypomania, defined by RDC criteria, when treated with monoamine oxidase inhibitors, and similarly concluded that SAD, or a subset of SAD, may be part of a bipolar spectrum (Himmelhoch, 1998). Further, it has been suggested that this bipolar connection may explain much of the comorbid alcoholism associated with SAD (Perugi et al, 2002). A recent multicenter study of patients with bipolar I or II disorder found a 22% lifetime rate of SAD, which was significantly higher than the 13% rate of SAD reported in the NCS; SAD was not limited to patients with bipolar II disorder (Simon et al, submitted). More research is needed to better understand the association of bipolar disorder and SAD, and how it interacts with and impacts on treatment.

Comorbid anxiety disorders are also quite common, and include panic disorder, posttraumatic stress disorder (PTSD), generalized anxiety disorder (GAD), and obsessive compulsive disorder (OCD). Data from the NCS revealed the presence of comorbid posttraumatic stress disorder in 16% of individuals with SAD, whereas panic disorder was present in 11%, and generalized anxiety disorder was present in 13% (Magee et al, 1996). In treatment-seeking populations, the rates of comorbid anxiety disorders are often higher, with rates of comorbid SAD in primary panic samples reported near 45% (Montejo & Liebowitz, 1994). In primary social phobia, comorbid GAD has been reported near 24% (Mennin et al, 2000). Some data support the notion that SAD may occur secondarily to trauma or PTSD (Orsillo et al, 1996; Engdahl et al, 1998). The precise relationship between SAD and PTSD, however, remains unclear, and further research is necessary to examine whether exposure to traumatic events is a risk factor for SAD. One study of group cognitive behavioral therapy suggests that, at least for this modality of SAD treatment, comorbid anxiety disorders cause less interference with SAD treatment outcomes than comorbid MDD (Erwin et al, 2002). Further, patients with comorbid GAD were found to be more impaired and suffer from greater cognitive symptoms, but again GAD did not impair SAD treatment outcomes with group CBT (Mennin et al, 2000).

Individuals with SAD are also at substantially increased risk for alcohol abuse and dependence, and other substance abuse disorders. Individuals with SAD frequently use alcohol to self-medicate in order to decrease anticipatory anxiety and reduce avoidance of feared social and/or performance situations. The presence of a binge pattern of drinking in particular may be predictive of the presence of SAD (Wells et al, 1994). In the NCS, the lifetime prevalence rate for alcohol dependence associated with social anxiety was 24% (Magee et al, 1996); consequently there is a two to three time greater risk that someone with SAD will develop alcohol abuse or dependence compared with the general population. Rates of comorbid alcohol dependence approaching 40% have been reported in treatment-seeking populations. In one study, 43% of patients with comorbid SAD and panic disorder met criteria for alcohol dependence (Otto et al, 1992). As with other comorbidities, SAD onset typically precedes alcohol abuse. In the ECA study, the onset of SAD preceded the onset of alcohol abuse 85% of the time (Schneier et al, 1992). A follow-up prospective study of individuals without baseline heavy drinking but with social phobia or subclinical social fears similarly found that the risk of the developing alcohol abuse or dependence was more than twice that of the general population without such fears (Crum & Pratt, 2001). The precise etiology of this comorbidity remains debated. A recent genetic study examining familial inheritance did not find support for co- inheritance of SAD and alcoholism, leading the authors to support the self-medication hypothesis (Merikangas et al, 1998). However, whether alcohol use actually decreases social anxiety remains unclear (Abrams et al, 2001; Himle et al, 1999).

Nonetheless, the early age of onset for SAD, generally prior to other mood, anxiety or substance use disorders, suggests that SAD may be a risk factor for the development of other psychopathology. Further, individuals with SAD and comorbid psychiatric disorders may be more severely affected and the consequences of the comorbidity may include more severe impairment in social and occupational functioning (Magee et al, 1996), higher rates of suicide ideation (Schneier et al, 1992) and suicide attempts (Davidson et al, 1993), and poorer outcome (Davidson et al, 1993). Comorbidity may also influence response to SAD treatment. However, controlled data examining pharmacotherapy for SAD comorbid with MDD is lacking. The presence of SAD, particularly early onset SAD, should raise suspicion and result in screening for the presence of comorbidity, with special attention to alcohol abuse/dependence and depressive disorders. The early recognition and treatment of SAD is important, and it is hoped that such early intervention may help to prevent or minimize the occurrence of other disorders, although more research is needed to clarify this association and the precise impact of early intervention. Further study regarding the influence of SAD on the development and persistence of comorbid psychiatric disorders, and the impact of comorbidity on treatment selection and outcome is necessary.

Conclusion

Prevalence rates indicate that SAD is the most commonly occurring anxiety disorder, and one of the most common psychiatric disorders to affect the general population. SAD is a significant public health concern associated with substantial economic costs (Greenberg et al, 1999). Further studies are necessary to ascertain more accurate assessment of the rates and impact of comorbidity of mood, anxiety and substance use disorders, as well as to better understand the natural course and risk factors associated with the development of SAD. This information would facilitate the creation and implementation of optimal treatment interventions for individuals with SAD and ultimately preventative interventions for those at risk for its development.

References

Abrams K, Kushner M, Medina KL, Voight A. The pharmacologic and expectancy effects of alcohol on social anxiety in individuals with social phobia. *Drug Alcohol Depend*. 2001;Oct 1;64(2):219-31

Alpert JE, Uebelacker LA, McLean NE, Nierenberg AA, Pava JA, Worthington JJ, Tedlow JR, Rosenbaum JF, Fava M. Social phobia, avoidant personality disorder and atypical depression: co-occurrence and clinical implications *Psychol Med*. 1997;27:627-633.

American Psychiatric Association: Diagnostic and Statistical Manual of Mental Disorders (3rd edition). American Psychiatric Press; 1980 Washington, DC.

American Psychiatric Association: Diagnostic and Statistical Manual of Mental Disorders (3rd edition revised). American Psychiatric Press; 1987; Washington, DC, pp. 241-243.

American Psychiatric Association: Diagnostic and Statistical Manual of Mental Disorders. 1994. In: 4th ed. American Psychiatric Press, Washington, DC, pp. 416-417.

Biederman J, Hirshfeld-Becker DR, Rosenbaum JF, Hérot C, Friedman D, Snidman N, Kagan J, Faraone SV. Further evidence of association between behavioral inhibition and social anxiety in children. *Am J Psychiatry*. 2001; 158:1673-1679.

Bourdon KH, Boyd JH, Rae DS, Burns BJ, Thompson JW, Locke BZ. Gender differences in phobias: results of the ECA community survey. *J Anxiety Disord*. 1988;2:227-241.

Breslau N, Schultz L & Peterson E. Sex differences in depression: a role for preexisting anxiety. *J Psychiatry Research*. 1995;58(1):1-12.

Chartier MJ, Waker JR, Stein MB. Social phobia and potential childhood risk factors in a community sample. *Psychol Med*. 2001;31:307-315.

Crum RM & Pratt LA. Risk of heavy drinking and alcohol use disorders in social phobia: a prospective analysis. *Am J Psychiatry*. Oct, 2001; 158(10):1693-700.

Davidson JRT, Hughes DL, George LK, Blazer DG. The epidemiology of social phobia: findings from the Duke Epidemiology Catchment Area Study. *Psychol Med*. 1993;23:709-718.

DeWit DJ, Ogborne A, Offord DR, MacDonald K. Antecedents of the risk of recovery from DSM-III-R social phobia. *Psychol Med*. 1999;29:569-582.

Engdahl B, Dikel TN, Eberly R et al. Comorbidity and course of psychiatric disorders in a community sample of former prisoners of war. *Am J Psychiatry*. 1998;155:1740-1745.

Erwin BA, Heimberg RG, Juster H & Mildlin M. Comorbid anxiety and mood disorders among persons with social anxiety disorder. *Behaviour Research and Therapy*. 2002;40:19-35.

Furmark T. Social phobia: overview of community surveys. *Acta Psychiatr Scand*. 2002;105:84-93.

Greenberg PE, Sisitsky T, Kessler RC, Finkelstein, SN, Berndt ER, Davidson JRT, Ballenger JC, Fryer AJ. The economic burden of anxiety disorders in the 1990s. *J Clin Psychiatry*. 1999;60:427-435.

Himle JA, Abelson JL, Haghightgou H, Hill EM, Nesse RM, Curtis GC. Effect of alcohol on social phobic anxiety. *Am J Psychiatry*. 1999 Aug; 156(8):1237-43.

Himmelhoch JM. Social anxiety, hypomania and the bipolar spectrum: data, theory and clinical issues. *J Affect Disord*. 1998;50(2-3):203-13.

Kessler RC, Nelson CB, et al. Comorbidity of DSM-III-R major depressive disorder in the general population: results from the US National Comorbidity Survey. *Br J Psychiatry*. 1996;168(suppl 30):17-30.

Kessler RC, McGonagle KA, Zhao S, Nelson CB, Hughes M, Eshleman S, Wittchen HU, Kendler KS. Lifetime and 12-month prevalence of DSM-III-R psychiatric disorders in the United States: Results from the National Comorbidity Survey. *Arch Gen Psychiatry*. 1994;51:8-19.

Kessler RC, Stang P, Wittchen HU, Stein M, Walters EE. Lifetime comorbidities between social phobia and mood disorders in the US National Comorbidity Survey. *Psychol Med*. 1999;29: 555-567.

Kessler RC, Stein MB, Murray B, Berglund P. Social phobia subtypes in the National Comorbidity Survey. *Am J Psychiatry*. 1998;155:613-619.

Lecrubier Y, Weiller E. Comorbidities in social phobia. *Int Clin Psychopharmacol*. 1997;12(suppl):17-21.

Magee WJ, Eaton WW, Wittchen H, McGonagle KA, & Kessler RC. Agoraphobia, simple phobia, and social phobia in the national comorbidity survey. *Arch Gen Psychiatry*. 1996;53:159-168.

Mennin DS, Heimberg RG, Jack MS. Comorbid generalized anxiety disorder in primary social phobia: symptom severity, functional impairment, and treatment response. *J Anxiety Disord*. 2000;14:325-343.

Merikangas KR, Angst J. Comorbidity and social phobia: evidence from clinical, epidemiological, and genetic studies. *Eur Arch Psychiatry Clin Neurosci.* 1995;244:297-303.

Merikangas KR, Stevens DE, Fenton B, Stolar M, O'Malley S, Woods SW, Risch N. Co-morbidity and familial aggregation of alcoholism and anxiety disorders. *Psychol Med.* 1998 Jul;8(4):773-88.

Montejo J, Liebowitz MR. Social phobia: anxiety disorder comorbidity. *Bull Menninger Clin.* 1994;58(2 suppl A):A1-A42.

Narrow WE, Rae DS, Robbins LN, Regier DA. Revised prevalence estimates of mental disorders in the United States: Using a clinical significance criterion to reconcile 2 survey's estimates. *Arch Gen Psychiatry.* 2002;59:115-123.

Orsillo SM, Heimberg RG, Juster HR, et al. Social phobia and PTSD in Vietnam war veterans. *J Trauma Stress.* 1996;9:235-252.

Otto MW, Pollack MH, Sachs GS, O'Neil CA, Rosenbaum JF. Alcohol dependence in panic disorder patients. *J Psychiat Res.* 1992;26:29-38.

Perugi G, Akiskal HS, Ramacciotti S et al. Depressive comorbidity of panic, social phobic, and obsessive-compulsive disorders re-examined: is there a bipolar II connection? *J Psychiatr Res.* 1999;33:53-61.

Perugi G, Akiskal HS, Toni C, Simonini E, Gemignani A. The temporal relationship between anxiety disorders and (hypo)mania: a retrospective examination of 63 panic, social phobic and obsessive-compulsive patients with comorbid bipolar disorder. *J Affect Disord.* 2001;67(1-3):199-206.

Perugi G, Frare F, Madaro D, Marammani I, Akiskal H. Alcohol abuse and social phobic patients: is there a bipolar connection?. *J Affect Disord.* 2002; 68:33-39.

Perugi G, Frare F, Toni C, Mata B, Akiskal HS. Bipolar II and unipolar comorbidity in 153 outpatients with social phobia. *Compr Psychiatry.* 2001;42(5):375-81.

Pine D, Cohen P, Gurley D, Brook J, Ma Y. The risk for early-adulthood anxiety and depressive disorders in adolescents with anxiety and depressive disorders. *Arch Gen Psychiatry*. 1998;55:56-64.

Schneier FR, Johnson J, Hornig CD, Liebowitz MR, Weissman MM. Social phobia. Comorbidity and morbidity in an epidemiological sample. *Arch Gen Psychiatry*. 1992;49:282-288.

Simon NM, Otto MW, Wisniewski S, Fossey M, Sagduyu K, Frank E, SachsG, Nierenberg A, Pollack MH. Comorbid Anxiety Disorders Associated with Additional Morbidity and Impairment In Patients with Bipolar Disorder: Baseline Data from the Systematic Treatment Enhancement in Bipolar Disorder (STEP-BD) Study. Submitted.

Stein MB, Chavira DA. Subtypes of social phobia and comorbidity with depression and other anxiety disorders. *J Affect Disord*. 1998;50(Suppl): S11-S16.

Stein MB, Fuetsch M, Müller N, Höfler M, Lieb R, Wittchen HU. Social anxiety disorder and the risk of depression: a prospective community study of adolescents and young adults. *Arch Gen Psychiatry*. 2001;58:251-256.

Stein MD, Walker JR, Forder DR. Public speaking fears in a community sample: prevalence, impact on functioning, and diagnostic classification. *Arch Gen Psychiatry*. 1996;53:169-174.

Weinstock LS. Gender differences in the presentation and management of social anxiety disorder. *J Clin Psychiatry*. 1999;60 (Suppl 9):9-13.

Wells JC, Tien AY, Garrison R, Eaton WW. Risk factors for the incidence of social phobia as determined by the Diagnostic Interview Schedule in a population-based study. *Acta Psychiatr Scand*. 1994 Aug;90(2):84-90.

Wittchen HU, Stein, MB, Kessler RC. Social fears and social phobia in a community sample of adolescents and young adults: prevalence risk factors and co-morbidity. *Psycholl Med*. 1999;29: 309-323.

Yonkers KA, Dyck IR, Keller MB. An eight-year longitudinal comparison of clinical course and characteristics of social phobia among men and women. *Psychiatr Serv*. 2001;52:637-643.

Chapter 2
Early Antecedents of Social Anxiety Disorder: From Risk to Prevention

Dina R. Hirshfeld-Becker, Ph.D., Aude Henin, Ph.D., Stephanie R. Racette, M.A., Lynette Dufton, B.A., and Jordan W. Smoller, M.D., Sc.D.

Introduction

Social anxiety disorder is estimated to afflict 13% of adults at some point during their lives making it the most common of the anxiety disorders and the third most common psychiatric disorder (Kessler et al, 1994). Comprising a spectrum of problems ranging from isolated performance phobias to generalized fears of all social encounters, it can be severely debilitating, leading to impairment in academic, social, occupational, and familial functioning, as well as to comorbid mood disorders and alcohol and substance use. Although mainly studied in adults, social anxiety disorder has recently been recognized as a potentially debilitating problem in children and adolescents as well. The concerns of socially phobic youth mirror those of adults. They include fears, in social or performance situations, of being confused, blushing, doing something embarrassing, being judged stupid or weak, or having a panic attack (Essau et al, 1999). Among a sample of adolescents with lifetime diagnoses of social phobia, nearly all reported severe impairment in daily activities at some point (Essau et al, 1999). Moreover, regardless of current diagnoses, more than half of these adolescents continued to have impairments at school or work and during social activities. The impairment associated with early-onset social phobia may be especially pronounced, because of the disruptive effects of psychopathology during the formative years or the elevated risks of childhood adversity in anxious individuals (Panella & Henggeler, 1986). Clearly, it would be of great benefit to find ways to intervene early with this disorder.

However, in order to intervene early and prevent morbidity, it is necessary to understand some of the precursors and risk factors for the disorder, both to enable the ready identification of individuals at risk, and to understand approaches by which to intervene. Over the past fifteen years, progress has been made in identifying developmental antecedents to social anxiety disorder, as well as in developing treatments for children with the disorder, making it promising that early intervention efforts might ultimately become feasible. In the present chapter, we outline some of these hypothesized antecedents, discuss what further research is needed, and sketch some directions preventive interventions might take. Among these factors, family genetic, temperamental, parental, information processing, social learning, and peer relationship influences have shown the greatest promise in highlighting the multiple pathways implicated in the development and maintenance of social anxiety.

The Genetics of Social Anxiety

Two lines of inquiry have provided strong evidence that genes contribute to the risk of social phobia. The first has explored the familial and genetic influences on the clinical diagnosis of social phobia and the second has examined the genetic basis of personality and temperamental traits that are related to social anxiety. We will review each of these briefly as well as molecular studies aimed at identifying the specific genes involved.

Family studies of social phobia have documented an excess risk of the disorder among first-degree relatives of affected individuals. In family studies involving direct interviews of family members, the risk of social phobia was 15 – 26% among first-degree relatives of affected individuals (Fyer et al, 1993; Fyer et al, 1996; Fyer et al, 1995; Stein et al, 1998), three to ten-fold greater than the risk among relatives of unaffected probands. The generalized subtype appears to be more familial than discrete or non-generalized social phobia (Mannuzza et al, 1995; Stein et al, 1998). Manuzza and colleagues (1995) found that the prevalence of social phobia was significantly greater among relatives of probands with the generalized subtype (16%) than among relatives of never-mentally-ill controls (6%) or probands with non-generalized social phobia (6%). Stein and colleagues (1998) found that first-degree relatives of probands with generalized social phobia were significantly (9.7-fold) more likely to have generalized social phobia than were relatives of unaffected controls; however, the prevalence of performance-only (discrete) or non-generalized social phobia was not significantly elevated.

The generalized subtype of social phobia is phenomenologically similar to avoidant personality disorder (APD), and, not surprisingly, familial risk for these disorders appears to overlap. In their family study, Stein and colleagues found that 74% of probands with generalized social phobia met criteria for APD. The prevalence of APD in relatives of probands with generalized social phobia was higher than among relatives of probands without social phobia (19.8% vs. 0%), but the likelihood of a relative having APD was not associated with the presence of APD in the probands with generalized social phobia. In a population-based sample (N = 1202) from Sweden surveyed with a DSM-IV based diagnostic questionnaire, Tillfors et al (2001) found that a parental history of excessive social anxiety similarly increased the risk of both social phobia and APD, supporting the hypothesis that the two disorders are manifestations of a single underlying spectrum of social anxiety.

Although they have demonstrated the transmissibility of social phobia, family studies cannot resolve how much genes contribute to familial risk. Twin studies, however, can parse the relative contributions of genetic and environmental influences and provide estimates of heritability (the proportion of phenotypic variance due to genetic factors). In a population-based study of more than 1000 female twin pairs, Kendler and colleagues (1992) estimated the heritability of social phobia to be 30%. A subsequent analysis of nearly 1200 male twin pairs (Kendler, 2001) provided similarly modest evidence of heritability (20%). In both men and women, the best fitting models indicated that the environmental contribution to social phobia derived from individual-specific factors rather than shared family environment. In an analysis of data from two assessments 8 years apart, Kendler and colleagues (1999) were able to correct for the unreliability of cross-sectional assessments and estimated a heritability of 50% for social phobia. The absence of an important contribution of shared family environment weighs against the hypothesis that social anxiety is acquired through modeling or social learning within the family (Kendler et al, 1999). Instead, Kendler and colleagues (1999) have suggested that phobias develop when an inherited phobia proneness is activated by exposure to specific (probably evolutionarily salient) environmental stimuli. A recent analysis by this group using data from a large sample of twins group examined the "stress-diathesis" model of phobia acquisition and was unable to find support for the hypothesis that environmental experiences or learning are required for the expression of phobias (Kendler et al, 2002). It should be noted that other studies have suggested a role for shared family environment in the development of social phobia; for example, in a prospective longitudinal study, Lieb and colleagues (2000) found that parental anxiety and parenting style were associated with the development of social phobia in offspring (see also the section below on parenting and family environment).

Family and twin studies have also addressed the boundaries of the transmitted phenotype. Social phobia is commonly comorbid with other phobic disorders, with panic disorder, and with major depression (Merikangas & Angst, 1995). How much, if any, of this comorbidity is due to a shared genetic diathesis? In a small study using a high-risk design, children of parents with social phobia appeared to be at risk for overanxious disorder and separation anxiety in addition to social phobia (Mancini et al, 1996). With respect to panic disorder and phobic disorders, Fyer and colleagues (1993; 1996; 1995) have provided evidence that social phobia, at least among relatives of probands with non-comorbid social phobia, "breeds true"—that is, relatives are at increased risk for social phobia but not other anxiety disorders. However, in the female twin sample described above, Kendler and colleagues (1992) reported evidence for an inherited "phobia proneness" dimension reflecting shared genetic influences on agoraphobia, social phobia, and specific phobias. For social phobia, 21% of the variance was attributable to genetic factors specific to the disorder while another 10% (approximately one-third of the genetic variance) was attributable to genetic factors common to all phobias. Subsequent analyses suggested that the genetic liability to phobic disorders overlaps with that of panic disorder and bulimia (Kendler et al, 1995).

The familial aggregation of social phobia and panic disorder was also examined by Horwath and colleagues (1995) in a family study of probands with either panic disorder alone, panic disorder with major depression, early onset major depression or no mental disorder. The relatives of probands with panic disorder (without comorbid major depression) were 5 - 6 times more likely to have social phobia than were relatives of never mentally ill controls while relatives of the other two proband groups did not have excess rates of social phobia. However, across the three ill proband groups, first-degree relatives with panic disorder had an elevated risk of social phobia, and the strength of this association did not differ significantly by proband group. The investigators concluded that the familial aggregation of panic disorder and social phobia may be due to the familial aggregation of panic disorder in relatives of probands with panic disorder combined with the tendency of social phobia to be a comorbid disorder.

In another analysis, Fyer and colleagues (1996) compared relatives of probands with either 1) panic disorder alone, 2) social phobia alone, 3) comorbid PD and social phobia, or 4) never ill controls. They found that relatives of probands with comorbid PD and social phobia had elevated rates of PD but not social phobia and resembled relatives of PD-alone probands. The relatives of probands with social phobia alone had elevated rates of social phobia but not PD. They concluded that social phobia in individuals who have PD or later develop PD exhibits different familial transmission from social phobia alone and that familial aggregation of PD is not affected by comorbidity with social phobia.

The frequent comorbidity between depression and social phobia raises the question of whether these conditions might also share genetic determinants. Findings from family studies have been mixed, with some analyses indicating an elevated risk of major depression in relatives of social phobia probands (Fyer et al, 1993; Reich & Yates, 1988) and others finding no increased risk (M. Stein et al, 1998). Twin data from Kendler's female twin sample suggest a modest correlation between genetic factors influencing social phobia and major depression (r = 0.30). In the best-fitting model, the proportion of the comorbidity between social phobia and depression due to genetic factors that influence both disorders was 48%. More recently, Nelson and colleagues (2000) reported findings from the population-based Missouri Adolescent Female Twin Study, including 1344 twins. In their best-fitting model, the heritability of social phobia was 28% and the additive genetic contribution to social phobia and depression appeared to overlap completely (genetic r = 1.0).

Overall, then, family studies have suggested that social phobia is transmitted separately from panic disorder and other phobic disorders, while twin studies suggest overlapping genetic influences. Studies of anxious temperament ("behavioral inhibition to the unfamiliar," discussed later) and certain molecular genetic findings also suggest a possible shared diathesis for panic and phobic disorders (Gratacos et al, 2001; Smoller et al, 2001). Evidence for a genetic relationship between social phobia and depression is conflicting, but there is the suggestion that at least some of heritable liability is shared.

The issue of the boundaries of the heritable phenotype is a crucial one for genetic studies of social phobia (and for other psychiatric disorders) (Smoller & Tsuang, 1998). The consensus diagnostic categories defined by DSM-IV are not based on pathogenetic mechanisms and are unlikely to optimally capture the heritable features of anxiety disorders. To the extent that our phenotype definitions deviate from the underlying genetically influenced traits, the genetic basis of disorders like social phobia will be more difficult to characterize. One important question is whether social anxiety is best characterized as a categorical phenotype (ie, disorder present or absent), a spectrum (eg, including subsyndromal phobic fears), a quantitative trait (eg, shyness) or some combination of these. One integrative view suggests that social phobia is part of a continuum bounded by shyness at one pole and avoidant personality disorder at the other (Stein et al, 2002). Family and twin studies that have demonstrated the familial and genetic transmission of the clinical diagnosis of social phobia support the validity of a categorical definition. But should the phenotype definition be expanded to include social phobic fears that do not meet the threshold for disorder? In their family study of social phobia, Fyer and colleagues (1993) found no evidence that subsyndromal irrational social fears were themselves familial or carried an increased risk of social phobia in first degree relatives compared to relatives of probands without social fears. Consistent with this, Kendler and colleagues (1999) found that including unreasonable social fears that did not reach their threshold for a diagnosis of phobia (ie, objective evidence of interference with one's life) did not materially alter the estimated heritability of social phobia. On the other hand, several twin studies have found that the heritability of social anxiety symptoms and phobic fears is at least comparable to that of phobic disorders (Rose, & Ditto, 1983; Neale & Fulker, 1984; Phillips et al, 1987; Skre et al, 2000; Torgersen, 1979; Warren et al, 1999).

An alternative approach has focused on the genetic basis of anxiety traits and temperaments that may be underlie or predispose to anxiety symptoms and disorders (Goldsmith & Lemery, 2000; Stein et al, 2002). Some of these are thought to be quantitative traits or dimensions along which individuals with and without disorders vary. Temperaments and anxiety traits related to social anxiety include behavioral inhibition to the unfamiliar (Biederman et al, 2001; Kagan et al, 1984) (reviewed below), shyness/sociability (Plomin & Daniels, 1986), fear of negative evaluation (Stein et al, 2002) and harm avoidance (Cloninger, 1986). In their family study sample, Stein and colleagues (2001) found that first degree relatives of generalized social phobia probands scored significantly higher on quantitative trait measures of social anxiety, harm avoidance, and trait anxiety. Factor analysis identified a single factor that accounted for 84% of the variance in these intercorrelated measures. These data support the hypothesis that the heritable phenotype involves temperamental risk factors for social phobia. In a sample of 437 twin pairs, Stein and colleagues (Stein et al, 2002) estimated the heritability of one of these traits, fear of negative evaluation, at 42% and found a strong genetic correlation (r = 0.80) between this trait and avoidant personality traits.

Shyness and behavioral inhibition (BI) in particular are phenomenologically related to social phobia and may also be familial and developmental risk factors for that disorder. Twin and adoption studies have documented that genes contribute to shyness and BI in children (DiLalla et al, 1994; Emde et al, 1992; Matheny, 1989; Plomin & Daniels, 1986; Plomin et al, 1993; Robinson et al, 1992). In the MacArthur Longitudinal Twin Study, estimated heritability was 18–60% for measures of shyness and 41% for BI in twins at ages 14 and 20 months (Cherny et al, 1994; Plomin et al, 1993). Furthermore, the stability of shyness and BI between these two ages appeared to be mediated by genetic factors. Additional analyses of subsamples of this cohort suggest that extreme BI is highly heritable (heritability > 70% at 2 years of age), although the precision of these estimates is unclear because of the relatively small sample sizes involved (DiLalla et al, 1994; Robinson et al, 1992).

Harm avoidance was defined by Cloninger and colleagues (1993) as a heritable temperament encompassing "pessimistic worry in anticipation of future problems, passive avoidant behaviors such as fear of uncertainty and shyness of strangers, and rapid fatigability." Elevated harm avoidance has been observed in patients with OCD (Richter et al, 1996), panic disorder and GAD (Starcevic et al, 1996), and in patients with social phobia (Kim & Hoover, 1996) and their first degree relatives (Stein et al, 2001).

Taken together, the evidence clearly suggests that genes influence social phobia (especially the generalized subtype), but the precise nature of the heritable phenotype requires further investigation. In particular, quantitative and temperamental social anxiety traits also appear to be familial and heritable. It may be that such temperamental traits are more proximal to the genetic substrate than is the DSM-IV category of social phobia itself. Ultimately, the resolution of this question may follow the identification of specific genes related to the expression of social anxiety.

Thus far, molecular genetic studies have had limited success in identifying such genes. At this writing, there have been no published genome scans for the phenotype of social phobia. No evidence of linkage to either of two candidate gene—the serotonin transporter and the serotonin 5HT2A receptor—

was found in a study of 17 families of probands with generalized social phobia (Stein et al, 1998). Genes involved in the dopamine system have also
been of interest because of evidence of dopaminergic dysregulation in social
phobia (Mathew et al, 2001). In the same sample of 17 generalized social
phobia families, Kennedy and colleagues (2001)found no evidence of linkage to three dopamine receptor genes (D2, D3, D4) or the dopamine transporter (DAT). In one study of children, however, a polymorphism in the
DAT gene was associated with a quantitative count of social phobia symptoms measured by parental ratings (Rowe et al, 1998). Another study found
that female carriers of the trinculeotide repeat mutation in the FMR-1 gene
(responsible for Fragile X syndrome) had an elevated rate of social phobia
and avoidant personality disorder (Franke et al, 1998).

Recent gene mapping studies have supported the potential utility of
expanding phenotype definitions beyond the DSM categories and considering the potential shared features of panic and phobic anxiety disorders. In
a linkage analysis of a large extended pedigree, Smoller and colleagues
(2001) observed suggestive evidence of linkage (lod = 2.38) to a locus on
chromosome 10 for a phenotype definition that included panic and phobic
disorders and was derived from studies of BI. A more remarkable finding
was reported by a group of investigators from Spain who investigated the
genetic basis of panic and phobic anxiety disorders and their co-occurrence
with joint laxity (a syndrome of increased distensibility and hypermobility
of joints) (Gratacos et al, 2001). They identified a segmental duplication of
chromosome 15q24-26 (named DUP25) which appeared to be strongly
associated with a phenotype comprising panic disorder, phobic disorders
(including social phobia) and joint laxity in 7 extended pedigrees. A lod
score of 5.0 was observed under a model of complete penetrance with the
phenotype of "panic disorder/agoraphobia/social phobia/joint laxity."
Further analyses indicated that there was mosaicism (the presence within
an individual of cell lines with and without the duplication) and non-
Mendelian inheritance of DUP25. These investigators suggest that the phenotypic effect of DUP25 derives from overexpression or disruption of genes
in the DUP25 region that affect panic and phobic anxiety disorders and
joint laxity, although the identity of such genes is unknown.

In keeping with the hypothesis that the genetically transmitted phenotype is
more likely to be a temperamental social anxiety proneness, a number of
investigators have begun to use such traits in genetic linkage and association

studies. Candidate gene association studies of shyness and BI have begun to appear, but results to date have been largely negative (Henderson et al, 2000; Jorm et al, 1998; Jorm et al, 2000; Smoller et al, 2001). While some studies have found evidence of association or linkage between the trait of harm avoidance and a polymorphism in the serotonin transporter gene (Katsuragi et al, 1999; Lesch et al, 1996; Mazzanti et al, 1998), others have not (Ebstein et al, 1996; Gelernter et al, 1998; Herbst et al, 2000; Jorm et al, 2000). Harm avoidance was also linked to a locus on the short arm of chromosome 8 in a large genome scan of more than 750 sibling pairs (Cloninger et al, 1998).

Research aimed at identifying specific genes involved in the development of social phobia is clearly still in its early stages. The few positive findings noted above require further study and replication before they can be considered established. A number of factors are likely to complicate the search for genes influencing social anxiety including the modest heritability of social phobia and uncertainties about optimal phenotype definition. The inheritance of social phobia is likely to be complex in most cases and reflect multiple genes interacting with environmental factors. The effect of any one genetic locus may be modest and therefore require large samples to be detectable. Other strategies that may be important to the success of gene mapping studies include further validation of phenotype definitions, the identification of biological "endophenotypes," and making use of genetic findings from animal models of anxiety and fear behavior (Smoller et al, 2001; Smoller & Tsuang 1998). Despite the clear need for further studies to identify the specific genetic factors involved, the research to date establishes that in identifying individuals at risk for social anxiety disorder, particularly its more debilitating generalized presentation, family history of the disorder itself, and possibly of related disorders (panic, phobias, or depression), are important indicators.

Temperamental Precursor: Behavioral Inhibition

As noted above, one promising avenue in identifying individuals at risk for social phobia is to study temperamental factors that may be associated with the disorder. An advantage to studying such indicators is that they can be observed very early in development, well before the diagnosis of social phobia itself can be made. The best studied of these potential temperamental precursors is "behavioral inhibition to the unfamiliar." First described by Jerome Kagan and colleagues at Harvard University, behavioral inhibition (BI) represents an enduring tendency to exhibit caution, restraint, and reticence in situations that are novel or unfamiliar (Kagan, 1989; Kagan, 1994;

Kagan, Reznick, & Snidman, 1988). Because of the rapid developmental changes that occur over the first years of life, BI manifests differently in toddlers, preschoolers, and older children. Inhibited toddlers react to unfamiliar settings with distress, fear, and avoidance. They may cling to parents when faced with unfamiliar adults or peers, or refuse to approach new toys or new settings. As children mature, they are less likely to display overt fear or distress, but tend to show quiet restraint and hesitancy to smile, approach, or initiate spontaneous conversations with new peers or adults. In preschoolers, such tendencies are evident in interactions with individual peers or adults, whereas older children exhibit inhibition more commonly in group situations, for example, remaining solitary in settings such as birthday parties or new classrooms (Gersten, 1989). Older children may also develop anxious anticipation of new situations.

Kagan and colleagues studied two cohorts of youngsters originally selected in toddlerhood as extremely inhibited or uninhibited based on repeated laboratory observations of their reactions to novel settings, people, and toys. They found inhibition to be preserved to a moderate degree through early childhood, with about three quarters of children preserving their inhibited tendencies from ages 21 months through 7.5 years (Kagan et al, 1984; Kagan et al, 1988; Reznick et al, 1986). Other longitudinal studies, using varied observational means of assessing inhibition, have supported the impression of moderate stability of BI (Asendorpf, 1994; Asendorpf, 1990; Broberg, Lamb, & Hwang, 1990; Fordham & Stevenson-Hinde, 1999; Scarpa et al, 1995; Stevenson-Hinde & Shouldice, 1995), with the suggestion that children extreme in inhibition are more likely to remain inhibited over the course of childhood (Kagan et al, 1988; Kerr et al, 1994). Several longer-term studies have suggested that inhibited children maintain their cautiousness and restraint as adults (Caspi, Bem, & Elder, 1989; Caspi & Silva, 1995; Gest, 1997). In addition, Kagan and others have extended their observations to early infancy, and found that "high reactivity" at age four months, defined as a tendency to respond to surprising events with distress and high motor activity, tends to moderately predict BI in toddlerhood and shy or fearful behavior in early childhood (Calkins, Fox, & Marshall, 1996; Kagan et al, 1999; L. A. Schmidt et al, 1997).

Kagan and colleagues have hypothesized that BI reflects a lowered threshold to limbic and sympathetic nervous system arousal in response to novelty; that is, higher reactivity of the basolateral and central nuclei of the amygdala and their projections to the striatum, hypothalamus, sympathetic chain, and cardiovascular system. In one small cohort they found correlations between BI and increased urinary MHPG (at age 5.5 years), increased baseline morning salivary cortisol levels (at age 5.5 and 7.5 years), and high and stable heart rates (at ages 21 months, 4 and 5.5 years) with a tendency for heart rate to accelerate across laboratory batteries and for the highest heart rates to be associated with highest stability of inhibition (Kagan, Reznick, & Snidman, 1988). These findings have not been consistently replicated in other cohorts or by other groups. However, the tendency for heart rate to increase across batteries is similar to responses observed in children with test anxiety in social evaluative situations (Beidel, 1988) as well as in socially phobic adults (Beidel, Turner, & Dancu, 1985; Heimberg, Hope, & Dodge, 1990). Others explain the neuropsychiatric basis of behavioral inhibition in terms of Gray's "behavioral inhibition system"(Gray, 1982; Gray, 1991; Gray & McNaughton, 1996), which responds to signals of novelty, danger, or punishment with increased arousal, inhibition of ongoing behaviors, and passive avoidance. This system is thought to be based in the septo-hippocampal system, its noradrenergic afferents from the locus coeruleus and serotonergic inputs from the raphe nucleus, and the frontal cortex, with more recent formulations recognizing the influence of the amygdala and hypothalamus as well. Others have suggested that BI might reflect increased activation of "withdrawal centers" such as areas of the right frontal region, the amygdala, and the temporal polar region, and decreased activation of "approach centers" such as the left dorsolateral prefrontal cortex, basal ganglia, amygdala, and projections to the hypothalamus (Davidson, 1994). Indeed, several small studies have suggested that inhibited children show increased right cerebral hemisphere or decreased left hemisphere activation (Calkins et al, 1996; Davidson, 1994; Schmidt et al, 1999). Similar patterns of activation have been observed in adults with social phobia. For example, social phobics anticipating making a speech showed a large increase in right anterior temporal activation compared to control subjects (Davidson, 1996).

Several lines of evidence have suggested that BI in children is associated with risk for social phobia. First, and most compelling, longitudinal studies comparing children identified by Kagan and colleagues in toddlerhood as extremely inhibited or uninhibited have suggested that the inhibited youngsters are significantly more likely to develop social anxiety disorder. Thus, when 41 children from one cohort were evaluated at age 7.5-8 years using diagnostic interviews (the Diagnostic Interview for Children and Adolescents- Parent Version, or DICA-P, for DSM-III) administered to mothers, the inhibited children had significantly higher lifetime rates of "phobic disorder" (Biederman et al, 1990). Although the DICA-P did not distinguish between social and specific phobias, the most commonly feared situations among phobic children were speaking in front of the class, strangers, being called on in class, and crowds. Children who remained persistently inhibited when assessed at ages 21 months, and 4.5, 5.5, and 7.5 years carried the highest risk for these disorders (Hirshfeld et al, 1992). The same sample of children was combined with children from a second cohort selected in toddlerhood (total N=79) and assessed at age 13 by direct psychiatric interview, using modules adapted from the Diagnostic Interview Schedule for Children (DISC) to assess specific fears, separation anxiety, performance anxiety, and generalized social anxiety (Schwartz, Snidman, & Kagan, 1999). Youngsters who had been classified as inhibited as toddlers were found to have significantly higher rates of current general social anxiety than uninhibited youngsters, whereas no other category of anxiety, including performance anxiety, differed between groups. Generalized social anxiety associated with impairment was significantly more prevalent in inhibited versus uninhibited youngsters (34% vs. 9%, p<.05), and was particularly elevated in inhibited girls (44% vs. 6%, p<.05).

Other studies have supported this association. In a longitudinal study of over 2,000 high school students, Hayward and colleagues found that BI reported in 9th grade using the Retrospective Self-Report of Inhibition (RSRI), which queries behaviors recalled from grades 1-6, significantly predicted new onset of social phobia over the next four years (Hayward et al, 1998). Ninth graders who scored in the top 15th percentile on both social avoidance and fearfulness scales of the RSRI were found to have a greater than five-fold increased risk of developing social phobia over the next four years compared with students who were not high on either measure. Although the study did not use early childhood observations, it did suggest that retrospectively reported BI among 9th graders can predict onset of social phobia during high school.

In a study which did use laboratory observations of temperament, Biederman and colleagues examined correlates of BI among offspring at risk for panic disorder and depression and comparison offspring of parents without mood or anxiety disorders (Biederman et al, 2001). Temperament was assessed using standard laboratory protocols for children between ages 2 to 6 years. Diagnostic assessments were conducted on all children who attained the age of 5 years within the initial 5-year-study period, using K–SADS–E (DSM-III-R) with mothers supplemented with a DICA–P module assessing DSM-III-R avoidant disorder of childhood. Although many of the assessments done in this study were cross-sectional, approximately half of the children had their diagnostic assessments over a year after their temperamental assessment. BI was significantly associated with social anxiety disorder (defined as either social phobia or avoidant disorder) and with avoidant disorder alone. Rates of all other anxiety disorders did not differ between inhibited and non-inhibited children. Although the interaction between temperament and family risk status was not significant, the association between BI and social anxiety disorder was noted only among the offspring of parents with panic disorder and/or depression. These three studies, then, using different methodologies, converge in finding specific associations between BI and social anxiety disorder.

Given the familial nature of social phobia, if BI is indeed a risk factor for social anxiety disorder, we would expect the parents of inhibited children to have increased rates of social anxiety disorder. Indeed, when the parents of children selected as inhibited by Kagan and colleagues were interviewed with the Diagnostic Interview Schedule (DIS), they were found to have increased rates of social phobia (Rosenbaum et al, 1991), again with the effect most pronounced among the parents of children who had remained most persistently inhibited from toddlerhood to the early elementary school years (Hirshfeld et al, 1992). In a related study (Cooper & Eke, 1999), mother- or teacher-reported shyness among 4-year-olds (N=43) was found to be significantly associated with maternal social phobia. Shy children who had no other comorbid problems had mothers with a nearly eight-fold increase in lifetime social phobia compared with normal control children.

Additionally, several retrospective studies of adolescents or young adults have confirmed the link between BI and social anxiety. In a community sample of 3021 German adolescents and young adults, Wittchen and colleagues (1999) found retrospectively reported BI (using a translated RSRI) to be related to social phobia in general (odds ratio with 95% confidence interval: 4.54 [3.38-6.09]) and especially to generalized social phobia (odds ratio: 23.73 [10.12-56.68]). Additionally, a retrospective study by Mick and

Telch (1998) found that undergraduates with social anxiety (with or without generalized anxiety) scored significantly higher on retrospectively reported BI (total RSRI score and social inhibition subscale) than those with generalized anxiety or with minimal social anxiety. Moreover, BI as assessed on the RSRI was significantly correlated with the Social Phobia and Anxiety Inventory measuring current social anxiety.

Taken as a whole, the studies reviewed in this section suggest that BI in early childhood may represent a precursor to social phobia, and in particular, generalized social phobia. However, several caveats must be considered in interpreting these studies. First, although recent studies in two different samples have demonstrated impressive specificity of the BI-social anxiety disorder link (Biederman et al, 2001; Schwartz et al, 1999), other data suggest we remain cautious about this conclusion. For example, risk for BI in children has also been found to be conferred by parental panic disorder and possibly major depression (Kochanska, 1991; Kochanska & Radke-Yarrow, 1992; Rosenbaum et al, 1988; Rosenbaum et al, 2000). A small study found associations with parental alcoholism, as well (Hill et al, 1999), although another study found no association (Biederman et al, 2001). Similarly, adults with anxiety and mood disorders other than social anxiety disorder endorse elevated childhood BI in retrospective reports (Reznick et al, 1992; van Ameringen et al, 1998). Also, whereas non-clinically referred children who describe themselves as inhibited score most highly on self-report measures of social anxiety, they also endorse other symptoms of anxiety and mood disorders (Muris et al, 1999). Additionally, in their study of a birth cohort from Dunedin, New Zealand, Caspi and colleagues found that children rated by examiners as inhibited at age 3 were significantly more likely than well-adjusted 3 year-olds to have current depression at age 21 (using the DIS for DSM–III–R), but had no excess risk for current anxiety disorders (although lifetime prevalences were not rated) (Caspi et al, 1996). It should be borne in mind that the children in the longitudinal studies mentioned were still well within the age of risk for other psychiatric disorders. It may be that BI predisposes to a developmental series of anxiety or mood disorders, the earliest of which is social phobia.

Finally, another important point is that in each of the studies described, the majority of inhibited children did not develop social phobia. Therefore, BI may be a predisposing factor, but by no means does having this temperamental marker ensure that a child will develop social anxiety disorder.

Parenting and Family Environment Factors

The data on parental influences on social anxiety are quite sparse (Masia & Morris, 1998). Certainly there is no evidence that parental behaviors "cause" social anxiety disorder; however, parents may be able to influence its course. For example, by encouraging their child to take small risks when facing feared situations, parents may be able to reduce a child's anxiety and avoidance, whereas by avoiding feared situations themselves, parents might teach their child to avoid uncomfortable situations. That parental behaviors may influence the maintenance or remission of childhood anxiety disorders in general can be inferred from treatment studies suggesting that adding a parent component to cognitive behavioral treatment for childhood anxiety disorders can improve outcome (Barrett, 1998; Barrett et al, 1996). In particular, one study demonstrated that the efficacy of cognitive-behavioral treatment of children with anxious parents can be compromised unless the anxious parent also receives parent anxiety-management training (Cobham et al, 1998).

The direct study of etiologic effects of parental behaviors on social anxiety relies largely upon retrospective reports by adults, correlational studies of parent-child interactions or relationship factors, and inferences from studies of parents of peer-neglected children. Often, interpretations of studies of parent-child relationships are complicated by bi-directional influences between child and parent behaviors, as well as by potential confounds (eg, a parent who models social avoidance may also confer genetic risk for social anxiety disorder). It has long been recognized that children's temperamental tendencies and behaviors may actively contribute to shaping their social environment and parental responses through eliciting particular reactions (Lerner & Lerner, 1987). As an illustration, in an experiment where a child confederate was trained to behave anxiously or oppositionally with adult female study participants, the women responded with more helping and rewarding behavior towards the "anxious" child (Brunk & Henggeler, 1984). In this way, then, a child's temperamental style can be self-reinforcing, by eliciting particular social responses and, in turn, by influencing the child's typical reactions to them (Caspi et al, 1989). For example, an inhibited preschooler may become silent, avoidant, and clingy when meeting new people, leading well-meaning and responsive parents to comfort and protect the child (allowing or facilitating the avoidance), which in turn may reinforce the child's anxious and avoidant responses and interfere with the child's development of skills both for coping with the anxiety and for meeting new people. Therefore, even when particular parental responses in infancy are noted to be associated with later child behaviors, we cannot assume that these parental behaviors "caused" the child outcomes. In addition, although the discussion above of genetic factors has cited studies modeling the environmental variance in social phobia as primarily due to factors "unshared" by siblings in a family, it should be noted that influences such as parental protectiveness or parental modeling of avoidance may actually be "unshared" by virtue of the nature of their associations to a particular child's temperamental tendencies. Thus, parents may be more solicitous to an anxious child than to a bolder child in the same family. Similarly, it can be hypothesized that an anxious parent's avoidance might be more likely to be imitated by a temperamentally anxious than a non-anxious child. The variance in child anxiety explained by parental behaviors is likely to be low (Rapee, 1997). Despite all of these limitations, it can still be helpful to review some of the ways parental behaviors have been hypothesized to influence social anxiety. If confirmed empirically, these parental behaviors might be good candidates for preventive intervention.

Children learn from their parents' actions, behaviors, and attitudes. Thus, parents of socially anxious children may influence their children's social anxiety and avoidant behaviors by modeling social avoidance, limiting social opportunities, providing little guidance or supervision of peer encounters, reinforcing avoidant behaviors, and influencing the child's beliefs and expectancies in ways that might increase social evaluative anxiety. We will consider each of these in turn.

Studies suggest that individuals with social phobia are more likely to have observed social avoidance in their parents. In a study comparing social phobic adults and non-anxious controls, Bruch and Heimberg (1994) found that social phobics reported that their families of origin were more isolated and were less likely to socialize. This effect was noted especially among individuals with generalized social phobia. Generalized social phobics also rated their mothers as significantly more fearful and avoidant in social situations than the other groups. Similarly, in a large study of young children, investigators found an inverse association between family intellectual and recreational orientations (ie, encouragement of social and cultural involvement) and child shyness at ages 12 and 24 months (Plomin & Daniels, 1986). In addition, shyness in adoptive parents had a low but significant correlation with shyness in adopted children (Daniels & Plomin, 1985). These studies support the hypothesis that modeling of social avoidance by parents may influence a child's social avoidance.

Parents often play an active role in facilitating children's social interactions, particularly when the children are young (Masia & Morris, 1998). More and more in urban or suburban settings where parents hesitate to allow children to play outside unsupervised, parents are called upon to arrange play dates, supervise youngsters' peer interactions, and monitor ongoing play. Parents who themselves fear social interactions might be expected to be compromised in some of these roles. Clinically we have commonly encountered preschoolers or early elementary school children who have few playdates because their parents are phobic of telephoning other parents to arrange them.

Beyond simply limiting interactions, parents who are socially anxious themselves may be less skillful in facilitating their young child's play when social opportunities do occur. In this regard, studies of parents of peer-neglected versus popular children may be relevant, since anxious or inhibited children are more likely than non-anxious children to be neglected by peers (Masia & Morris, 1998). Mothers of preschoolers typically tend to assist children with social interactions through modeling, direct instruction, and prompting specific actions (Finnie & Russell, 1988). Using a laboratory interaction in which mothers of peer-neglected or popular children had to help their child join in the play of a dyad of unfamiliar peers, Finnie & Russell (1988) found that mothers of peer-neglected children were not as skillful as mothers of popular children. Whereas mothers of the popular children tried to assess the other children's frame of reference and encourage the child to integrate without disrupting the play, mothers of neglected children were more likely either to avoid the supervisory task or to use their authority to gain entry for their child. Moreover, the mothers of peer-neglected children were less knowledgeable about skillful responses to hypothetical child social situations.

There is also evidence that parents of anxious children in general (including but not limited to socially anxious children) may influence their children to use more avoidant coping strategies. Barrett and colleagues (1996) observed 7-14-year-old children engaged in laboratory discussions with their parents about how they would cope with hypothetical potentially threatening situations. They compared children with anxiety disorders, behavior disorders, or no disorders (31 of the 152 children had social phobia). Of the two hypothetical situations, one involved a potential social threat (walking up to children playing a game, wanting to join in, and noticing that they are laughing). Children were interviewed about how they would cope with these situations both before and after their family discussions. After discussing the situations with their parents, children with anxiety disorders were more likely than non-anxious children to adopt more avoidant coping strategies. Analysis of the transcripts of the discussions revealed that parents of anxious children were more likely than parents of non-clinic controls to respond to the child's proposed avoidant responses by suggesting their own avoidant response, whereas they were less likely to agree to pro-social plans proposed by the child (Dadds et al, 1996). The child's ultimate decision to use an avoidant response was positively correlated with the probability that the parent reciprocated avoidance and negatively correlated with the chance that the parent agreed to a prosocial plan. Preliminary data from another group, using a similar approach with a small sample including both clinical and non-clinical children also revealed that parents' anxious statements were associated with children's change in coping plans (Chorpita et al, 1996).

It is possible, moreover, that certain types of parental behaviors may indirectly influence children's expectations of critical responses from others or of negative outcomes to their own efforts at socialization or performance. Many studies of parenting behavior have focused on dimensions of control and warmth, with the idea that the combination of high control and low warmth represents a risk factor for psychopathology (Parker, 1983; Rapee, 1997). For example, Chorpita and Barlow (1998) have argued that parents who exert maximal control over a child's activities and decisions might negatively influence the child's sense of being able to control his or her own environment. Similarly, Krohne (1990, 1992) has suggested that parental restrictiveness, punitiveness, and inconsistency may contribute to a child's expectation of negative outcomes and a diminished perception of control over such outcomes. In addition, Spence (2001) has proposed that parents may foster children's tendency to overestimate threats. Others have focused on the nature of the attachment developed between and infants and parents, noting that infants whose parents are appropriately responsive (eg, warm, engaged) develop secure attachments with good outcome (eg, self-confidence, good peer relations) later in childhood, while children whose parents display rejecting, interfering, or ignoring behavior may develop insecure or "anxious attachment" (Ainsworth, 1982; Blehar, Lieberman, & Ainsworth, 1977).

Indeed, when asked about their parents' behaviors, socially anxious adolescents and adults report rejection, overprotection, and lower affection (Arrindell et al, 1989; Parker, 1979), although at least one study has found that parents' emotional warmth and rejection were unrelated to social fears in children (Bögels et al, 2001). For example, a study of a large sample of adolescents in Germany (N=1047) found that parental anxiety and youth-reported parenting style (rejection and overprotection) were independently associated with social phobia and that these parental attitudes were more pronounced when the parents had psychopathology themselves (Lieb et al, 2000). In another study, BI in 7-12-year-old children of mothers with history of anxiety disorder was associated with maternal attitudes of criticism and dissatisfaction, measured from five-minute-speech samples in which the mothers discussed the children (Hirshfeld et al, 1997). An observational study also found critical attitudes on the part of parents of socially anxious children (Hummel & Gross, 2001). When compared to normal controls during an observed parent-child puzzle task, parents of socially anxious children tended to speak less, use fewer explanations, and to be more critical of their child's performance, using more negative than positive feedback. Therefore, links have been found between parental criticism, rejection, and overprotection and childhood BI or social anxiety. It must be underscored, however, that high control or rejection and low warmth are associated with anxiety and depressive disorders in general and not specifically with social phobia. Poor parental relationships may represent a risk factor for psychopathology in general (Parker, 1983).

Studies have also found associations between insecure attachment, observed in laboratory in infancy, and later social anxiety. For example, insecure attachment in infancy predicted timidity, submissiveness, low popularity, and tendency to be victimized in preschool (LaFreniere & Sroufe, 1985; Troy & Sroufe, 1987). In addition, Warren and colleagues showed that adolescents who had insecure (anxious-ambivalent) attachment as infants were twice as likely to develop anxiety disorders by late adolescence (Warren et al, 1997). Of the adolescents who developed anxiety disorders in this study, over a third had social phobia. Whereas the construct of attachment as measured in the laboratory is a relational variable which may be contributed to by the child's temperament (Calkins & Fox, 1992) as well as by parental characteristics such as anxiety (Manassis et al, 1994), this association from infancy to adolescence is impressive and warrants further study. Once again, however, the association with anxious-ambivalent attachment was not specific to social anxiety, but applied to anxiety disorders in general.

Other studies examine factors perhaps more linked to the development of social evaluative anxiety per se. Thus, youths and adults with social anxiety report that their parents evinced high concern with the opinions of others, shame of their shyness and poor performance (Caster, Inderbitzen, & Hope, 1999) and a tendency to use shaming as a discipline technique (Bruch & Heimberg, 1994). Children who experience criticism, rejection, or shaming may become preoccupied with evaluative comments, leading to generalized fear of negative evaluation, self-consciousness, and avoidance of social scrutiny (Bruch, 1989).

With the exception of Warren's study, all of the studies cited have been retrospective or correlational. To properly examine parental influences on children's social anxiety, more prospective observational studies are needed. Such studies would be most informative about environmental influences if they compared adopted children with their adoptive and biological parents.

Although we are not aware of any prospective observational studies of social anxiety disorder, two studies to date have prospectively explored parental influences on BI. Arcus (1991) conducted naturalistic home observations of a small sample of infants classified as "high reactive" at 4 months. She found that infants whose mothers held them proportionately more often when crying or fretting at ages 5-7 months were more likely to show BI at age 14 months, whereas infants whose mothers set firmer limits (issued firm prohibitions and removed objects) at ages 9-13 months were less likely to become inhibited. She hypothesized that by subjecting infants to mild stress, mothers may have facilitated their developing strategies for coping with stress. In a larger study of 125 first-born boys, Belsky and colleagues (1998) found that among children who had been observed to show higher negative affect in infancy, a father's tendency to display more sensitivity, positive affect, cognitive stimulation, and absence of detachment in the second year and to display less intrusiveness and negative affect in the second and third years predicted BI at age 3 years, with parenting variables accounting for 27% of the variance in BI. The authors suggest that by pushing the child to change (thus appearing insensitive and intrusive to raters), fathers may have influenced sons to become less inhibited. They caution, however, that it is not known whether such fathering methods might have other negative influences. Moreover, since BI was not rated at ages earlier than 3 years, it is not known whether child BI may have influenced or elicited fathers' behaviors. In both of these naturalistic studies, therefore, it is possible that other factors (eg, parental anxiety, parental behaviors elicited by stable infant tendencies) may have contributed to the associations.

Cognitive Risk Factors

Cognitive and information processing models of anxiety have proven especially useful in understanding the internal factors that may serve to maintain social anxiety. Although there are no studies that we know of that suggest that pre-existing cognitive tendencies are temporal precursors to social anxiety disorder, the way "anxiety sensitivity," for example, is emerging as a potential precursor to panic disorder (Schmidt et al, 1997; Schmidt et al, 1999), this possibility is one that ought to be explored. For at-risk youth, cognitive factors may interact with developmental processes and other risk factors in the expression of anxious distress.

In the model offered by Beck and his colleagues (1997; 1985) anxious cognitions are viewed as resulting from the interaction of biological, social and psychological systems (Beck et al, 1985) and are thought to determine or maintain anxiety. According to this model, when individuals fail to accurately appraise their anxious thoughts and feelings, anxiety escalates and then subsides only following an avoidant or defensive response (Beck & Clark, 1997). Anxious individuals therefore learn that an avoidance response reduces anxiety, and since the maintenance of avoidance behavior is reinforced by this reduction, avoidance behaviors become established and strengthened (Mowrer, 1960). Anxiety is also maintained by avoidance since this prevents the discomfirmation of negative beliefs and expectations (Otto, 1999).

Rapee and Heimberg (1997) have integrated and extended some of these earlier cognitive-behavioral models of anxiety (eg, Beck et al, 1985; Clark & Wells, 1995). Their model conceptualizes shyness, specific social phobia, generalized social phobia, and avoidant personality disorder along a continuum of "concerns about social evaluation," with similar cognitive antecedents. Within this model, the authors propose that individuals with social phobia assume that others are inherently critical and likely to view them negatively. At the same time, socially anxious individuals attach great importance to being viewed positively by others. Upon entering a social situation, socially phobic individuals form a mental representation of their external appearance and behavior, as an audience might see them. They simultaneously focus attention on this internal representation, salient aspects of their self-image, and any perceived threat in the environment (eg, signs of disapproval or rejection). The imagined audience serves as the primary threat stimulus in social phobia, and is derived from information retrieved from long-term memory, internal cues, and external cues. As such, the individual's evaluation is not objective, but is prone to distortion or bias. The perceived image also changes from moment to moment depending on internal (eg, proprioceptive cues) and external feedback (eg, verbal and nonverbal feedback from the audience). Given that much of this feedback is subtle and ambiguous, it also lends itself to distortion and negative bias (Rapee & Heimberg, 1997).

Support for this model has come from the finding that compared to nonclinical subjects, social phobics perceive their performance in social situations more negatively. Socially phobic individuals are also more likely to rate themselves more negatively in social situations than individuals with depression or other anxiety disorders. These biases actually represent the fluid interaction of several cognitive processes, including attention, memory, and cognitive constructs (eg, perfectionism; anxiety sensitivity), which we summarize briefly in turn.

Adult social phobics demonstrate attentional biases, reflected in hypervigilance to social-evaluative threat words, with specific speech phobics showing this effect for speech stimuli words and generalized social phobics showing this effect for general social threat words (Hope et al, 1990; Maidenberg et al, 1996; Mattia et al, 1993; McNeil et al, 1995). Social phobics also evince speech disturbances, such as longer and more frequent pauses and poorer eye contact (Lewin et al, 1996), suggesting that the speaker's attention is being allocated to stimuli other than speech content (Hofmann et al, 1997). Although socially phobic individuals may display rapid automatic activation of threat-relevant information, they have been observed to strategically attempt, with additional processing time, to inhibit the threat meaning (Amir et al, 1998). The rapid threat evaluation followed by avoidance of strategic processing may be especially problematic in anxiety disorders by preventing habituation or objective evaluation of threatening material (Mogg et al, 1997).

Although there have been very few studies of socially phobic children, information processing studies have identified biased attention in youth with a variety of anxiety disorders (eg, separation anxiety, social phobia, generalized anxiety disorder). These have found support for a cognitive bias towards threat in anxious children (Martin et al, 1992; Moradi et al, 1999; Vasey & MacLeod, 2001). For example, Vasey and colleagues (2001) demonstrated that children (ages 9-14) diagnosed with a variety of anxiety disorders exhibited a mood-congruent bias towards threatening stimuli, compared to a group of same-aged, nonanxious children. Nonanxious children did not show a bias away from threatening stimuli, but instead attended equally to both threat and neutral words. A second study (Vasey et al, 1996) replicated many of the above findings. Twenty high-test-anxious children (ages 12-14) were compared to 20 low test-anxious children. Results indicated a significant interaction between group status and gender. Both anxious boys and girls showed a significant amount of attention towards threat. However, in the nonanxious group, boys showed a bias away from threatening stimuli, while girls showed no bias in either direction.

Although small in sample size, these studies suggest that clinically anxious children demonstrate an attentional bias towards threat-relevant stimuli. Although interference tasks may need to be age adapted (eg, using pictorial rather than verbal Stroop tasks; increasing viewing time to accommodate reading differences), this biased cognitive processing has been observed in children as young as 6 years of age. The magnitude of the observed cognitive bias does not appear to change significantly over the entire age range (Martin et al, 1992), and appears to be specific to anxiety disorders in youth (Taghavi et al, 1999). Moreover, the magnitude of the effects found in studies of anxious youth are very similar to those reported for adults, suggesting that attentional bias for threatening stimuli appears at a relatively early age and remains stable across various developmental periods.

During anxiety-provoking social situations, socially phobic adults may experience more negative self-evaluation and negative other-focused thoughts (Stopa & Clark, 1993), accompanied by increases in inwardly-focused attention, using what has been termed the "observer perspective" (Hope et al, 1989; Stopa & Clark, 1993). For example, when individuals with social phobia are asked to recall an anxiety provoking situation, they tend to report images or memories in which they see themselves from the observer's perspective (Hackmann et al, 2000; Hackmann et al, 1998; Wells et al, 1998; Wells & Papageorgiou, 1999). In contrast, normal controls or individuals with nonsocial concerns tend to recall the situation from a field perspective (as though seen with their own eyes). These images tend to be associated with specific memories involving unpleasant social occurrences. Thus, early, negative social experiences might contribute to the development of negative, observer-perspective images among socially phobic individuals, that may subsequently be reinforced through social interactions, mediate emotional responses when similar threat-related stimuli occurs again, and be resistant to discomfirmatory feedback (Hackmann et al, 2000). The observer perspective is likely to be distorted, and associated with dispositional (internal, stable, and global) attributions for negative behaviors or anxiety-provoking events. For instance, Coles and colleagues (2001) observed that, as the social situation became increasingly threatening, the attributions of socially phobic patients became more stable, global, and internal. In contrast, nonanxious controls displayed a "self-serving bias," whereby their attributions became more situational (external, unstable, and specific). Improvement during cognitive-behavioral treatment for social anxiety has been associated with decreases in negative self-focused attention before and during social interactions (Hofmann, 2000; Woody et al, 1997) and increases in positive self-focused thoughts and neutral other-focused thoughts (Hofmann, 2000).

Memory bias for threat-relevant information has not consistently been observed in social phobia (Rapee et al, 1994), with some studies finding enhanced memory for threat-related verbal information (Foa et al, 2000; Hope et al, 1990) and others finding none (Cloitre et al, 1995; Rapee et al, 1994). However, recent studies using pictorial, or ecologically valid stimuli, have more consistently observed memory biases among socially phobic adults. For example, Lundh and Ost (1996) found that socially phobic subjects later recalled more faces that they had initially rated as "critical" than faces they had rated as "accepting," whereas control subjects displayed the reverse pattern. Similarly, Foa and colleagues (2000) observed that patients with generalized social phobia, but not controls, displayed a bias towards recognition of negative facial expressions (anger and disgust), compared to nonnegative expressions. In one study that required participants to recall a social interaction a day later, the memories of socially phobic individuals tended to be biased in favor of negative self-related, as opposed to external information (Mellings & Alden, 2000).

Memory biases, in what Clark and Wells (1995) have called the "post-mortem," may also exacerbate memory biases. Individuals with high levels of social anxiety often experience numerous, highly intrusive and interfering thoughts about past, unsatisfactory social events, which lead them to recall the events as more negative than they were (Fehm & Margraf, 2002; Rachman et al, 2000). Subsequently, prior to social events, the individual may engage in anticipatory processing, with thought patterns dominated by "recollections of past failures," and anticipated poor performance. In turn, this increases the likelihood of a negative social outcome.

Estimations of the probability of harm and the severity of the negative consequences of the threat have been hypothesized to be critical determinants of anxiety (Beck et al, 1985). Across multiple anxiety disorders, anxious individuals tend to rate the probability and consequences of threat as significantly higher than nonanxious individuals. Moreover, individuals high in anxiety interpret ambiguous situations in a manner consistent with their threat concerns (Butler & Matthews, 1983; McNally, 1996). The types of events that may lend themselves to this type of biased processing in social phobia tend to be ambiguous social events (where there is no or little direct social feedback) (Alden & Wallace, 1995). Socially anxious subjects have been found to interpret ambiguous social events in a more negative fashion than either nonanxious controls or patients with other anxiety disorders (Dreessen et al, 1999; Stopa & Clark, 2000). This tendency has recently been observed in socially anxious youth as well. In a study conducted by Muris and colleagues (2000), socially anxious children, when told stories involving a wide range of social encounters, perceived more stories to be threatening, made this judgment more rapidly, and had more negative feelings and cognitions about the stories.

Socially phobic individuals may tend to underestimate the effectiveness of their social behavior, while overestimating negative aspects of their performance (Stopa & Clark, 1993). Interestingly, Alden and Wallace (1995) observed that social phobic outpatients rated their own nonverbal behavior more negatively than did objective observers, whereas they displayed a positive bias when evaluating the behavior of their partner. This was observed even when their interactions were objectively rated as successful.

In addition to negative interpretations of ambiguous stimuli, socially phobic patients tend to subject mildly negative social events to catastrophic interpretations (Beck et al, 1985). For example, compared to either nonclinical controls or anxious control participants, social phobics are more likely to attribute negative social events to stable personal characteristics (eg, "I am incompetent") and to assume that these negative outcomes will have disastrous long-term consequences (Stopa & Clark, 2000). These interpretations are important as they undoubtedly increase state anxiety and may lead to avoidance or safety-seeking behaviors. In turn, these behaviors and associated decreases in self-efficacy may increase the likelihood of negative social outcomes, thus perpetuating the cycle. Estimates of harm may also be mediated by perceptions of control over negative events (Barlow, 1991; Beck et al, 1985; Heimberg et al, 1989). For example, anxious individuals rate themselves as lower on measures of perceived control over threat, when compared to nonanxious individuals (Cloitre et al, 1992; Rapee et al, 1996). Experimental manipulations of control have also been found to impact levels of anxiety (Sanderson et al, 1989), and fears of social harm appear to be predicted by both the anticipated consequences of the threat and perceived control over threat (Rapee, 1997).

Reduced perceptions of control over events in social phobia may be related, at least in part, to accompanying difficulties with self-worth and self-criticism (Cox et al, 2000). Although self-criticism and internal, global, and stable attributions for negative events have been associated with depression, two studies suggest that these may be equally prominent in the cognitive style of socially phobic individuals (Cox et al, 2000; Heimberg et al, 1989). These studies also suggest that global disturbances in self-image are important in social phobia, and may extend beyond social situations (Clark & Wells, 1995). Moreover, self-criticism may serve as a vulnerability factor for comorbid depression in socially phobic individuals (Cox et al, 2000).

Social phobia has also been associated with elevated self-ratings on measures of self-consciousness (Bruch & Heimberg, 1994; Bruch et al, 1989; Hope & Heimberg, 1988), perfectionism (Juster et al, 1996; Lundh & Ost, 1997; Lundh & Ost, 1996; Saboonchi et al, 1999), and anxiety sensitivity (Maidenberg et al, 1996). Anxiety sensitivity refers to a fear of anxiety-related bodily sensations in which the sensations are interpreted as having potentially harmful consequences (eg, social, physical, or psychological consequences) (Muris, 2002). Most closely associated with panic, it has recently also been implicated in the pathogenesis of social phobia (Maidenberg et al, 1996). For example, social phobics tend to obtain highest scores on the Social Concerns subscale of the Anxiety Sensitivity Index, a widely accepted measure of anxiety sensitivity (Zinbarg et al, 1997), and to overestimate the visibility of their anxiety (Stopa & Clark, 1993). Many social phobics fear displaying visible anxiety symptoms (Safren et al, 1998), interpret these in a catastrophic fashion (Mulkens et al, 1999; Wells & Papageorgiou, 2001), and attribute these to negative causes such as intense anxiety, personal failure, or mental illness (Otto, 1999; Roth et al, 2001). In one study, providing patients with negative feedback about their physiological responses during a social encounter was associated with increased anxiety, negative beliefs, and self-focused attention (Wells & Papageorgiou, 2001).

Although these cognitive processes are thought to originate in childhood, only a handful of studies have examined the role of cognitive and social factors in childhood social phobia. Kendall has proposed that it is the absence of negative self-statements, rather than the presence of positive self statements, that differentiates anxious from nonanxious youth, a finding which he has termed, the "power of non-negative thinking" (Kendall & Chansky, 1991; Treadwell & Kendall, 1996). In all but one study (Beidel, 1991), clinical samples of anxious youth have been found to display higher levels of negative cognitions in threatening or ambiguous situations (Bogels & Zigterman, 2000; Chanksy & Kendall, 1997; Kendall & Chansky, 1991; Prins et al, 1994; Rabiner et al, 1993; Treadwell & Kendall, 1996). Similarly, among nonclinical samples of children, trait anxiety is strongly related to threatening interpretations of ambiguous stimuli (Chorpita et al, 1996). During interactions with peers, socially anxious children have been found to experience more negative expectancies than nonanxious children, to view social interactions as more threatening and competitive (Rabiner et al, 1993) and to report a higher frequency of cognitions about negative evaluation, failure, humiliation, and inadequacy (Beidel & Turner, 1998; Epkins, 1996). Similarly, shy boys report more public self-consciousness, and experience more negative and less positive thoughts than non-shy boys (Johnson & Glass, 1989). Compared to children who have either no diagnoses or disruptive behavior disorders, anxious children also report elevated anxiety sensitivity (Chorpita et al, 1996; Muris et al, 2001; Rabian et al, 1993). In an analysis of the revised Child Anxiety Sensitivity Index, the dimension of "fear of publicly observable anxiety reactions" was most strongly associated with symptoms of social anxiety (Muris, 2002).

Barrett et al (1996) examined the cognitive style of children with overanxious disorder, simple phobia, or social phobia on a task in which they were presented with an ambiguous situations having to do with potential physical or social threat. The responses of these anxious youth were compared to those of a group of children with oppositional defiant disorder and a group of nonclinical children. Anxious and oppositional children both tended to interpret ambiguous situations as more threatening than the nonclinical children. However, anxious children tended to choose avoidant solutions whereas the oppositional children chose more aggressive responses.

In one of the only studies of socially phobic youth, Spence and colleagues (1999) examined the interaction of social skills, social anxiety, and cognitive features in a group of 27 children with social phobia and a matched control group of 27 nonphobic children. Results suggested that socially anxious youth displayed a pattern of negative cognition in social evaluative situations, which resembled that previously reported in adults. They tended to anticipate negative outcomes in social situations and evaluated their own performance more negatively than their nonanxious counterparts (Spence et al, 1999). Interestingly, socially anxious youth also displayed poorer social behaviors, were less likely to have favorable outcomes in their social interactions, and were rated less highly on measures of social competence by several reporters. For example, they were less likely to select assertive responses, initiate social interactions, or participate in social interactions at school. Thus, their poor self-ratings were at least partially justified. However, even in situations where there were no observable performance deficits, socially anxious youth continued to rate themselves more negatively, suggesting that poor self-evaluations may generalize beyond situations where the children actually evince poorer performance. Supporting Kendall's assertion of "the power of non-negative thinking," there were no differences between groups in frequency of positive cognition (Spence et al, 1999).

If socially anxious children anticipate negative scrutiny and evaluation, they may seek evidence of this during social interactions, and behave accordingly (eg, avoid social interactions) (Chanksy & Kendall, 1997). Chansky and Kendall (1997) examined the expectancies of anxiety-disordered children in unfamiliar social situations and their perceptions of their social anxiety and adequacy. As hypothesized, anxious children rated themselves as more socially impaired than controls; they reported lower perceived social competence and higher social anxiety and expected to be disliked and rejected by unfamiliar peers. Negative self-perceptions were associated with negative expectancies of being liked and accepted by peers, suggesting a relationship between social anxiety and perceived social competence. Although parents and teachers of anxious children rated them as more socially anxious, shy, and less socially competent than control children, the two groups did not differ in the frequency of having a best friend. Moreover, negative social expectancies were unrelated to the ability to make friends or to the number of current friendships. However, having a best friend was associated with less social anxiety only for control children. It appeared that nonanxious children were able to generalize the experience of a positive social experience, whereas the negative social schemas of anxious children were not impacted by positive interactions. Although in this study, negative social expectancies were unrelated to poor peer status, for some children, negative peer status may occur if their negative expectancies and anxiety lead to ineffective social behavior.

Clearly, these findings suggest developmental continuity in the cognitions of socially phobic individuals. Across the entire age range, these individuals display biased attention to threat, schemas concerning the exaggerated likelihood and consequences of social failure, decreased perceptions of social efficacy and control, and hypersensitivity to physical symptoms of anxiety. It has been proposed that these cognitive biases may emerge over development from the interaction of temperamental and physiological predispositions, peer and family experiences, and normal developmental processes. From a developmental perspective, social anxiety disorder emerges in childhood during the period when active anticipation and elaboration of possible negative outcomes increase dramatically (Vasey, 1996; Vasey & Borkovec, 1992; Vasey et al, 1994; Vasey & MacLeod, 2001). Among normal children, worries increase significantly in children ages 8 and older, especially about behavioral competence, social evaluation, and psychological well-being. Cognitive distortions concerning the probability of harm, and one's control over preventing it, entail both the ability to anticipate future outcomes and the development of a concept of self. In this regard, significant changes in the child's self-understanding (Damon &

Hart, 1982) and anticipatory capabilities (Piaget & Inhelder, 1966) appear after about age 8, and may impact the development of schemas regarding harm. Anxiety-related phenomena such as worry require the simultaneous consideration of multiple outcomes and the elaboration of potential catastrophic outcomes in threatening situations (Vasey & Borkovec, 1992). These abilities have been shown to increase significantly during middle childhood and adolescence (Magnusson, 1985; Vasey et al, 1994). During middle childhood, children also display thinking that is more organized and less stimulus-bound than their younger-aged peers, and display an increased ability to take others' perspectives and to compare one's abilities with others, as well as concerns about social evaluation (Flavell, 1977). Given these important cognitive changes, this may be a period in development in which distorted schemas of social threat and efficacy become more salient, automatic, and stable.

Although the mere presence of these biases cannot lead to the conclusion that they are necessarily involved in the development or maintenance of social anxiety, the above-described findings clearly link information processing biases with concurrent anxious distress. The finding that these information processing biases are present at the youngest ages at which anxiety can be detected leads to the hypothesis that these biases may predate and serve as risk factors for anxiety, rather than reflect a consequence of prolonged illness exposure. Moreover, information processing biases such as attentional biases may moderate other risk factors such as temperament in the course of anxiety disorders (Lonigan & Phillips, 2001). Cognitive studies of at-risk youth, prior to their developing clinically-significant levels of anxiety, would be invaluable in determining the temporal sequence of these various aspects of anxiety. Moreover, observations of the course of information processing biases in these at-risk youth, and comparisons with normative samples, would enable the analysis of the multidirectional associations between genetic or temperamental vulnerabilities, cognitive styles, and environmental experiences in the expression of social anxiety.

Conditioning Experiences   Many socially phobic individuals report a specific embarrassing or humiliating experience associated with the onset of their disorder. In one study, Ost (1985) found that 58% of social phobics recalled a traumatic social experience near or at the onset of their symptoms. Similarly, Stemberger and colleagues (1995) found that 44% of social phobics reported a traumatic conditioning experience that started or exacerbated their symptoms. Furthermore, 56% of specific social phobics who feared one or several specific situations (eg, speaking in front of large groups, eating or writing in public, or using public restrooms) associated a traumatic conditioning experience with their disorder, compared with 40% of those with a generalized subtype. Social phobia may also be conditioned through repetitive or cumulative experiences, such as shame-inducing discipline by parents or extensive teasing by peers (Beidel & Turner, 1998). Social phobics most often recall their conditioning traumatic experiences as occurring during adolescence, a time where individuals commonly feel more socially awkward and vulnerable to embarrassment.

In addition to direct experience, indirect experience may also lead to conditioned fears. Individuals may acquire phobias by observing others reacting fearfully, or by simply hearing about other's experiences (Rachman, 1991). Ost reported that in a sample of 32 socially anxious individuals, 13-16% reported they developed their phobia by observing others undergoing traumatic social experiences, and 3% of the sample reported acquiring social phobia after hearing about another's traumatic experience (Ost, 1985; Ost & Hughdahl, 1981). Among children, modeling occurs most often when the child's model is of particular salience and importance, such as a parent. Therefore, socially phobic parents who consistently respond with fear to particular phobic stimuli may then "teach" their child to also avoid these stimuli.

It is important to consider that when evaluating evidence for social learning hypotheses, retrospective reports of a patient's attributed etiology may not be accurate. Recalled incidents may represent early manifestations of the disorder rather than causal events (Mattick et al, 1995), and, as discussed above, social phobics may have a memory bias for negative episodes. In addition, as discussed earlier, Kendler's twin study of phobias (1992) suggested that social learning mechanisms do not affect social phobia unless individuals learn from people outside their immediate family (so that the conditioning experience represents unshared vs. shared environmental variance). However, as discussed in the section on parenting and family environment, it can also be argued that influences within the family may be unshared as well if the experiences of these events or relationships with other families differ between siblings.

Even in cases where conditioning plays a role, factors other than the traumatic event itself contribute to the origin of social phobia. Stemberger and colleagues (1995) showed that 20% of controls without social phobia also reported traumatic social experiences. Therefore, conditioning experiences may result in social phobia only in those who have a vulnerability to develop the disorder (Mineka & Zinbarg, 1995). The temperamental factors and possible cognitive biases discussed above may be important factors that lead to this vulnerability.

Peer Influences

Among the types of life events or learning experiences that have been associated with the development of social phobia, peer relations in childhood have been proposed as significant contributors. Studies examining the impact of peer relationships on social phobia have examined the transactional relationships among peer neglect or rejection, developmental factors, social anxiety, social withdrawal, and social skills deficits. As we shall see then, as with parenting factors, hypothesized associations between social anxiety and peer relations are reciprocal, with social anxiety and its manifestations both contributing to neglectful or rejecting responses by peers and also influencing the child's response to these peer behaviors in directions that maintain or exacerbate the social anxiety.

By way of background, it is helpful to summarize developmental features of peer relations. The early school years are a period during which children develop social competencies that influence later social outcomes (Taylor, 1989). Establishing positive peer relationships and gaining acceptance into the peer group are important features of social relationships at this age, and are key for developing social feelings and a progressive understanding of social events (Taylor, 1989). Thus, children's social attributions are largely dependent on their peer experiences during development (Crick & Ladd, 1993). During middle childhood, self-awareness and self-consciousness become more salient, and shyness and withdrawal come to be recognized and considered problems by peers (Bukowski et al, 1993; Hymel et al, 1990). During this developmental period, children begin to attribute behavior to internal traits, and become increasingly aware of the transactional nature of relationships. This is also a time when peer teasing and stigmatization increase dramatically (Younger & Piccinin, 1989). As children enter adolescence, their interactions are characterized by peer conformity, high positive affect, and verbal reciprocity (Panella & Henggeler, 1986). During this time, peer relationships play an increasingly important role by influencing social skills, emotional functioning, and social understanding. In fact, peer relationships in adolescence are strongly related to concurrent and later psychological functioning (Panella & Henggeler, 1986).

Studies of the peer relationships of socially anxious children, of the symptoms shown by neglected or rejected children, and of the childhood histories reported by socially anxious adults all suggest associations between social anxiety and peer neglect or rejection. For example, shy adults report that their childhood histories were marked by negative social incidents, including episodes of being teased, picked on, or ridiculed. Although perhaps biased in their reporting, these adults report that these unpleasant peer experiences colored their attitudes towards social interactions (Ishiyama, 1984). Recent cross-sectional studies have also found that children and adolescents with social anxiety report or experience greater peer neglect and rejection (La Greca, 2001; LaGreca & Lopez, 1998; Strauss et al, 1988). For example, high socially anxious children perceived their social acceptance to be low and reported more negative interactions with peers (eg, being teased; having an enemy at school) than low-anxious children (Ginsburg, La Greca, & Silverman, 1998). Social impairments were especially pervasive in children with high levels of generalized social avoidance (Ginsburg et al, 1998). Similarly, very shy or withdrawn children were viewed by their peers as less approachable, less socially competent, and less socially desirable (Evans, 1993). Strauss et al (1986) found that in an elementary school sample, children identified by teachers as socially withdrawn received fewer positive peer nominations, and more negative nominations from their peers than children rated "outgoing" by teachers. They were also less preferred as playmates. Adolescents who described high levels of social anxiety reported feeling less accepted and supported by their classmates and less romantically attractive to others (La Greca & Lopez, 1998). Socially anxious adolescent girls with high levels of generalized social anxiety and distress reported having fewer best friends, and friendships that were lower in companionship, intimacy and emotional support. For adolescent boys, generalized social anxiety and avoidance were associated with less perceived support and competency in their close friendships (La Greca & Lopez, 1998). In addition, Vernberg and colleagues (1992) found that for adolescents who had recently moved to a new school, social anxiety was negatively associated with developing intimacy and companionship with new peers, and was positively correlated with peer exclusion and aggression.

There is evidence as well that peer rejection or victimization is linked with subsequent social anxiety and withdrawal. Active social rejection by peers tends to be stable over time, and has been associated with subsequent social adjustment difficulties, mental health problems, internalizing symptoms, social isolation, social evaluative concerns, and perceived social incompetence (Coie et al, 1992; DeRosier et al, 1994; Hymel et al, 1990; La Greca et al, 1988 ; La Greca & Lopez, 1998). A meta-analysis suggested that victims of peer victimization were more generally and socially anxious than non-victims, with a mean effect size of r=.25 (Hawker & Boulton, 2000). However, it was clear that the suffering of youth victimized by peers was not confined to the social domain, but extended also to feeling anxious, depressed, and lonely. Moreover, peer rejection has also been found to be associated with aggressive behaviors, academic dysfunction, and other problems (French, 1990). Therefore, although peer rejection and victimization is associated with social anxiety, the association is clearly not specific, either cross-sectionally or longitudinally (Woodward & Fergusson, 1999).

In many cases, the symptoms of social anxiety themselves may contribute to some of these difficulties with peers. Studies have found that children and adolescents with social phobia often experience greater social difficulty, including difficulty forming friendships (Panella & Henggeler, 1986; Rubin et al, 1990). Anxiety, depression, and loneliness may be associated with peer relationship difficulties such as submissiveness and withdrawal (Parkhurst & Asher, 1992; Strauss et al, 1988) and associations between these symptoms and peer victimization may be mediated by similar peer interaction difficulties (Boivin et al, 1995; Perry et al, 1988; Schwartz et al, 1993). For example, anxiety disordered children age 6 to 13-years were rated by parents and teachers as less assertive, more shy, and more withdrawn than children with other disorders (Strauss et al, 1989). Similarly, very shy or withdrawn children were found to participate less frequently in verbal interactions, and to be viewed by their peers as less socially competent (Evans, 1993). Approaching the issue from the other direction, adolescent youths nominated as submissive by their peers reported greater social anxiety, greater fear of negative evaluation and social inhibition, and rated themselves as higher on social avoidance and distress than students rated as dominant. The submissive group also obtained very low acceptance ratings by peers, were rated as most "easily pushed around," and received low nominations for the descriptors "sense of humor," "best leader," and "most cooperative." These results suggest that socially anxious adolescents have relationships characterized by submissiveness and nondominance behaviors. Moreover, they seem to be viewed by peers as targets of exclusion, ridicule, and aggression (Walters & Inderbitzen, 1998). However, the finding that socially anxious individuals display poorer social competency in general is somewhat controversial. Among adults, socially-phobic individuals have been observed to perform fewer cooperative and dominance behaviors during social interactions than normal controls (Walters & Inderbitzen, 1998). Although several studies have reported poorer social skills or competence among anxious youth (Alden & Wallace, 1995; La Greca et al, 1988; Panella & Henggeler, 1986; Rabiner et al, 1993), others have found no difference among socially anxious and nonanxious groups of children (Chanksy & Kendall, 1997). This may in part, depend on the severity of the anxiety, the level of social withdrawal, and the reporter (eg, parents versus self report). Nevertheless, a significant body of literature suggests that at least for some youth, social anxiety is associated with lower social competence.

Once neglect, rejection, or victimization occur, they in turn affect the targeted child's self-worth, social evaluative anxiety, and avoidance. Thus, in the meta-analytic study cited earlier, victims of peer rejection and victimization tended to display negative views of themselves socially, with a mean effect size for victimization and self-reported self-worth of r=.46. (Hawker & Boulton, 2000). Lower peer status has been associated with internal attributions for negative social outcomes, and external attributions for positive outcomes (Ames et al, 1977; Crick & Ladd, 1993). A history of peer rejection or teasing during the time when children are developing social attributions might lead, in the absence of disconfirming evidence, to self-blame for negative social interactions (Graham & Juvonen, 1998). In turn, self-blame and negative outcome might be associated with social withdrawal and passivity (Graham & Juvonen, 1998). Indeed, attributing social failures to internal and stable factors has been associated with increased loneliness in middle childhood (Renshaw & Brown, 1993). A study of children in 6th and 7th grade found that students who perceived themselves as victimized by peers had increased loneliness, social anxiety, and low self-worth. These symptoms were mediated by attributing peer difficulties to internal (characterlogical) deficiencies (Graham & Juvonen, 1998). Blaming one's character for these difficulties implies that the difficulties will be persistent and uncontrollable, which may lead to feelings of helplessness and expectations of continued victimization. In contrast, attributing peer victimization to one's behavior was not associated with adjustment difficulties (Graham

& Juvonen, 1998). Interestingly, self-reports of victimization were associated with internal consequences (eg, distress, social anxiety), whereas peer-reports of victimization were related to interpersonal consequences (eg, peer rejection) (Graham & Juvonen, 1998).

Moreover, as a result of aversive social experiences, socially anxious youth may develop avoidance as a coping strategy (Vernberg et al, 1992). The avoidance and negative coping responses that typically accompany social anxiety in youth has been well-documented (Beidel, 1991; Beidel & Randall, 1994), and these youth have been found to demonstrate increased social withdrawal, and less approach behaviors (Beidel, 1991). Clearly, social anxiety negatively impacts the development of companionship and intimacy in newly formed friendships in adolescence. General social avoidance and distress, rather than avoidance and distress in new social situations seems to be the aspect of social anxiety most associated with difficulty interacting with friends early in the school year, and with less frequent interactions with friends later in the year. Withdrawal and avoidance hinder friendship development, which in turn may enhance fears of negative evaluation and social avoidance in new situations because of early rejection experiences. General social avoidance and distress may be more vulnerable to shaping by negative peer influences, and more resistant to positive peer friendship experiences (Vernberg et al, 1992). Negative peer experiences may increase feelings of social anxiety and increase socially avoidant behaviors in children. As avoidance restricts the opportunity for positive peer interactions and decreases assertiveness, a circular pattern of poorer peer relationships and impairment may ensue. Over time, social avoidance and impairment may become more ingrained (Ginsburg et al, 1998; La Greca & Lopez, 1998; Vernberg et al, 1992).

Some studies have supported hypotheses about potential protective or mitigating factors affecting outcome of socially anxious children. For example, some studies have reported that having at least one friend is associated with more-positive outcomes (Crick & Ladd, 1993; Fordham & Stevenson-Hinde, 1999; Harter, 1985). For example, Fordham and Stevenson-Hynde (1999) observed that having at least one high-quality friendship by age 10 was associated with a greater sense of classmate support, decreased anxiety, and improved self-worth, even among shy, at-risk children (Fordham & Stevenson-Hinde, 1999). In addition, social skill at age 4 was found to improve the outcomes and buffer children identified as high in BI (Asendorpf, 1994). These studies suggests that at least for shy children, friendship may be key in buffering them from the impact of social isolation and withdrawal on mood and self-worth.

Despite these promising findings, little is known about the longitudinal peer outcomes of socially anxious youth. Although cross-sectional studies have identified that socially anxious youth are at-risk for peer relationship difficulties, rejection, and social isolation, the impact of these difficulties over time remains somewhat unclear. More work is also needed to tease out the degree to which peer-relationship difficulties add to a child's risk for social phobia. Equally importantly, the psychosocial factors that may contribute to the resiliency of at-risk youth also merit greater attention. Recently, several researchers have begun to report the outcomes of long-term follow-up studies of these children, examining both the normative changes in self-reports of social anxiety and peer difficulties, and the impact of social anxiety on the development and maintenance of peer-sociometric status (Morris, 2001). This line of research will no doubt clarify the developmental trajectories of peer relationships and inform the development and refinement of preventive interventions for at-risk youth.

From Risk to Prevention: Clinical Implications

As can be gleaned from our summary of the work to date, further research into vulnerability factors is needed in order to test the hypotheses put forward about risk factors for social anxiety disorder. Whereas the evidence of genetic factors is compelling, the relatively low heritability of social anxiety disorder suggests that multiple other factors are involved. Additionally, much more work will be needed to elucidate the specific genetic factors involved. The temperamental evidence is suggestive, but more work is needed to examine the specificity of the link between BI and social anxiety disorder. It would be especially helpful to conduct studies of offspring of parents with social anxiety disorder (generalized and discrete, early and late onset), and to compare rates of BI within these groups as well as with those of comparison parents with panic disorder, depression, and no anxiety or mood disorders. It would also be helpful to conduct twin and adoption studies that examined both BI and DSM-IV anxiety disorders and the degree to which their associations are accounted for by shared genetic factors. Studies of parenting factors, cognitive and conditioning factors, and peer influences are really at the hypothesis-generating level, and require much more study, most particularly in prospective longitudinal studies of children at high-risk (eg, offspring of social phobic adults, with and without BI). It might also be informative to attempt experimental (intervention) studies that targeted specific cognitive, peer-related, or parental risk factors by attempting to modify them in randomly assigned groups of children and observing whether these changes affected the maintenance or onset of the disorder.

At the same time, we also believe that it is not too early to begin working toward early or preventive interventions (Hirshfeld-Becker & Biederman, 2002). Children who carry familial risk for anxiety disorder and/or depression who are behaviorally inhibited appear already to have significantly elevated rates of social anxiety disorder as early as age 6 (over 20% in one study) (Biederman et al, 2001). Such children could most likely benefit from intervention to prevent worsening dysfunction. Ironically, because social anxiety disorder tends to run in families, the youngsters who may be at highest risk genetically and temperamentally are also more likely to grow up with parents who may be unskilled in helping them manage social anxiety. Even parents not afflicted themselves are often at a loss as to how to help children who, from infancy or toddlerhood on, show intense fear and distress when faced with unfamiliar peers or adults and struggle with the kinds of everyday social situations typical for young children (eg, birthday parties, crowded playgrounds, transitions to new classrooms). Parents may err on the side of being too accommodating, inadvertently reinforcing social avoidance. Alternatively, they may pressure a child too harshly to face feared situations, perhaps inadvertently increasing the child's shame or self-consciousness and sensitizing the child further.

Fortunately, promising general (Kendall et al, 1997; Kendall, 1994) and specific (Beidel et al, 2000) cognitive behavioral and psychopharmacological (Compton et al, 2001; Isaacs et al, 2001) treatments for social anxiety in children are being developed and researched. For example, an approach including skills training, individual and group in vivo exposure practice, and the inclusion of a peer component in which children practice social skills with non-anxious peers appears promising (Beidel et al, 2000). Studies have suggested that some of the same cognitive-behavioral methods (Kendall, 1994) used to treat childhood anxiety disorders may also show efficacy as preventive interventions during the school-age years (Dadds et al, 1999; Dadds et al, 1997). These results suggest that it may become possible to identify children at risk for social anxiety disorder and to offer interventions to help them manage social anxiety, reduce avoidance, and improve social skills, in order to prevent the debilitating effects of the disorder.

Recently, at least two groups have begun work on early interventions delivered to preschool or early school-age children at risk for social anxiety disorder because of having BI (Rapee, 2002), or at risk for anxiety disorders in general because of a profile of risk factors including parental psychopathology, BI, or anxiety disorders (Hirshfeld-Becker & Biederman, in press; Hirshfeld-Becker et al, 2002). The advantage to intervening early with children at risk is that one can reduce social anxiety before it begins adversely to affect academic and social functioning (Hirshfeld-Becker & Biederman, in press). Interventions with very young children necessarily incorporate strong parent components, teaching parents to help the child manage anxiety through presenting coping skills and facilitating gradual exposure to feared social situations. In this way, the parents may be helped to find a middle ground between allowing avoidance and pressuring the child to face the feared situation, perhaps by identifying mild-to-moderately stressful situations and having the child practice successive approximations to the desired goal, with much praise and reinforcement. While the full results of these studies have yet to be seen, they suggest directions for future efforts that may ultimately succeed in reducing the debilitating impact of social anxiety disorder.

References

Ainsworth MDS. Attachment: retrospect and prospect. In: *The Place of Attachment in Human Behavior.* Parkes, CM and Stevenson-Hinde, J. New York: Basic Books, Inc.; 1982,3-30.

Alden LE, Wallace ST. Social phobia and social appraisal in successful and unsuccessful social interactions. *Behav Res Ther.* 1995;33: 497-505.

Ames R, Ames C, Garrison W. Children's casual ascriptions for positive and negative interpersonal outcomes. *Psychol Rep.* 1977;41: 595-602.

Amir N, Foa EB, Coles ME. Automatic activation and strategic avoidance of threat-relevant information in social phobia. *J Abnorm Psychol.* 1998;107: 285-290.

Arcus, DM. The experiential modification of temperamental bias in inhibited and uninhibited children. Unpublished doctoral dissertation, Harvard University, 1991.

Arrindell W, Kwee M, Methorst G, Van der Ende J, Pol E, Moritz B. Perceived parental rearing styles of agoraphobic and socially phobic inpatients. *Br J Psychiatry.* 1989;155: 526-535.

Asendorpf J. The malleability of behavioral inhibition: a study of individual developmental functions. *Dev Psychol.* 1994;30: 912-919.

Asendorpf JB. Development of inhibition during childhood: evidence for situational specificity and a two-factor model. *Dev Psychol.* 1990;26: 721-730.

Barlow DH. The nature of anxiety: anxiety, depression and emotional disorders. In: *Chronic Anxiety: Generalized Anxiety Disorder and Mixed Anxiety-Depression.* Barlow, DH. New York, NY: Guilford Press; 1991, 1-28.

Barrett PM. Evaluation of cognitive-behavioral group treatments for childhood anxiety disorders. *J Clin Child Psychol.* 1998;27: 459-468.

Barrett PM, Rapee RM, Dadds MM, Ryan SM. Family enhancement of cognitive style in anxious and aggressive children. *J Abnorm Child Psychol.* 1996;24: 187-203.

Barrett PM, Rapee RM, Dadds MR. Family treatment of childhood anxiety: a controlled trial. *J Consult Clin Psychol.* 1996;64: 333-342.

Beck AT, Clark DA. An information processing model of anxiety: automatic and strategic processes. *Behav Res Ther.* 1997;35: 49-58.

Beck AT, Emery G, Greenberg RL. *Anxiety Disorders and Phobias: A Cognitive Perspective.* New York: Basic Books, Inc.; 1985.

Beidel D. Psychophysiological assessment of anxious emotional states in children. *J Abnorm Psychol.* 1988;97:80-82.

Beidel D. Social phobia and overanxious disorder in school-age children. *J Am Acad Child Adolesc Psychiatry.* 1991;30:545-552.

Beidel DC. Social phobia and overanxious disorder in school-age children. *J Am Acad Child Adolesc Psychiatry*. 1991;30: 545-552.

Beidel DC, Randall, J. Social Phobia. In: *International Handbook of Phobic and Anxiety Disorders in Children and Adolescents*. Yule, W. New York, NY: Plenum Press; 1994:111-129.

Beidel DC, Turner, SM. Shy children, phobic adults: nature treatment of social phobia. *ADAA Reporter*. 1998;9, 19-20.

Beidel DC, Turner SM, Dancu CV. Physiological, cognitive and behavioral aspects of social anxiety. *Behav Res Ther*. 1985;23: 109-117.

Beidel DC, Turner SM, Morris TL. Behavioral treatment of childhood social phobia. *J Consult Clin Psychol*. 2000;68:1072-1080.

Belsky J, Hsieh K-H, Crnic K. Mothering, fathering, and infant negativity as antecedents of boys' externalizing problems and inhibition at age 3 years: differential susceptibility to rearing experience? *Dev Psychopathol*. 1998;10:301-319.

Biederman J, Hirshfeld-Becker DR, Rosenbaum JF, Herot C, Friedman D, Snidman N, Kagan J, Faraone SV. Further evidence of association between behavioral inhibition and social anxiety in children. *Am J Psychiatry*. 2001;158:1673-1679.

Biederman J, Hirshfeld-Becker DR, Rosenbaum JF, Perenick SG, Wood J, Faraone SV. Lack of association between parental alcohol or drug addiction and behavioral inhibition in children. *Am J Psychiatry*. 2001;158:1731-1733.

Biederman J, Rosenbaum JF, Hirshfeld DR, Faraone, SV, Bolduc EA, Gersten M, Meminger SR, Kagan, J, Snidman, N, Reznick, JS. Psychiatric correlates of behavioral inhibition in young children of parents with and without psychiatric disorders. *Arch Gen Psychiatry*. 1990;47:21-26.

Blehar MC, Lieberman AF, Ainsworth, MDS. Early Face-to-Face Interaction and its relation to later infant-mother attachment. *Child Dev*. 1977;48:182-194.

Bögels SM, van Oosten A, Muris P, Smulders D. Familial correlates of social anxiety in children and adolescents. *Behav Res Ther.* 2001;39:273-287.

Bögels SM, Zigterman D. Dysfunctional cognitions in children with social phobia, separation anxiety disorder, and generalized anxiety disorder. *J Abnorm Child Psychol.* 2000;28:205-211.

Boivin M, Hymel S, Bukowski W. The roles of social withdrawal, peer rejection, and victimization by peers in predicting loneliness and depressed mood in childhood. *Dev Psychopathol.* 1995;7:685-765.

Broberg A, Lamb M, Hwang, P. Inhibition: its stability and correlates in sixteen- to forty-month-old children. *Child Dev.* 1990;61:1153-1163.

Bruch B, Heimberg R. Differences in perceptions of parental and personal characteristics between generalized and nongeneralized social phobics. *J Anxiety Disord.* 1994;155-168.

Bruch M. Familial and developmental antecedents of social phobia: sssues and findings. *Clin Psychol Rev.* 1989;9: 37-47.

Bruch MA, Heimberg RG, Berger P, Collins TM. Social phobia and perceptions of early parental and personal characteristics. *Anxiety Res.* 1989;2: 57-65.

Brunk MA, Henggeler SW. Child influences on adult controls: an experimental investigation. *Dev Psychol.* 1984;20:1074-1081.

Bukowski WM, Hoza B, Boivin M. Popularity, friendship, and emotional adjustment during early adolescence. *New Dir Child Dev.* 1993; Summer 60:23-37.

Butler G, Matthews A. Cognitive processes in anxiety. *Adv Behav Res Ther.* 1983;5:51-62.

Calkins S, Fox, N. The relations among infant temperament, security of attachment, and behavioral inhibition at twenty-four months. *Child Dev.* 1992;63:1456-1472.

Calkins SD, Fox NA, Marshall, TR. Behavioral and physiological antecedents of inhibited and uninhibited behavior. *Child Dev.* 1996;67:523-540.

Caspi A, Bem DJ, Elder GH. Continuities and consequences of interactional styles across the life course. *J Pers.* 1989;57:375-406.

Caspi A, Moffitt TE, Newman DL, Silva PA. Behavioral observations at age 3 years predict adult psychiatric disorders. *Arch Gen Psychiatry.* 1996;53:1033-1039.

Caspi A, Silva PA. Temperamental qualities at age 3 predict personality traits in young adulthood: longitudinal evidence from a birth cohort. *Child Dev.* 1995;66:486-498.

Caster JB, Inderbitzen HM, Hope D. Relationship between youth and parent perceptions of family environment and social anxiety. *J Anxiety Disord.* 1999;13:237-251.

Chanksy TE, Kendall PC. Social expectancies and self-perceptions in anxiety-disordered children. *J Anxiety Disord.* 1997;11:347-363.

Cherny SS, Fulker DW, Corley RP, Plomin R, DeFries JC. Continuity and change in infant shyness from 14 to 20 months. *Behav Genet.* 1994;24:365-79.

Chorpita B, Albano A, Barlow D. Cognitive processing in children: relation to anxiety and family influences. *J Clin Child Psychol.* 1996;25:170-176.

Chorpita B, Collica T, Litt S, Albano A, Barlow D. *Microsocial analysis of the influence of parent verbalizations on children's negative cognitive style and bias for threat.* Paper presented at the Association for the Advancement of Behavior Therapy, 29th Annual Convention, NY, 1996.

Chorpita BF, Albano AM, Barlow DH. Child anxiety sensitivity index: considerations for children with anxiety disorders. *J Clin Child Psychol.* 1996;25:77-82.

Chorpita BF, Barlow DH. The development of anxiety: the role of control in the early environment. *Psychol Bull.* 1998;124:3-21.

Clark D, Wells A. A cognitive model of social phobia. In: *Social Phobia: Diagnosis, Assessment, and Treatment.* Heimberg R, et al. New York: The Guilford Press; 1995:69-93.

Cloitre M, Cancienne J, Heimberg RG, Holt CS, Liebowitz M. Case histories and shorter communications: memory bias does not generalize across anxiety disorders. *Behav Res Ther.* 1995;33:305-307.

Cloitre M, Heimberg RG, Liebowitz MR, Gitow A. Perceptions of control in panic disorder and social phobia. *Cogn Ther Res.* 1992;16:569-577.

Cloninger C. A unified biosocial theory of personality and its role in the development of anxiety states. *Psychiatr Dev.* 1986;3:167-226.

Cloninger CR, Svrakic DM, Przybeck TR. A psychobiological model of temperament and character. *Arch Gen Psychiatry.* 1993;50:975-990.

Cloninger CR, Van Eerdewegh P, Goate A, Edenberg HJ, Blangero J, Hesselbrock V, Reich T, Nurnberger Jr. J, Schuckit M, Porjesz B, Crowe R, Rice JP, Foroud T, Przybeck TR, Almesy L, Bucholz K, Wu W, Shears S, Carr K, Crose C, Willig C, Zhao J, Tischfield J, Li TK, Conneally PM, et al. Anxiety proneness linked to epistatic loci in genome scan of human personality traits. *Am J Med Genetics (Neuropsychiatric Genetics).* 1998;81:313-317.

Cobham V, Dadd, M, Spence S. The pole of parental anxiety in the treatment of childhood anxiety. *J Cons Clin Psychol.* 1998;66:893-905.

Coie JD, Lochman JE, Terry R, Hyman, C. Predicting early adolescent disorder from childhood aggression and peer rejection. *J Consult Clin Psychol.* 1992;60:783-792.

Coles ME, Turk CL, Heimberg RG, Fresco DM. Effects of varying levels of anxiety within social situations: relationship to memory perspective and attributions in social phobia. *Behav Res Ther.* 2001;39:651-665.

Compton SN, Grant PJ, Chrisman AK, Gammon PJ, Brown VL, March JS. Sertraline in children and adolescents with social anxiety disorder: an open trial. *J Am Acad Child Adolesc Psychiatry.* 2001;40:564-567.

Cooper PJ, Eke M. Childhood shyness and maternal social phobia: A Community Study. *Br J Psychiatry.* 1999;174:439-443.

Cox BJ, Recto, NA, Bagby M, Swinson RP, Levitt AJ, Joffe RT. Is self-criticism unique for depression? A comparison with social phobia. *J Affect Disord.* 2000;57:223-228.

Crick NR, Ladd GW. Children's perceptions of their peer experiences: attributions, loneliness, social anxiety, and social avoidance. *Dev Psychol.* 1993;29:244-254.

Dadds MH, Holland DE, Laurens KR, Mullins M, Barrett PM and Spence, SH. Early intervention and prevention of anxiety disorders in children: results at 2-year follow-up. *J Consult Clin Psychol.* 1999;67:145-50.

Dadds MH, Spence SH, Holland DE, Barrett PM and Laurens KR. Early intervention and prevention of anxiety disorders: a controlled trial. *J Consult Clin Psychol.* 1997;65:627-635.

Dadds MR, Barrett PM, Rapee RM, Ryan S. Family process and child anxiety and aggression: an observational analysis. *J Abnorm Child Psychol.* 1996;24:715-734.

Damon W, Hart D. The development of self-understanding from infancy through adolescence. *Child Dev.* 1982;53:841-864.

Daniels D, Plomin R. Origins of individual differences in infant shyness. *Dev Psychol.* 1985;21:118-121.

Davidson R. Asymmetric brain function, affective style, and psychopathology: the role of early experience and plasticity. *Dev Psychol.* 1994;6:741-758.

Davidson R. *Cerebral asymmetry and affective style: Developmental and individual differences*. Paper presented at the 43rd Annual Meeting of the American Academy of Child and Adolescent Psychiatry, Philadelphia, PA, 1996.

DeRosier ME, Kupersmidt JB, Patterson CJ. Children's academic and behavioral adjustment as a function of the chronicity and proximity of peer rejection. *Child Dev*. 1994;65:1799-1813.

DiLalla LF, Kagan J, Reznick JS. Genetic etiology of behavioral inhibition among 2-year-old children. *Infant Behav Dev*. 1994;17:405-412.

Dreessen L, Arntz A, Hendriks T, Keune N, van den Hout M. Avoidant personality disorder and implicit schema-congruent information processing bias: a pilot study with a pragmatic inference task. *Behav Res Ther*. 1999;37:619-632.

Ebstein RP, Novick O, Umansky R, Priel B, Osher Y, Blaine D, Bennett ER, Nemanov L, Katz M, Belmaker, RH. Dopamine D4 receptor (D4dr) exon Iii polymorphism associated with the human personality trait of novelty Seeking. *Nat Genet*. 1996;12:78-80.

Emde RN, Plomin R, Robinson J, Corley R, DeFries J, Fulker DW, Reznick JS, Campos J, Kagan J, Zahn-Waxler C. Temperament, emotion, and cognition at fourteen months: the Macarthur longitudinal twin study. *Child Dev*. 1992;63:1437-1455.

Epkins CC. Cognitive specificity and affective confounding in social anxiety and dysphoria in children. *J Psychopathol Behav Assess*. 1996;18: 83-101.

Essau CA, Conradt J, Petermann F. Frequency and comorbidity of social phobia and social fears in adolescents. *Behav Res Ther*. 1999;37:831-843.

Evans MA. Communicative competence as a dimension of shyness. In: Rubin KH, Asendorpf JB, (Eds). *Social Withdrawal, Inhibition, and Shyness in Childhood*. Hillsdale, NJ: Lawrence Erlbaum; 1993:189-212.

Fehm L, Margraf J. Thought suppression: specificity in agoraphobia versus broad impairment in social phobia? *Behav Res Ther*. 2002;40:57-66.

Finnie V, Russell, A. Preschool children's social status and their mother's behavior and knowledge in the supervisory role. *Dev Psychol.* 1988;24:789-801.

Flavell JH. *Cognitive Development.* Englewood Cliffs, NJ: Prentice-Hall; 1977.

Foa EB, Gilboa-Schechtman E, Amir N, Freshman M. Memory bias in generalized social phobia: remembering negative emotional expressions. *J Anxiety Disord.* 2000;14:501-519.

Fordham K, Stevenson-Hinde, J Shyness, friendship quality, and adjustment during middle childhood. *J Child Psychol Psychiatry.* 1999;40:757-768.

Franke P, Leboyer M, Gansicke M, Weiffenbach O, Biancalana V, Cornillet-Lefebre P, Croquette MF, Froster U, Schwab SG, Poustka F, Hautzinger M, Maier, W. Genotype-phenotype relationship in female carriers of the premutation and full mutation of fmr-1. *Psychiatry Res.* 1998;80:113-127.

French DC. Heterogeneity of peer-rejected girls. *Child Dev.* 1990:61.

Fyer A, Mannuzza S, Chapma, T, Liebowitz M, Klein, D. A direct interview family study of social phobia. *Arch Gen Psychiatry.* 1993;50:286-293.

Fyer A, Manuzza, S Chapman T, Lipsitz J, Martin, L, Klein, D. Panic disorder and social phobia: effects of comorbidity on familial transmission. *Anxiety.* 1996;2:173-178.

Fyer AJ, Mannuzza S, Chapman TF, Martin LY, Kelin DF. Specificity in familial aggregation of phobic disorders. *Arch Gen Psychiatry.* 1995;52:564-573.

Garcia-Coll C, Kagan J, Reznick JS. Behavioral inhibition in young children. *Child Dev.* 1984;55:1005-1019.

Gelernter J, Kranzler H, Coccaro EF, Siever LJ, New AS. Serotonin transporter protein gene polymorphism and personality measures in african American and European-American subjects. *Am J Psychiatry.* 1998;155:1332-8.

Gersten M. Behavioral inhibition in the classroom. In: *Perspectives on Behavioral Inhibition*. Resnick, J. Chicago: University of Chicago Press; 1989:71-91.

Gest SD. Behavioral inhibition: stability and associations with adaptation from childhood to early adulthood. *J Pers Soc Psychol*. 1997;72:467-475.

Ginsburg GS, La Greca AM, Silverman WK. Social anxiety in children with anxiety disorders: relation with social and emotional functioning. *J Abnorm Child Psychol*. 1998;26:175-185.

Goldsmith HH, Lemery KS. Linking temperamental fearfulness and anxiety symptoms: a behavior-genetic perspective. *Biol Psychiatry*. 2000; 48(12):1199-1209.

Graham S, Juvonen, J. Self-blame and peer victimization in middle school: an attributional analysis. *Dev Psychol*. 1998;34:587-599.

Gratacos M, Nadal M, Martin-Santos R, Pujana MA, Gago J, Peral B, Armengol L, Ponsa I, Miro R, Bulbena A, Estivill X. A polymorphic genomic duplication on human chromosome 15 is a susceptibility factor for panic and phobic disorders. *Cell*. 2001;106:367-79.

Gray J. *The Neuropsychology of Anxiety: An Enquiry into the Functions of the Septohippocampal System*. Oxford: Clarendon Press;1982.

Gray JA. Neural systems, emotion and personality. In: *Neurobiology of Learning, Emotion, and Affect*. Madden IV, J. New York: Raven Press, Ltd; 1991.

Gray JA, McNaughton, N. The neuropsychiatry of anxiety: reprise. *Nebr Symp Motiv*. 1996;43:61-134.

Hackmann A, Clark DM, McManus F. Recurrent images and early memories in social phobia. *Behav Res Ther*. 2000;38:601-610.

Hackmann A, Surawy C, Clark DM. Seeing yourself through others' eyes: a study of spontaneously occurring images in docial phobia. *Behav Cogn Psychother*. 1998;26:3-12.

Harter S. Manual for the self-perception profile for children. Denver, CO: University of Denver; 1985.

Hawker DSJ, Boulton MJ. Twenty years' research on peer victimization and psychosocial maladjustment: a meta-analytic review of cross-sectional studies. *J Child Psychol Psychiatry.* 2000;441-455.

Hayward C, Killen J, Kraemer K, Taylor C. Linking self-reported childhood behavioral inhibition to adolescent social phobia. *J Am Acad Child Adolesc Psychiatry.* 1998;37.

Heimberg R, Hope D, Dodge C. DSM-III-R subtypes of social phobia: comparison of generalized phobics and public speaking phobics. *J Nerv Mental Dis.* 1990;178:172-179.

Heimberg RG, Klosko JS, Dodge CS, Shadick R, Becker RE, Barlow DH. Anxiety disorders, depression, and attributional style: a further test of the specificity of depressive attributions. *Cogn Ther Res.* 1989; 13.

Henderson AS, Korten AE, Jorm AF, Jacomb PA, Christensen H, Rodgers B, Tan X, Easteal S. Comt and drd3 polymorphisms, environmental exposures, and personality traits related to common mental disorders. *Am J Med Genet.* 2000;96:102-107.

Herbst JH, Zonderman AB, McCrae RR, Costa PT Jr. Do the dimensions of the temperament and character inventory map a simple genetic architecture? Evidence from molecular genetics and factor analysis. *Am J Psychiatry.* 2000;157:1285-90.

Hill, SJ, Lowers, L, Locke, J, Snidman, N, Kagan J. Behavioral inhibition in children from families at high risk for developing alcoholism. *J Am Acad Child Adolesc Psychiatry.* 1999;38:410-420.

Hirshfeld DR, Biederman J, Brody L, Faraone SV, Rosenbaum JF. Expressed emotion toward children with and without behavioral inhibition: associations with maternal anxiety disorders. *J Am Acad Child Adolesc Psychiatry.* 1997;36:910-7.

Hirshfeld DR, Rosenbaum JF, Biederman J, Bolduc EA, Faraone SV, Snidman N, Reznick JS, Kagan J. Stable behavioral inhibition and its association with anxiety disorder. *J Am Acad Child Adolesc Psychiatry*. 1992;31:103-111.

Hirshfeld-Becker DR, Biederman J. Rationale and principles for early intervention with young children at risk for anxiety disorders. *Clin Child Fam Psychol Rev*. 2002;5:161-172.

Hofmann S, Gerlach A, Wender A, Roth W. Speech disturbances and gaze behavior during public speaking in subtypes of social phobia. *J Anxiety Disord*. 1997;11:573-585.

Hofmann SG. Self-focused attention before and after treatment of social phobia. *Behav Res Ther*. 2000;38:717-725.

Hope D, Rapee R, Heimberg R. Representations of self in social phobia: vulnerability to social threat. *Cogn Ther Res*. 1990;14:177-189.

Hope DA, Gansler DA, Heimberg RG. Attentional focus and causal attributions in social phobia: implications from social psychology. *Clin Psychol Rev*. 1989;9:49-60.

Hope DA, Heimberg RG. Public and private self-consciousness and social phobia. *J Pers Assess*. 1988;4:185-195.

Hope DA, Heimberg RG, Klein JF. Social anxiety and the recall of interpersonal information. *J Cogn Psychother*. 1990;4:185-195.

Horwath E, Wolk SI, Goldstein RB, Wickramaratne P, Sobin C, Adams P, Lish JD and Weissman MM. Is the comorbidity between social phobia and panic disorder due to familial cotransmission or other factors? *Arch Gen Psychiatry*. 1995;52:574-582.

Hummel RM, Gross AM. Socially anxious children: An observational study of parent-child interaction. *Child and Family Behavior Therapy*. 2001;23:19-41.

Hymel S, Rubin K, Rowden L, LeMare L. Children's peer relationships: longitudinal prediction of internalizing and externalizing problems from middle to late childhood. *Child Dev.* 1990;61:2004-2021.

Ishiyama F. Shyness: Anxious social sensitivity and self-isolating tendency. *Adolescence.* 1984;19:903-911.

Johnson RL, Glass CR. Hetersocial anxiety and direction of attention in high school boys. *Cogn Ther Res.* 1989;13:509-526.

Jorm AF, Henderson AS, Jacomb PA, Christensen H, Korten AE, Rodgers B, Tan X, Easteal S. An association study of a functional polymorphism of the serotonin transporter gene with personality and psychiatric symptoms. *Mol Psychiatry.* 1998;3(5):449-451.

Jorm AF, Prior M, Sanson A, Smart D, Zhang Y, Easteal S. Association of a functional polymorphism of the serotonin gene with anxiety-related temperament and behavior problems in children: a longitudinal study from infancy to the mid-teens. *Mol Psychiatry.* 2000;5:542-547.

Juster HR, Frost RO, Heimberg RG, Holt CS, Mattia JI, Faccenda K. Social phobia and perfectionism. *Pers Indiv Diff.* 1996;20:725-731.

Kagan J. Temperamental contributions to social behavior. *Am Psychol.* 1989; 44: 668-674.

Kagan J. Galen's Prophecy: Temperament in human nature. New York: BasicBooks; 1994:

Kagan J, Reznick JS, Clarke C, Snidman N, Garcia-Coll C. Behavioral inhibition to the unfamiliar. *Child Dev.* 1984;55:2212-2225.

Kagan J, Reznick JS, Snidman N. Biological bases of childhood shyness. *Science.* 1988;240:167-171.

Kagan J, Reznick JS, Snidman N, Gibbons J, Johnson MO. Childhood derivatives of inhibition and lack of inhibition to the unfamiliar. *Child Dev.* 1988;59:1580-1589.

Kagan J, Snidman N, Zetner M, Peterson E. Infant yemperament and snxious symptoms in school age children. *Dev Psychopathol.* 1999;11:209-224.

Katsuragi S, Kunugi H, Sano A, Tsutsumi T, Isogawa K, Nanko S, Akiyoshi J. Association between serotonin transporter gene polymorphism and anxiety- related traits. *Biol Psychiatry.* 1999;45:368-70.

Kendall P, Chansky T. Considering cognition in anxiety-disordered children. *J Anxiety Disord.* 1991;5:167-185.

Kendall P, Flannery-Schroeder E, Panichelli-Mindel S, Southam-Gerow M, Henin A, Warman M. Therapy for youths with anxiety disorders: a second randomized trial. *J Cons Clin Psychol.* 1997;65:366-380.

Kendall, PC. Treating anxiety disorders in children: results of a randomized clinical trial. *J. Consult. Clin Psychol.* 1994;62:100-110.

Kendler K, Neale M, Kessler R, Heath A, Eaves, L. The genetic epidemiology of phobias in women: the interrelationship of agoraphobia, social phobia, situational phobia, and simple phobia. *Arch General Psychiatry.* 1992;49:273-281.

Kendler K, Walters E, Neal, M, Kessler R, Heath A, Eaves L. The structure of the genetic and environmental risk factors for six major psychiatric disorders in women. *Arch Gen Psychiatry.* 1995;52:374-383.

Kendler KS, Karkowski LM, Prescott, CA. Fears and phobias: reliability and heritability. *Psychol Med.* 1999;29:539-553.

Kendler KS, Myers J, Prescott, CA. The etiology of phobias: an evaluation of the stress-diathesis model. *Arch Gen Psychiatry.* 2002;59:242-8.

Kendler KS, Myers J, Prescott CA, Neale, MC. The genetic epidemiology of irrational fears and phobias in men. *Arch Gen Psychiatry.* 2001;58:257-65.

Kennedy J, Neves-Pereira M, King N, Lizak M, Basile V, Chartier M, Stein M. Dopamine system genes not linked to social phobia. *Psychiatr Genet.* 2001;11:213-217.

Kerr M, Lambert WW, Stattin H, Klackenberg-Larsson I. Stability of inhibition in a dwedish longitudinal sample. *Child Dev.* 1994;65:138-146.

Kessler RC, McGonagle KA, Zhao S, Nelson CB, Hughes M, Eshleman S, Wittchen H, Kendler KS. Lifetime and 12-month prevalence of DSM-III-R psychiatric disorders in the united states. *Arch Gen Psychiatry.* 1994;51:8-19.

Kim SW, Hoover KM. Tridimensional personality questionnaire: assessment in patients with social phobia and a control group. *Psychol Rep.* 1996;78:43-9.

Kochanska G. Patterns of inhibition to the unfamiliar in children of normal and affectively ill mothers. *Child Dev.* 1991;62:250-263.

Kochanska G, Radke-Yarrow M. Inhibition in toddlerhood and the dynamics of the child's interaction with an unfamiliar peer at age five. *Child Dev.* 1992;63:325-335.

Krohne H. Parental child rearing and anxiety development. In: *Health Hazards in Adolescence: Prevention & Intervention in Childhood & Adolescence.* Hurrelmann, K and Losel, F. New York: DeGruyter; 1990, 115-130.

Krohne H. Developmental conditions of anxiety and coping: a two-process model of child-rearing effects. In: *Advances in Test Anxiety Research,* Vol. 7. Hagtvet K and Johnsen T. 7. Amsterdam: Swets & Zeitlinger; 1992, 143-155.

La Greca AM. Friends or foes? Peer influences on anxiety among children and adolescents. In: *Anxiety Disorders in Childen and Adolescents: Research, Assessment, and Intervention.* Cambridge Child and Adolescent Psychiatry. Silverman, WK and Treffers, PDA. New York, NY: Cambrdige University Press; 2001;159-186.

La Greca AM, Dandes SK, Wick P, Shaw Kea. Development of the social anxiety scale for children: reliability and concurrent validity. *J Clin Child Psychol.* 1988;17:84-91.

La Greca AM, Lopez N. Social anxiety among adolescents: linkages with peer relations and friendships. *J Abnorm Child Psychol.* 1998;26:83-94.

LaFreniere PJ, Sroufe LA. Profiles of peer competence in the preschool: interrelations between measures, influence of social ecology, and relation to attachment history. *Dev Psychol*. 1985;21:56-69.

Lerner RM, Lerner JV. Children in their contexts: a goodness-of-fit model. In: parenting across the lifespan. Lancaster J, Altman J, Possi A & Sherri L (Eds). New York: Aldive de Gruyter; 1987;377-403.

Lesch K-P, Bengel D, Heils A, Sabol S, Greenberg B, Petri S, Benjamin J, Muller C, Hamer D, Murphy D. Association of anxiety-related traits with a polymorphism in the serotonin transporter gene regulatory region. *Science*. 1996;274:1527-1531.

Lewin MR, McNeil DW, Lipson JM. Enduring without avoiding: pauses and verbal dysfluencies in public speaking. *J Psychopathol Behav Assess*. 1996;18:387-402.

Lieb R, Wittchen, HU, Hofler, M, Fuetsch, M, Stein, MB and Merikangas, KR. Parental psychopathology, parenting styles, and the risk of social phobia in offspring: a prospective-longitudinal community study. *Arch Gen Psychiatry*. 2000;57:859-866.

Lonigan CJ, Phillips BM. Temperamental influences on the development of anxiety disorders. In: *The Developmental Psychopathology of Anxiety*. Vasey MW, Dadds MR. NY: Oxford University Press; 2001;61-91.

Lundh LG, Ost LG. Explicit and implicit memory bias in social phobia: The Role of Subdiagnostic Type. *Behav Res Ther*. 1997;35: 05-317.

Lundh LG, Ost LG. Stroop interference, self-focus, and perfectionism in social phobics. *Pers Indiv Diff*. 1996;20:725-731.

Lundh LG, Ost LG. Memory bias for critical faces in social phobics. *Behav Res Ther*. 1996;34:787-794.

Magnusson D. Situational factors in research in stress and anxiety: sex and age differences. In: *Stress and Anxiety*. Defares PB. (Ed.) Washington, DC: Hemisphere; 1985, 69-78.

Maidenberg E, Chen E, Craske M, Bohn P, Bystritsky A. Specificity of Attentional Bias in Panic Disorder and Social Phobia. *J Anxiety Disord*. 1996;10:529-541.

Manassis K, Bradley S, Goldberg S, Hood J, Swinson R. Attachment in Mothers with Anxiety Disorders and Their Children. *J Am Acad Child Adolesc Psychiatry*. 1994;33:1106-1113.

Mancini C, van Ameringen M, Szatmari P, Fugere C, Boyle M. A high-risk pilot study of the children of adults with social phobia. *J Am Acad Child Adolesc Psychiatry*. 1996;35:1511-1517.

Mannuzza S, Schneier FR, Chapman TF, Liebowitz MR, Klein DF, Fyer AJ. Generalized social phobia: reliability and validity. *Arch Gen Psychiatry*. 1995;52: 230-237.

Martin M, Horder P, Jones GV. Integral bias in naming of phobia-related words. *Cogn Emotion*. 1992;6:483-490.

Masia C, Morris T. Parental factors associated with social anxiety: methodological limitations and suggestions for integrated behavioral research. *Clin Psychol Sci Prac*. 1998;5:211-228.

Matheny AP. Children's behavioral inhibition over age and across situations: genetic similarity for a trait during change. *J Pers*. 1989;57:215-235.

Mathew S, Coplan J, Gorman J. Neurobiological mechanisms of social anxiety disorder. *Am J Psychiatry*. 2001;158:1558-1567.

Mattia J, Heimberg R, Hope D. The revised stroop color-naming task in social phobics. *Behav Res Ther*. 1993;31:305-313.

Mattick RP, Page AC, Lampe L. Cognitive and behavioral aspects. In: *Social Phobia: Clinical and Research Perspectives*. Stein MB, (Ed.) Washington, DC: American Psychiatric Press, Inc.; 1995;189-229.

Mazzanti CM, Lappalainen J, Long JC, Bengel D, Naukkarinen H, Eggert M, Virkkunen M, Linnoila M, Goldman, D. Role of the serotonin transporter promoter polymorphism in anxiety-related traits. *Arch Gen Psychiatry.* 1998;55:936-40.

McNally RJ. Cognitive bias in the anxiety disorders. *Nebr Symp Mot.* 1996;43:211-250.

McNeil DW, Ries BJ, Taylor LJ, Boone ML, et al. Comparison of social phobia subtypes using Stroop tests. *J Anxiety Disord.* 1995;9:47-57.

Mellings TMB, Alden LE. Cognitive processes in social anxiety: the effects of self-focus, rumination, and anticipatory processing. *Behav Res Ther.* 2000;38:243-257.

Merikangas K, Angst J. Comorbidity and social phobia: evidence from clinical, epidemiologic, and genetic studies. *Eur Arch Psychiatry Clin Neurosci.* 1995;244:297-303.

Mick M, Telch M. Social anxiety and history of behavioral inhibition in young adults. *J Anxiety Disord.* 1998;12:1-20.

Mineka S, Zinbarg R. Conditioning and ethological models of social phobia. In: Social Phobia: Diagnosis, Assessment, and Treatment. Heimberg R, Liebowitz M, Hope D, Schneier F (Eds). New York: The Guilford Press; 1995, 134-162.

Mogg K, Bradley BP, Bono JD, Painter M. Time course of attentional bias for threat information in non-clinical anxiety. *Behav Res Ther.* 1997;35:297-303.

Moradi AR, Taghavi MR, Neshat-Doost HT, Yule W. Performance of children and adolescents with PTSD on the Streep colour-naming task. *Psychol Med.* 1999;29:415-419.

Morris TL. Social Phobia. In: *The Developmental Psychopathology of Anxiety.* Vasey, MW and Dadds, MR (Eds). New York: Oxford University Press; 2001, 435-458.

Mowrer O. Learning Theory and Behavior. New York: Wiley; 1960.

Mulkens S, deJong PJ, Dobbelaar A, Bogels SM. Fear of blushing: fearful preoccupation irrespective of facial coloration. *Behav Res Ther.* 1999;37:1119-1128.

Mullen M, Snidman N, Kagan J. Free-play behavior in inhibited and uninhibited children. *Infant Behav Dev.* 1993;16:383-389.

Muris P. An expanded childhood anxiety sensitivity index: Its factor structure, reliability, and validity in a non-clinical adolescent sample. *Behav Res Ther.* 2002;40:299-311.

Muris P, Merckelbach H, Damsma E. Threat perception bias in nonreferred, socially anxious children. *J Clin Child Psychol.* 2000;29:348-359.

Muris P, Merckelbach H, Wessel I, van de Ven M. Psychopathological correlates of self-reported behavioural inhibition in normal children. *Behav Res Ther.* 1999;37:575-84.

Muris P, Schmidt N, Merckelbach H, Schouten, E. Anxiety sensitivity in adolescents: Factor structure and its relationship to trait anxiety and symptoms of anxiety disorders and depression. *Behav Res Ther.* 2001;39:89-100.

Neale M, Fulker D. A bivariate path analysis of fear data on twins and their parents. *Acta Genet Med Gemellol.* 1984;33:265-271.

Nelson EC, Grant J, Bucholz K, Madden PAF, Glowinski A, Reich W, Heath AC. Social phobia in a population-based female adolescent twin sample: Co-morbidity and associated suicide-related symptoms. *Psychol Med.* 2000;30:797-804.

Ost L. Ways of acquiring phobias and outcome of behavioral treatments. *Behav Res Ther.* 1985;23:683-689.

Ost L, Hughdahl K. Acquisition of phobias and anxiety response patterns in clinic patients. *Behav Res Ther.* 1981;16:439-447.

Otto MW. Cognitive behavioral therapy for social anxiety disorder: model, methods, and outcome. *J Clin Psychiatry*. Supplement: New Frontiers in the Management of Social Anxiety Disorder: Diagnosis, Treatment, and Clinical Course. 1999;60:14-19.

Panella D, Henggeler SW. Peer interactions of conduct-disordered, anxious-withdrawn, and well-adjusted black adolescents. *J Abnorm Child Psychol*. 1986;14:1-11.

Parker G. Reported parental characteristics of agoraphobics and social phobics. *Br J Psychiatry*. 1979;135:555-560.

Parker G. Parental overprotection: a risk factor in psychosocial development. New York: Grune and Stratton, Inc.; 1983.

Parkhurst J, Asher, S. Peer rejection in middle school: subgroup differences in behavior, loneliness, and interpersonal concerns. *Dev Psychol*. 1992;28:231-241.

Perry D, Kusel S, Perry L. Victims of peer aggression. *Dev Psychol*. 1988;28:231-241.

Phillips K, Fulker D, Rose R. Path analysis of seven fear factors in adult twin and sibling pairs and their parents. *Genet Epidemiol*. 1987;4:345-355.

Piaget J, Inhelder B. The early growth of logic in the child. New York, NY: Harper & Row; 1966:

Plomin R, Daniels D. Genetics and shyness. In: *Shyness: Perspectives on Research and Treatment*. Jones W, et al. New York, NY: Plenum; 1986.

Plomin R, Emde R, Braungart J, Campos J, Corley R, Fulker D, Kagan J, Reznick J, Robinson J, Zahn-Waxler C, DeFries, J. Genetic change and continuity from fourteen to twenty months: the macarthur longitudinal twin study. *Child Dev*. 1993;64:1354-1376.

Prins PJM, Groot MJM, Hanewald, GJ. Cognition in test-anxious children: the role of on task and coping cognition reconsidered. *J Consult Clin Psychol* 1994;62:404-409.

Rabian B, Peterson RA, Richters J, Jensen, PS. Anxiety sensitivity among anxious children. *J Clin Child Psychol.* 1993;22:441-446.

Rabiner DL, Keane SP, MacKinnon-Lewis C. Children's beliefs about familiar and unfamiliar peers in relation to their socioeconomic status. *Dev Psychol.* 1993;29:236-243.

Rachman S. Neo-conditioning and the classical theory of fear acquisition. *Clin Psychol Rev.* 1991;11:155-173.

Rachman S, Gruter-Andrew J, Shafran R. Post-event processing in social anxiety. *Behav Res Ther.* 2000;38:611-617.

Rapee RM. Interventions for at-risk 4 year-olds: changing temperament. Paper presented at the ADAA Satellite Conference on "Learning and Unlearning Fears: Preparedness, Neural Pathways and Patients." Austin, Texas (2002).

Rapee RM. Perceived threat and perceived control as predictors of the degree of fear in physical and social situations. *J Anxiety Disord.* 1997;11:455-461.

Rapee RM. Potential role of childrearing practices in the development of anxiety and depression. *Clin Psychol Rev.* 1997;17:47-67.

Rapee RM, Craske M, Barlow DH. Measurement of perceived control over anxiety-related events. *Behav Ther.* 1996;27:279-293.

Rapee RM, Heimberg RG. A cognitive-behavioral model of anxiety in social phobia. *Behav Res Ther.* 1997;35:741-756.

Rapee RM, McCallum SL, Melville LF, Ravenscroft H, Rodney JM. Memory bias in social phobia. *Behav Res Ther.* 1994;32:89-99.

Reich J, Yates W. Family history of psychiatric disorders in social phobia. *Compr Psychiatry.* 1988;29:72-75.

Renshaw P, Brown P. Loneliness in middle childhood: concurrent and longitudinal predictors. *Child Dev.* 1993;64.

Research-Unit-on-Pediatric-Psychopharmacology-Anxiety-Study-Group. Fluvoxamine for the treatment of anxiety disorders in children and adolescents. *N Engl J Med.* 2001;344:1279-1284.

Reznick JS, Hegeman IM, Kaufman E, Woods SW, Jacobs M. Retrospective and concurrent self-feport of behavioral inhibition and their relation to adult mental health. *Dev Psychopathol.* 1992;4:301-321.

Reznick JS, Kagan J, Snidman N, Gersten M, Baak K, Rosenberg A. Inhibited and uninhibited behavior: a follow-up study. *Child Dev.* 1986;57:660-680.

Richter MA, Summerfeldt LJ, Joffe RT, Swinson RP. The tridimensional personality questionnaire in obsessive-compulsive disorder. *Psychiatry Res.* 1996;65:185-8.

Robinson JL, Kagan J, Reznick JS, Corley R. The heritability of inhibited and uninhibited behavior: a twin study. *Dev Psychol.* 1992;28:1030-1037.

Rose RJ, Ditto WB. A developmental-genetic analysis of common fears from early adolescence to early adulthood. *Child Dev.* 1983;54:361-368.

Rosenbaum JF, Biederman J, Gersten M, Hirshfeld DR, Meminger SR, Herman JB, Kagan J, Reznick JS, Snidman N. Behavioral inhibition in children of parents with panic disorder and agoraphobia: a controlled study. *Arch Gen Psychiatry.* 1988;45:463-470.

Rosenbaum JF, Biederman J, Hirshfeld DR, Faraone SV, Bolduc EA, Kagan J, Snidman N, Reznick JS. Further evidence of an association between behavioral inhibition and anxiety disorders: results from a family study of children from a non-clinical sample. *J Psychiat Res.* 1991;25:49-65.

Rosenbaum JF, Biederman J, Hirshfeld-Becker DR, Kagan J, Snidman N, Friedman D, Nineberg A, Gallery DJ, Faraone SV. A controlled study of behavioral inhibition in children of parents with panic disorder and depression. *Am J Psychiatry.* 2000;157:2002-2010.

Roth DA, Antony MM, Swinson RP. Interpretations for anxietysymptoms in social phobia. *Behav Res Ther.* 2001;39:129-138.

Rowe D, Stever C, Gard J, Cleveland H, Sanders M, Abramowitz A, Kozol S, Mohr J, Sherman S, Waldman I. The relation of the dopamine transporter gene (Dat1) to symptoms of internalizing disorders in children. *Behav Genet.* 1998;28:215-225.

Rubin K, LeMare L, Lollis, S. Social withdrawl in childhood: developmental pathways to peer rejection. In: Peer Rejection in Childhood. Coie, JD. New York, NY: Cambridge University Press; 1990, 217-249.

Saboonchi F, Lundh LG, Ost LG. Perfectionism and self-consciousness in social phobia and panic disorder with agoraphobia. *Behav Res Ther.* 1999;37:799-808.

Safren SA, Heimberg RG, Turk CL. Factor structure of the social phobia scale and the social interaction anxiety scale. *Behav Res Ther.* 1998;36:443-453. Sameroff A. Transactional models in early social relations. *Hum Dev.* 1975;18:65-79.

Sanderson WC, Rapee RM, Barlow DH. The influence of perceived control on panic attacks induced via inhalation of 5.5% CO_2-Enriched Air. *Arch Gen Psychiatry.* 1989;46:157-162.

Scarpa A, Raine A, Venables P, Mednick S. The stability of inhibited/uninhibited temperament from Ages 3 to 11 years in mauritian children. *J Abnorm Child Psychol.* 1995;23:607-618.

Schmidt LA, Fox NA, Rubin KH, Sternberg EM, Gold PW, Smith CC, Schulkin J. Behavioral and neuroendocrine responses in shy children. *Dev Psychobiol.* 1997;30:127-140.

Schmidt LA, Fox NA, Schulkin J, Gold, PW. Behavioral and psychophysiological correlates of self-presentation in temperamentally shy children. *Dev Psychobiol.* 1999;35:119-135.

Schmidt NB, Lerew DR, Jackson RJ. The role of anxiety sensitivity in the pathogenesis of panic: prospective evaluation of spontaneous panic attacks during acute stress. *J Abnorm Psychol.* 1997;106:355-364.

Schmidt NB, Lerew DR, Jackson RJ. Prospective evaluation of anxiety sensitivity in the pathogenesis of panic: replication and extension. *J Abnorm Psychol.* 1999;108:532-537.

Schwartz C, Snidman N, Kagan, J. Adolescent social anxiety as an outcome of inhibited temperament in childhood. *J Am Acad Child Adolesc Psychiatry.* 1999; 8:1008-1015.

Schwartz D, Dodge C, Coie JD. The emergence of chronic victimization in boys' peer groups. *Child Dev.* 1993;64:1755-1772.

Skre I, Onstad S, Torgersen S, Philos DR, Lygren S, Kringlen E. The heritability of common phobic fear: a twin study of a clinical sample. *J Anxiety Disord.* 2000;14:549-62.

Smoller JW, Acierno Jr. JS, Rosenbaum JF, Biederman J, Pollack MH, Memimger S, Pava JA, Chadwick LH, White C, Bulzacchelli M, Slaugenhaupt SA. Targeted genome screen of panic disorder and anxiety disorder proneness using homology to murine qtl region. *Am J Med Genetics (Neuropsychiatric Genetics).* 2001;105:195-206.

Smoller JW, Rosenbaum JF, Biederman J, Susswein LS, Kennedy J, Kagan J, Snidman N, Laird N, Tsuang MT, Faraone SV, Schwarz A, Slaugenhaupt SA. Genetic association analysis of behavioral inhibition using candidate loci from mouse models. *Am J Med Genetics (Neuropsychiatric Genetics).* 2001;105:226-235.

Smoller JW, Tsuang MT. Panic and phobic anxiety: defining phenotypes for genetic studies. *Am J Psychiatry.* 1998;155:1152-1162.

Spence SH, Donovan C, Brechman-Toussaint M. Social skills, social outcomes, and cognitive features of childhood social phobia. *J Abnorm Psychol.* 1999;108:211-221.

Spence SH, Rapee R, McDonald C, Ingram, M. The structure of anxiety symptoms among preschoolers. *Behav Res Ther.* 2001;39:1293-1316.

Starcevic V, Uhlenhuth EH, Fallon S, Pathak, D. Personality dimensions in panic disorder and generalized anxiety disorder. *J Affect Dis.* 1996;37:75-79.

Stein M, Chartier M, Hazen A, Kozak M, Tancer M, Lander S, Furer P, Chubaty D, Walker J. A direct-interview family study of generalized social phobia. *Am J Psychiatry*. 1998;155:90-97.

Stein MB, Chartier MJ, Kozak MV, King N, Kennedy, JL. Genetic linkage to the serotonin transporter protein and 5ht2a receptor genes excluded in generalized social phobia. *Psychiatry Res*. 1998;81:283-291.

Stein MB, Chartier MJ, Lizak MV, Jang KL. Familial aggregation of anxiety-related quantitative traits in generalized social phobia: clues to understanding "disorder" heritability? *Am J Med Genetics (Neuropsychiatric Genetics)*. 2001;105:79-83.

Stein MB, Jang KL, Livesley WJ. Heritability of social anxiety-related concerns and personality characteristics: a twin study. *J Nerv Ment Dis*. 2002;190:219-24.

Stemberger R, Turner S, Beidel D, Calhoun K. Social phobia: an analysis of possible developmental factors. *J Abnormal Psychol*. 1995;104:526-531.

Stevenson-Hinde J, Shouldice A. 4.5 to 7 years: fearful behaviour, fears and worries. *J Child Psychol Psychiatry*. 1995;36:1027-1038.

Stopa L, Clark D. Cognitive processes in social phobia. *Behav Res Ther*. 1993;31:255-367.

Stopa L, Clark DM. Cognitive processes in social phobia. *Behav Res Ther*. 1993;31:255-267.

Stopa L, Clark DM. Social phobia and the interpretation of social events. *Behav Res Ther*. 2000;38:273-283.

Strauss CC, Forehand R, Smith K, Frame CL. The association between social withdrawal and internalizing problems of children. *J Abnorm Child Psychol*. 1986;14:525-535.

Strauss CC, Lahey BB, Frick P, Frame CL, Hynd GW. Peer social status of children with anxiety disorders. *J Consult Clin Psychol*. 1988;56:137-141.

Strauss CC, Lahey BB, Frick P, Frame CL, Hynd GW. Peer social status of children with anxiety disorders. *J Consult Clin Psychol*. 1988;56:137-141.

Strauss CC, Lease C, Kazdin AE, Dulcan M, Last, C. Multimethod assessment of the social competence of children with anxiety disorders. *J Clin Child Psychol*. 1989;18:184-189.

Taghavi MR, Neshat-Doost HT, Moradi AR, Yule W, Dalgleish, T. Biases in visual attention in children and adolescents with clinical anxiety and mixed anxiety-depression. *J Abnorm Child Psychol*. 1999.

Taylor AR. Predictors of peer rejection in early elementary grades: roles of problem behavior, academic achievement, and teacher preference. *J Clin Child Psychol*. 1989;18:360-365.

Tillfors M, Furmark T, Ekselius L, Fredrikson, M. Social phobia and avoidant personality disorder as related to parental history of social anxiety: a general population study. *Behav Res Ther*. 2001;39:289-98.

Torgersen S. The nature and origin of common phobic fears. *Br J Psychiatry*. 1979;134:343-351.

Treadwell KR, Kendall PC. Self-talk in youth with anxiety disorders: states of mind, content specificity, and treatment outcome. *J Consult Clin Psychol*. 1996;64:941-950.

Troy M, Sroufe LA. Victimization among preschoolers: tole of attachment relationship history. *J Am Acad Child Adol Psychiatry*. 1987;26:166-172.

van Ameringen M, Mancini C, Oakman, J. The relationship of behavioral inhibition and shyness to anxiety disorder. *J Nerv Mental Dis*. 1998;186:425-431.

Vasey MW. Anxiety-related attentional biases in childhood. *Behav Change*. 1996;13:199-206.

Vasey MW, Borkovec TD. A catastrophizing assessment of worrisome thoughts. *Cogn Ther Res*. 1992;16:505-520.

Vasey M, Crnic KA, Carter WG. Worry in childhood: a developmental perspective. *Cogn Ther Res*. 1994;18:529-549.

Vasey MW, El-Hag N, Daleiden, EL. Anxiety and the processing of emotionally-threatening stimuli: distinctive patterns of selective attention among high- and low-test anxious children. *Child Dev*. 1996;67:1173-1185.

Vasey MW, MacLeod, C. Information-processing factors in childhood anxiety: a review and developmental perspective. In: *The Developmental Psychopathology of Anxiety*. Vasey MW, Dadds MR. New York: Oxford University Press; 2001, 253-277.

Vernberg EM, Abwender DA, Ewell KK, Beery, SH. Social anxiety and peer relationships in early adolescence: a prospective analysis. *J Clin Child Psychol*. 1992;21:189-196.

Walters KS, Inderbitzen HM. Social anxiety and peer relations among adolescents: testing a psychobiological model. *J Anxiety Disord*. 1998;12:183-198.

Warren S, Huston L, Egeland B, Sroufe L. Child and adolescent anxiety disorders and early attachment. *J Am Acad Child Adolesc Psychiatry*. 1997;36:637-644.

Warren SL, Schmitz S, Emde RN. Behavioral genetic analysis of self-reported anxiety at 7 years of age. *J Am Acad Child Adolesc Psychiatry*. 1999;38:1403-1408.

Wells A, Clark DM, Ahmad S. How do I look with my mind's eye: perspective taking in social phobic imagery. *Behav Res Ther*. 1998;36:631-634.

Wells A, Papageorgiou C. The observer perspective: biased imagery in social phobia, agoraphobia, and blood/injury phobia. *Behav Res Ther*. 1999;37:653-658.

Wells A, Papageorgiou C. Social phobic interoception: effects of bodily information on anxiety, beliefs, and self-processing. *Behav Res Ther*. 2001;39:1-11.

Wittchen HU, Stein MB, Kessler RC. Social fears and social phobia in a community sample of adolescents and young adults: prevalence, risk factors and co-morbidity. *Psychol Med.* 1999;29:309-323.

Woodward LJ, Fergusson DM. Childhood peer relationship problems and psychosocial adjustment in late adolescence. *J Abnorm Child Psychol.* 1999;27:87-104.

Woody SR, Chambless DL, Glass CR. Self-focused attention in the treatment of social phobia. *Behav Res Ther.* 1997;35:117-129.

Younger AJ, Piccinin AM. Children's recall of aggressive and withdrawn behaviors: recognition memory and likability judgments. *Child Dev.* 1989;60:580-590.

Zinbarg RE, Barlow DH, Brown T. The hierarchical structure and general factor saturation of the anxiety sensitivity index: evidence and implication. *Psychol Assess.* 1997;9:277-284.

Chapter 3
Quality of Life In Social Anxiety Disorder

Jitender Sareen, M.D., Murray B. Stein, M.D.

Introduction

Social Anxiety Disorder (SAD), also called Social Phobia, is an anxiety disorder that is characterized by an extreme fear and/or avoidance of situations that involve possible scrutiny by others. Although previously SAD was considered a "neglected anxiety disorder," this condition has been extensively studied over the last decade because of its high prevalence rates and significant comorbidity with other psychiatric disorders (Sareen and Stein 2000).

Considerable uncertainty has existed as to whether SAD should be considered a "serious" mental disorder per se from a public health perspective (Wittchen et al, 2000). This chapter will review the findings that have demonstrated that people with SAD have significant functional impairment and poor quality of life. To this end, we will 1) describe the concept of Quality of Life, 2) describe methods of measuring quality of life, 3) list common measures of quality of life, 4) review the clinical and epidemiologic studies investigating quality of life issues in people with SAD, and 5) review the impact of treatment on quality of life in SAD patients. What will become clear through reading this chapter is that individuals with SAD suffer tremendously due to their illness.

Quality of Life Concept

The concept of "Quality of Life" (QOL) has become very important in understanding human suffering related to medical conditions (Mendlowicz and Stein, 2000). QOL was first developed in the social sciences and applied in medical practice to determine if cancer treatments could not only increase the survival time of patients, but also improve their sense of well-being. Since then, measuring Quality of Life has become an important component of clinical investigation and patient care. QOL has been measured to distinguish different patients or groups of patients, to predict patient outcomes, and to evaluate therapeutic interventions (Gill and Geinstein, 1994).

According to Patrick and Erickson (1993), life has two dimensions: quantity and quality. Quantity of life can simply be measured in terms of mortality rates or life expectancy. However, measuring quality of life requires a more complex evaluation (Patrick and Erickson, 1993). Although there has been a proliferation of instruments to measure quality of life, there has been a lack of clarity or consistency about the meaning and measurement of quality of life (Gill and Geinstein, 1994). Most experts agree that the concept of quality of life should be centered on the individual's subjective perception of the quality of his or her own life (Mendlowicz and Stein, 2000) . There is also a general consensus in the literature that quality of life is best approached as a multidimensional construct. Aaronson and colleagues suggested that the assessment of quality of life should comprise at least four domains: 1) physical functional status, 2) disease- and treatment-related physical symptoms, 3) psychological functioning, and 4) social functioning. Additional domains may be useful to increase the breadth of coverage (Aaronson et al, 1988).

Measuring Quality of Life

There are three general methods of measuring quality of life: 1) General QOL measures that assess QOL without reference to specific impact of illness or symptoms 2) Health-Related QOL measures that assess the impact of illness on various life dimensions, and 3) Objective measures such as work, social functioning and living conditions (Mogotsi et al, 2000).

Objective QOL indicators are a crucial supplement to the subjective criteria in measuring QOL (Mogotsi et al, 2000). Variables included in objective QOL measures often overlap with measures of disability and functional impairment, such as income, work productivity, and social functioning. Education level, marital status and living situation have been used as objective measures of social functioning. With respect to work productivity, a common measure of functional impairment is the number of days of work missed due to illness. Such objective measures are simpler to measure and provide important information regarding an individual's QOL and functioning.

Health Related QOL instruments could be non-specific to a particular disorder (eg, Short Form-36) or specific to a particular disease (eg, Leibowitz Self-Rated Disability Scale for Social Anxiety Disorder) (Ware, Jr. and Sherbourne 1992; Schneier et al, 1994). The latter instrument aims to measure the specific impact of symptoms or illness on various life dimensions. This allows for a closer assessment of the individual's perception of how the illness directly affects his or her life.

An important caveat in studying QOL issues in mental disorders is to understand that dysfunction in social or occupational functioning is part of the definition of the disorder. Unlike physical illnesses, mental disorders do not as yet have biological markers that define the illness. For example, a person is defined as having cancer on the basis of a tissue sample, or diagnosed with diabetes on the basis of serum glucose measurements. However, to make a diagnosis of a DSM-IV mental disorder such as Social Anxiety Disorder, the individual by definition has to have social fears that cause impairment in social or occupational functioning. Thus, when studies report that people with DSM-IV social phobia have greater impairment in functioning related to social fears compared to healthy controls, this is a circular argument. Despite these limitations,

Figure 1

Measuring Quality of Life

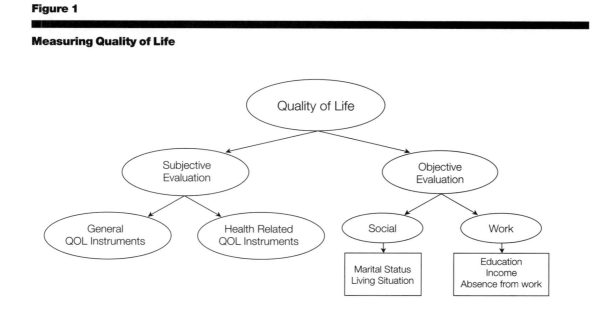

disease-specific QOL instruments are advantageous because the subject directly assesses the effect of the illness on his/her QOL. Also, such QOL instruments allow for comparison between different illnesses with respect to their impact on various life domains.

Quality of Life Instruments

Numerous Quality of Life instruments have been developed for studying patients with psychiatric and medical conditions (Gill and Geinstein, 1994). This section will describe some of the more commonly used, validated instruments available for use in studies and research. Few studies have directly compared QOL instruments. Weissman et al (2001) conducted one recent study to understand how three different QOL instruments would correlate with each other. Although there were significant correlations between the three QOL instruments (Medical Outcomes Short-Form 36, Social Adjustment Scale – Self-Report, and the Social Adaptation Self-Evaluation Scale), they concluded that the researcher or clinician would have to consider the specific items of the QOL instrument to carefully select the particular instrument that is most suitable for their work (Weissman et al, 2001). Also, they suggested that using multiple QOL instruments might provide a more comprehensive assessment compared to using only one.

In this section of the chapter, we will describe some of the more commonly used instruments in studying patients with mental disorders. We will highlight the important aspects of each of these instruments.

General (Non-Health Related)
The Quality of Life Inventory is based on a model of life satisfaction that assumes that an individual's overall life satisfaction consists of the sum of satisfaction in 17 areas of life deemed important. It is a brief self-report instrument that has been shown to be reliable in three non-clinical groups (alpha coefficients ranged from 0.77-0.89). This scale has demonstrated validity in that it has positive correlations with subjective well-being and the Satisfaction with Life Scale (Diener et al, 1985). It has also demonstrated negative correlations with the Beck Depression inventory (Beck et al, 1979) and the Symptom Checklist-90 item scale (Derogatis, 1983).

The Wisconsin Quality of Life Index (W-QLI) is a multidimensional non-health related QOL instrument (Diamond and Becker, 1999). This instrument assumes that QOL is comprised of nine dimensions: life satisfaction, occupational activities, psychological well-being, physical health, social relations, economics, activities of daily living, symptoms, and the patient's own goals. The W-QLI takes into account different perspectives of the patient, the patient's family, and the clinician. Rather than assume that each QOL dimension is equally important, the W-QLI allows both patients and staff to preference-weight the dimensions to get a relative ranking. The advantage of this scale is that it is multidimensional. However, it also leads to an issue of significant time being required to collect this data.

Health Related Quality of Life Instruments

Generic Health Related Quality of Life Instruments

The Medical Outcomes Study 36-item Short-Form Health Survey (SF-36) is a self-report instrument that measures health status, functioning, and well-being (McHorney et al, 1994; McHorney et al, 1993; Stewart et al, 1988). It takes approximately five minutes to administer. The time period covered by most items is four weeks. Eight health concepts are assessed: 1) physical functioning and limitations in physical activities because of health problems; 2) social functioning and limitations in social activities because of physical or emotional problems; 3) limitations in usual role activities because of physical health problems; 4) bodily pain; 5) mental health, psychological distress and well-being; 6) limitations in usual role activities because of emotional problems; 7) vitality, energy, and fatigue; and 8) perceptions of one's general health.

The reliability of the SF-36 is high, with alpha coefficients ranging from 0.68-0.96. Principal components analysis has identified two dimensions: 1) physical health and 2) mental health (Ware, Jr. et al, 1998). Scores on this scale can differentiate types and levels of medical and psychiatric conditions. The SF-36 has been validated in several clinical and normal populations (Homan et al, 2000) and also has validated translations for several other languages (Ware, Jr. et al, 1998; Bullinger et al, 1998).

The SF-36 often phrases questions in a way that requires a subject to rate the current disability compared with a prior normal level of functioning. Since many people with SAD never attain a normal level of functioning in certain domains (eg, interpersonal relationships), they may be unable to rate some SF-36 items meaningfully (Schneier et al, 1994).

The Illness Intrusiveness Rating Scale (IIRS) measures the concept of lifestyle disruptions, attributable to an illness and/or its treatment, that interfere with continued involvement in valued activities and interests (Devins,

1994). The IIRS examines 13 domains of functioning, each of which may be specifically affected by an illness or its treatment. The ratings are made along a 7-point Likert scale, ranging from one (not very much interference) to seven (very much interference). The reliability of the IIRS is high, with alpha coefficients ranging from 0.80-0.95. The 9-month test-retest correlations ranged from 0.80-0.85 in several groups of patients with chronic diseases. Devins and colleagues have administered the IIRS to a variety of chronically ill populations (multiple sclerosis (Devins et al, 1996), end-stage renal disease (Devins et al, 1984; Devins et al, 1990) neck cancer (Devins et al, 1994), insomnia (Devins et al, 1993)). In mental health populations, it has been used to study euthymic patients with bipolar affective disorder (Robb et al, 1997), panic disorder, obsessive compulsive disorder and SAD (Antony et al, 1998).

The Sheehan Disability Scale (SDS) includes three self-rated items regarding family, work and social impairment resulting from emotional symptoms (Sheehan 1983; Leon et al, 1992). The reliability of the SDS was measured in untreated and treated patients with panic disorder. The alpha coefficients for the SDS range from 0.56-0.86. A one-factor model was sufficient to account for the covariance structure among scale items. The SDS has been found to be capable of discriminating between subjects who had panic attacks during the past two weeks and those who had not. The SDS also demonstrated sensitivity to change in treated and untreated patients with panic disorder. The major advantage of this scale is that it is not time consuming to administer. However, due to the fact that it only covers three domains of QOL, it does not provide much information.

The Social Adjustment Scale – Self Report (SAS-SR) is also a self-report instrument that requires approximately 15-20 minutes to complete (Weissman and Bothwell 1976; Weissman et al, 1978). It contains 42 questions covering role performance in six areas of role functioning: work, social/leisure activities, relationships with extended family, roles as spouse, parent and member of family unit. This SAS-SR has an alpha internal consistency coefficient of 0.74 and a test-retest correlation of 0.80. It has demonstrated the capacity to differentiate between responses of community residents from patients with schizophrenia, depression, and alcoholism. It has shown statistically significant correlations with ratings for depression (Hamilton Depression Rating scale: 0.36-0.72), and for general psychopathology (Symptom Checklist 90:0.59-0.84) (Derogatis, 1983).

The Quality of Life Enjoyment and Satisfaction Questionnaire (QLES-Q) is a self-report instrument conceived as an outcome measure (Endicott et al, 1993). It contains 93 items measuring the degree of enjoyment and satisfaction experienced by subjects in eight areas of daily functioning. The alpha coefficients for this scale range from 0.90-0.96. The test-retest correlations range from 0.73-0.82. The summary scores on this scale correlate with the Clinical Global Impression severity of illness (-0.34 to -0.68) and the Hamilton Depression Rating Scale (-0.29 to -0.72).

The Social Adaptation Self-Evaluation Scale is a 21-item self-rating scale developed to detect presumed treatment differences in social motivation and behavior that may not be discernible in psychiatric assessment (Bosc et al, 1997). The scale was validated in a large general population survey, and its external and internal validity, test-retest reliability, and sensitivity to change have been described (Bosc et al, 1997). The time period of assessment is current. The first two items (interest in one's occupation and one's home-related activities) are mutually exclusive for scoring purposes. A total of 20 items are summed for a possible score from 0 to 60. Higher scores indicate higher functioning.

The Quality of Well-Being questionnaire is a preference-weighted measure that obtains observable levels of functioning at a point in time (usually the previous 6 days) from three separate scales: 1) mobility, 2) physical activity, and 3) social activity (Kaplan et al, 1998). These scales contain a variety of items. The QWB also requires the subject to identify his/her most undesirable symptom or problem from a list of 27 items. Then, the observed level of function and the subjective symptomatic complaint are weighted by preference, or utility for the state to determine a point in–time expression of well-being. The score of the QWB ranges from 0 (for dead) to 1.0 (for optimum function).

The QWB has been used in clinical and population studies (Kaplan et al, 1998). It has been used in clinical trials and studies to evaluate therapeutic interventions. The validity and reliability of the QWB have been demonstrated in a variety of samples. One of the constraints of using the QWB is that it must be administered by a trained interviewer. Recently, Kaplan et al have developed a Quality of Well-Being Self-Administered (QWB-SA) form that can be completed within 10-15 minutes. The QWB-SA has demonstrated validity and reliability in a sample of older adults (Kaplan et al, 1997) (Andresen et al, 1998).

Although there are no specific questions related to mental health in the QWB, empirical evidence has supported the use of the QWB in studying mentally ill individuals (Patterson et al, 1997; Pyne et al, 1997a; Pyne et al, 1997b; Patterson et al, 1996). This scale has not been used to study people with Social Anxiety Disorder.

Recently, Kaplan et al reviewed the similarities and differences between the SF-36 and the QWB (Kaplan et al, 1998). Compared to the SF-36, the QWB provides less information on health profiles. Ceiling effects are a common problem for some SF-36 subscales, whereas perfect scores on the QWB are rare. The QWB has a normal distribution for the population of adults and provides a metric that can be used for cost-utility and cost-effectiveness. Kaplan et al conclude that the SF-36 and the QWB provide alternate comprehensive measures of health outcomes (Kaplan et al, 1998).

Lastly, the General Well-Being (GWB) Schedule is a brief but broad–ranging indicator of subjective feelings of psychological well-being and distress for use in community surveys (McDowell and Newell, 1987). It covers seven domains: 1) energy, 2) state of morale, 3) control over emotions, 4) interest in life, 5) perceived stress, 6) perceived health status, and 7) satisfaction about relationships. This instrument has been validated in many samples and has demonstrated high levels of internal consistency (McDowell and Newell, 1987). It has also demonstrated validity with significant correlations with self-reported and interviewer ratings of depression. The GWB was used in the Mental Health Supplement to the Ontario Health Survey (Stein and Kean, 2000). Cronbach's alpha coefficient for this scale in this sample was 0.85.

Health-Related Quality of Life Instruments for Social Anxiety Disorder
The Disability Profile is a clinician-rated instrument with items assessing current (ie, over the past 2 weeks) and most severe life impairment due to Social Anxiety Disorder (Schneier et al, 1994). This instrument covers eight domains: school, work, family, marriage/dating, friendships, other interests, activities of daily living, and suicidal behavior. The internal reliability of this instrument is high, with alpha coefficients of current rating as 0.87 and lifetime rating as 0.90. However, the establishment of test-retest and inter-rater reliability have not been reported. Scores on this scale were significantly higher for patients with SAD than for normal comparison subjects on all items except current suicidal behavior and current school functioning.

The Leibowitz Self-Rated Disability Scale (LSRDS) is a self-rated instrument with 11 items assessing current (past 2 weeks) and most severe lifetime impairment due to Social Anxiety Disorder (Schneier et al, 1994). The domains are the same as the Disability Profile with additional items for alcohol abuse, drug abuse and mood dysregulation. The alpha coefficients for the LSRDS were 0.92 for current and lifetime ratings. The scores on this scale were significantly higher for the patients with SAD than with a comparison group of controls. Similar to the Disability Profile, this scale requires further validation for test-retest reliability.

Quality of Life in Social Anxiety Disorder

Clinical Studies of QOL in SAD

A number of studies in clinical samples have investigated the impact of SAD on quality of life. Schneier and colleagues compared 32 patients diagnosed with DSM-III-R social phobia to 14 healthy controls using a self-rated (Liebowitz Self-Rated Disability Scale) scale and a clinician rated (Disability Profile) scale (Schneier et al, 1994). Patients were excluded from the study if they had a current diagnosis of depression or if their principal diagnosis was not social phobia. On each scale, more than half of all patients reported at least moderate impairment in areas of school/education, work/employment, family relationships/social network, and other interests. The social phobics were more likely to demonstrate at least moderate impairment in activities of daily living, and suicidal thoughts or behavior. On the LSRDS, the majority of people with social phobia reported at least moderate impairment in self-regulation of alcohol use.

Safren et al reported data on 44 subjects seeking treatment at a University based anxiety clinic (Safren et al, 1997). All carried a principal diagnosis of social phobia. Comorbidity with bipolar, psychotic disorder, or active substance use within 3 months of entering the study were exclusion criteria. Persons with social phobia reported overall lower life satisfaction ratings on the Quality of Life Inventory (QOLI) compared to a normative sample. This study also demonstrated that QOL was inversely related to severity of social phobia.

Antony et al studied patients referred to a University based anxiety disorders clinic (Antony et al, 1998). They compared patients with Social Phobia (n=49) to Obsessive Compulsive Disorder (n=51), and Panic Disorder with or without agoraphobia (n=35), on the Illness Intrusiveness Rating Scale (IIRS). Patients with a current diagnosis of substance use disorder, psychotic disorder, or bipolar disorder were excluded from the analysis.

The three groups did not differ significantly with respect to the total scores on the IIRS. However, patients with SAD reported more impairment with respect to social relationships and self-expression/self-improvement compared to the other two anxiety disorder groups. Interestingly, patients with anxiety disorders had greater mean scores on the IIRS compared to previously reported mean IIRS scores on other chronic illnesses (euthymic Bipolar Disorder, end stage renal disease, insomnia, laryngeal cancer, multiple sclerosis, rheumatoid arthritis) (Antony et al, 1998).

To avoid help-seeking bias, Wittchen et al recruited subjects from newspaper advertisements (Wittchen and Beloch 1996; Wittchen et al, 2000). They compared generic quality of life, work productivity, and various other disorder-specific social impairments in current cases with pure (n=65), comorbid (n=51), and subthreshold (n=34) DSM-IV social phobia and controls with no social phobia. The controls had a history of herpes infection. All three of the social phobia groups had reduced scores on the SF-36 compared to the control group. The subscales of vitality, general health, mental health, role limitations due to emotional health, and social functioning were particularly affected by having any social phobia diagnosis. To measure disease specific impairments, the Leibowitz Self-Rated Disability Scale was also administered. Subjects with SAD reported dysfunction in most areas of their lives, especially education, career, and romantic relationships. The presence of past or current comorbid conditions increased the frequency and severity of disease-specific impairments. Subthreshold social phobia revealed slightly lower overall impairments than comorbid social phobics (Wittchen et al, 2000).

Wittchen et al also used the Work Productivity and Impairment Questionnaire (WPAI) of Reilly et al to quantify the effect of general health and symptom severity on work productivity (Reilly, 1993; Wittchen et al, 2000). Using this latter instrument, Wittchen et al, demonstrated that the pure and comorbid social phobics were significantly less productive at work than the controls and subthreshold social phobics. Interestingly, unemployment rates for all three social phobia groups were much higher than the controls. The highest rate of unemployment, 21.6%, was seen in the comorbid social phobia group. The pure social phobia group and subthreshold social phobia had similar unemployment rates of 10.8% and 11.8%, respectively. The control group only had an unemployment rate of 3.1%.

Stein et al studied Social Anxiety Disorder in the Primary care setting (Stein et al, 1999b). They compared people with SAD to those without mental illness on the Sheehan Disability Scale (SDS). The patients with SAD had significant comorbidity including panic disorder in 27.8% of cases, Generalized Anxiety Disorder in 30.6% of cases and Major Depressive Disorder in 58.3% of cases. People with SAD had significantly higher ratings on each of three SDS domains compared to the not mentally ill group. They also reported findings that people with SAD had greater number of days missed or cut down in the past 30 days due to emotional problems.

In summary, clinical studies comparing SAD patients to other groups have demonstrated significant dysfunction and poor quality of life associated with social phobia.

Community Surveys of Quality of Life in Social Anxiety Disorder

Psychiatric epidemiology has made remarkable advances over the last 20 years (Regier et al, 1998). The availability of widely accepted diagnostic criteria and development of reliable instruments have led to a greater appreciation of the high prevalence and significant impact of psychiatric disorders on the community. Most of the large epidemiologic surveys focused on identifying prevalence rates, comorbidity, and risk factors for psychiatric disorders without much attention to quality of life issues (Kessler et al, 1994). The only large epidemiologic survey that estimated prevalence rates of psychiatric disorders and an empirically validated quality of life instrument was the Mental Health Supplement to the Ontario Health Survey (MHS-OHS) (Offord et al, 1996). Prior to reviewing the findings from this survey, we will also consider the quality of life findings for people with SAD from the Epidemiologic Catchment Area Study and the National Comorbidity Survey.

One caveat to keep in mind is that the estimated prevalence of social phobia in the community has varied significantly depending on what criteria were used to define the threshold (Stein et al, 1994; Stein, 1996). While the Epidemiologic Catchment area study found that the lifetime prevalence was 1.8%-3.8%, the National Comorbidity Survey and the MHS-OHS found a lifetime prevalence of approximately 13.0%. Therefore, when Davidson et al, compared social phobics with "subthreshold social phobia" and non-ill comparison subjects from the ECA Study, it is important to note that the people classified as 'subthreshold social phobia' in the ECA might have been considered social phobics in the NCS and MHS-OHS samples (Davidson et al, 1994).

Davidson and colleagues (1994) analyzed data from the Duke University ECA study site (Sullivan et al, 1994). They found that people considered to have subthreshold social phobia ("SSP") were more likely to be female and unmarried than the control groups. The SSP group was also more likely to report work attendance problems, poor grades in school, symptoms of conduct disturbance, impaired subjective social support, lack of self-confidence, lack of a close friend, and use of psychotropic drugs in the past year. The SSP group also reported a greater number of life changes, chronic medical problems, and mental health visits within the past six months. The SSP group was very similar in dysfunction to the social phobia group leading Davidson and colleagues to argue that the original ECA estimated prevalence of less than 4% was unrealistically low. When the SSP group was combined to the SP group, the prevalence rate was greater than 10%. These rates were similar to the findings of the more recent NCS and OHS-MHS samples (Kessler et al, 1994; Sareen et al, 2001; Offord et al, 1996).

Magee and colleagues (1996) reported findings from the NCS regarding the impact of social phobia. Similar to Davidson's findings from the ECA sample, people with social phobia were more likely to be never married, and have lower education and income than those without social phobia. Eighty one percent of the individuals with social phobia had at least one other psychiatric disorder in their life. Approximately 50% of people with SAD reported at least one outcome indicative of severity at some time in their lives. Severity was defined as the subject reporting either significant role impairment, professional help seeking, or use of medications more than once. In this study, having SAD was also associated with low social support (Magee et al, 1996).

As mentioned previously, the MHS-OHS was the only large community survey that used an empirically validated instrument for measuring Quality of Life in conjunction with diagnosing mental disorders. This survey is contemporaneous to the NCS, conducted in early 1990s. Similar to the NCS that surveyed 8098 people in the US, the MHS-OHS surveyed 8116 people in Ontario (Boyle et al, 1996). Both used the University of Michigan revised Composite International Diagnostic Interview (UM-CIDI) to make DSM-

III-R based psychiatric diagnosis. Stein and Kean (2000) reported disability and QOL measures for people with and without SAD. Since the majority of people with SAD have a comorbid psychiatric disorder during their lifetime, some authors have argued that the functional impairment and poor QOL is better accounted for by the comorbid disorders than by SAD alone. Stein and Kean attempted to address this issue by reporting findings in all persons with SAD, persons with SAD without major depression, and all persons with major depression (Stein and Kean, 2000). On the General Well-Being Schedule, a diagnosis of SAD was associated with a significantly greater likelihood of reporting poor quality of well-being. These findings remained highly significant after adjustment for age, gender, and lifetime major depression.

The MHS-OHS had non-disease related QOL questions regarding respondents' satisfaction with main activities, family life, friends, leisure, and income. Each of these questions was scored on a 6-point scale (extremely satisfied, quite satisfied, fairly satisfied, fairly dissatisfied, quite dissatisfied, extremely dissatisfied). Any of three negative responses were coded as the person having dissatisfaction with that particular domain of life. Persons with a lifetime diagnosis of SAD showed significant dissatisfaction in each of the five domains. Again these findings were significant after controlling for a lifetime diagnosis of major depression, age, gender and social class. The odds of dissatisfaction with friends were slightly higher for persons with lifetime SAD than lifetime major depression: 5.95 (95% CI = 2.5-14.15) and 5.51 (95% CI = 2.36-12.84), respectively. In the other domains, main activity, family life, leisure and income, people with major depression had slightly higher odds of dissatisfaction than people with SAD. A past-year diagnosis of SAD was associated with a greater likelihood of reporting dysfunction in one's interpersonal relationships. However, this effect failed to attain statistical significance after adjusting for age, gender, and social class.

Stein and Kean also investigated the effects of SAD on a number of measures of disability (Stein and Kean 2000). A past-year diagnosis of SAD was associated with a significantly greater likelihood of 1) being unable to perform one's usual activities for at least one day in the past 30 days, 2) being unable to perform activities or accomplishing less at least one day in the past 30 days, and 3) requiring extreme effort to perform one's usual activities for at least one day in the past 30 days. These findings remained significant after adjusting for age, gender and socioeconomic status. Current major depressive disorder had a more profound impact on each of these indexes than did current SAD, but these differences did not reach statistical significance.

With respect to scholastic difficulties, a lifetime diagnosis of SAD was associated with a significantly greater likelihood of failing a grade, and leaving school prior to graduating from high school. A total of 38.1% of people with SAD did not complete high school, compared to 30.1% of people without SAD (adjusted odds ratio =1.77, 95% CI =1.39-2.26, p<0.0001). The presence or absence of comorbid lifetime major depressive disorder did not significantly impact on these outcomes. The likely reason for these findings is that SAD usually occurs in latency or adolescence in contrast to major depressive disorder, which usually occurs in adulthood.

Although the investigators made efforts to control for the effects of comorbid mental disorders (Stein and Kean, 2000), the respondents were not asked to attribute disability/quality of life measures to any particular disorder. (It is doubtful, of course, that respondents could reliably make such a determination, had they been asked.) They were queried whether "problems with your emotions, nerves or mental health, or with your use of alcohol or drugs" affected their functioning. At best, Stein and Kean's findings can be interpreted to mean that a diagnosis of SAD is associated with, though not necessarily a determinant of, poor quality of life and disability.

To examine whether people with SAD attribute poor QOL and disability specifically to excessive social fears, Stein and colleagues conducted a telephone survey in 1,956 individuals in Midwestern Canada (Stein et al, 2000). The population of each of the cities — Edmonton, Calgary and Winnipeg — ranged between 550,000-650,000. The survey employed the Composite International Diagnostic Interview - version 2.1 (CIDI 2.1) module for DSM-IV Social Phobia. Similar to the UM-CIDI that was used in the NCS and the MHS-OHS, the CIDI 2.1 asks respondents whether they were afraid of or avoided six social situations. To obtain a more comprehensive evaluation, Stein and colleagues added six other social phobic situational probes. At the end of the diagnostic module, a series of questions were asked focusing on specific functional impairment related to social anxiety (Table 1). Figure 2 demonstrates that people with SAD had significant impairment in various domains of their lives. Overall, 38% of people with SAD reported substantial (ie, a great deal of) interference with at least one of the life domains.

Table 1

**Social Anxiety Specific Functional Impairment Questions
in the Midwestern Canadian Community Survey**

**Response options for questions 1 through 4 were a lot, some, a little, or none. For questions 1a and
2a, the options were yes or no.**

1. How much has/have excessive fear(s) of being the center of attention or interacting with other people interfered
with your education?

　1a. Because of the concerns, have you actually ever dropped out of a class, not taken a particular course or not
　taken advanced education?

2. How much has/have excessive fear(s) of being center of attention or interacting with other people hindered you in
getting the kind of job you want?

　2a. Have you actually turned down a job offer or a job promotion because it might involve being the center of attention
　or interacting with other people?

3. How much does/do excessive fear(s) of being the center of attention or
of interacting with other people interfere with your ability to have the kind of personal life you would like to have?

4. How much does/do this/these concern(s) interfere with other aspects of your life?

Stein et al, 2000

**Social Anxiety Disorder
Subtypes and Severity**

Kessler et al used latent cluster analysis in the NCS dataset and demonstrated that SAD can be reliably distinguished into two subtypes: a speaking
subtype where respondents have social fears limited to speaking in small or
large groups; and a "generalized" subtype that involves fear and avoidance
of multiple situations (Kessler et al, 1998). Overall, SAD characterized by
pure speaking fears was found to be less persistent, less impairing, and less
highly comorbid than SAD characterized by generalized social fears. Stein
and Kean's analysis of the MHS-OHS replicated the findings that people
with SAD who have generalized social fears have significantly higher rates
of dysfunction in daily activities, and more troubled relationships, than
those with pure speaking fears (Stein and Kean 2000).

Figure 2

Functional impairment specifically due to social fears in a community survey

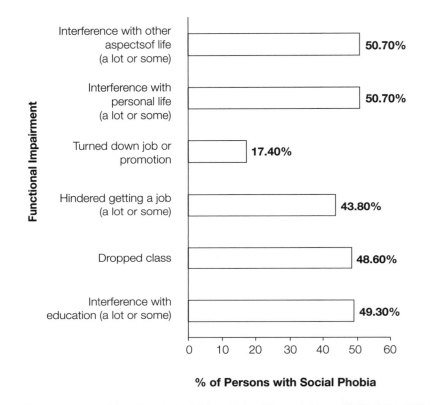

Stein et al, 2000

The community survey by Stein and colleagues, which included probes for 12 social situations compared to the six in the NCS and MHS-OHS, was not able to show an empirical basis for the SAD subtypes (Stein et al, 2000). However, as one would expect, people who endorsed fear of 7 or more social situations had much greater functional impairment than those who endorsed fear of 1-3 and 4-6 social situations.

Impact of Treatment on Quality of Life in Social Anxiety Disorder

There is a dearth of literature on the impact of treatment on quality of life in SAD. With respect to pharmacotherapy, a double-blind, placebo controlled trial of SAD patients with fluvoxamine investigated quality of life with the Sheehan Disability Scale (SDS) (Stein et al, 1999a). This 12 week study showed that compared to placebo, fluvoxamine provided significantly greater improvement in all three domains of the SDS.

With respect to cognitive behavior therapy, Safren et al (1997) used the Quality of Life Inventory (QOLI). At pre-treatment, persons with SAD had lower scores on the QOLI. After completion of the cognitive behavior therapy, there was a significant improvement in quality of life. However, the post-treatment scores remained lower than the control group (Safren et al, 1997).

Further studies on how treatment affects QOL for SAD persons are required. We hypothesize that in order to determine a true estimate of how a treatment will affect people with SAD, one would have to do long-term follow-up. Most treatment studies in social phobia have had a duration of 12 weeks. Whether it is medication or psychotherapy, if the person responds to the treatment, he/she is likely to gain skills in social interaction over a much longer period than 12 weeks. Based on our clinical experience, we estimate that improvements in QOL would continue to occur for at least the first year after the treatment.

Conclusions

This chapter illustrates that Social Anxiety Disorder is, indeed, a serious mental disorder. Whether one considers clinical studies or community surveys, the finding that SAD is associated with substantial impairment in functioning is consistent. Together with data suggesting that most people with SAD never receive treatment, these findings underscore the requirement of strategic public health policies to identify and treat this disorder at an early age (Weiller et al, 1996; Magee et al, 1996).

References

Aaronson NK, Bullinger M, Ahmedzai S. A modular approach to quality-of-life assessment in cancer clinical trials. *Recent Results Cancer Res*. 1988; 111:231-249.

Andresen EM, Rothenberg BM, Kaplan RM. Performance of a Self-Administered Mailed Version of the Quality of Well-Being (QWB-SA) Questionnaire Among Older Adults. *Med Care*. 1998;36:1349-1360.

Antony MM, Roth D, Swinson RP, Huta V, Devins GM. Illness intrusiveness in individuals with panic disorder, obsessive-compulsive disorder, or social phobia. *J Nerv Ment Dis*. 1998;186:311-15.

Beck AT, Rush AJ, Shaw BF, and Emery G. Cognitive Therapy for Depression. 1979. New York, Guilford Press.

Bosc M, Dubini A, Polin V. Development and validation of a social functioning scale, the Social Adaptation Self-Evaluation Scale. *Eur Neuropsychopharmacol*. 1997;7:S57-S70.

Boyle MH, Offord DR, Campbell D, Catlin G, Goering P, Lin E, Racine YA. Mental health supplement to the Ontario Health Survey: methodology. *Can J Psychiatry*. 1996;41:549-558.

Bullinger M, Alonso J, Apolone G, Leplège A, Sullivan M, Wood-Dauphine S, Gandek B, Wagner A, Aaronson NK, Bech P, Fukuhara S, Kaasa S, Ware JE, Jr. Translating health status questionnaires and evaluating their quality: the IQOLA Project approach. *Med Care*. 1998;51:913-923.

Davidson JR, Hughes DC, George LK, Blazer DG. The boundary of social phobia. Exploring the threshold. *Arch Gen Psychiatry*. 1994;51:975-983.

Derogatis LR. SCL-90-R: Administration, scoring, and procedures manual for the revised version. 1983. Towson, MD, Clinical Psychometric Research.

Devins GM. Illness intrusiveness and the psychosocial impact of lifestyle disruptions in chronic life-threatening disease. *Adv Renal Repl Ther*. 1994;1:283.

Devins GM, Berman L, Shapiro CM. Impact of sleep apnea and other sleep disorders on marital relationships and adjustment (abstract). *Sleep Res.* 1993; 22:550.

Devins GM, Binik YM, Hutchinson TA, Hollomby DJ, Barre PE, Guttmann RD. The emotional impact of end-stage renal disease: importance of patients' perception of intrusiveness and control. *Int J Psychiatry Med.* 1984; 13:327-343.

Devins GM, Mandin H, Hons RB, Burgess ED, Klassen J, Taub K, Schorr S, Letorneau P, Buckle S. Illness intrusiveness and quality of life in end-stage renal disease: comparison and stability across treatment modalities. *Health Psychol.* 1990;9:117-142.

Devins GM, Stam HJ, Koopmans JP. Psychosocial impact of laryngectomy mediated by perceived stigma and illness intrusiveness. *Can J Psychiatry.* 1994;39:608-616.

Devins GM, Styra R, O'Connor P, Gray T, Seland TP, Klein GM, Shapiro CM. Psychosocial impact of illness intrusiveness moderated by age in multiple sclerosis. *Psychol Health Med.* 1996;1:179-191.

Diamond R, Becker M. The Wisconsin Quality of Life Index: A Multidimensional Model for Measuring Quality of Life. *J Clin Psychiatry.* 1999;60:29-31.

Diener E, Emmons RA, Larsen RJ, Griffin S. The Satisfaction with Life Scale. *J Personal Assess.* 1985;49:71-75.

Endicott J, Nee J, Harrison W, Blumenthal R. Quality of Life Enjoyment and Satisfaction Questionnaire: a new measure. *Psychopharmacol Bull.* 1993; 29:321-6.

Gill TM, Geinstein AR. A Critical Appraisal of Quality of Quality-of-Life Measurements. *JAMA.* 1994;272:619-626.

Homan WM, Towheed T, Anastassiades T, Tenenhouse A, Poliquin S, Berger C, Joseph L, Brown JP, Murray TM, Adachi JD, Hanley DA, Papadimitropoulos E. Canadian Multicentre Osteoporosis Study Research Group: Canadian normative data for the SF-36 health survey. *CMAJ.* 2000; 163:265-271.

Kaplan RM, Ganiats TG, Sieber WJ, Anderson JP. The Quality of Well-Being Scale: critical similarities and differences with SF-36. *Int J Qual Health Care.* 1998; 10:509-520.

Kaplan RM, Sieber WJ, Ganiats TG. The Quality of Well-Being Scale: comparison of the interviewer-administered version with a self-administered questionnaire. *Psychol Health.* 1997;12:783-791.

Kessler RC, McGonagle KA, Zhao S, Nelson CB, Hughes M, Eshleman S, Wittchen H-U, Kendler KS. Lifetime and 12-month prevalence of psychiatric disorders in the United States: results from the National Comorbidity Survey. *Arch Gen Psychiatry.* 1994;51:8-19.

Kessler RC, Stein MB, Berglund PA. Social phobia subtypes in the National Comorbidity Survey. *Am J of Psychiatry.* 1998;155:613-619.

Leon AC, Shear MK, Portera L, Klerman GL. Assessing impairment in patients with panic disorder: the Sheehan Disability Scale. *Soc Psychiatry and Psychiatric Epid.* 1992;27:78-82.

Magee WJ, Eaton WW, Wittchen HU, McGonagle KA, Kessler RC. Agoraphobia, simple phobia, and social phobia in the National Comorbidity Survey. *Arch Gen Psychiatry.* 1996;53:159-168.

McDowell I and Newell C. Measuring health: a guide to rating scales and questionnaires. 125-133. 1987. New York, Oxford University Press.

McHorney CA, Ware JE Jr, Lu JFR, Sherbourne CD. The MOS 36-item short-form health survey (SF-36): III. Tests of data quality, scaling assumptions, and reliability across diverse patient groups. *Med Care.* 1994;32:40-66.

McHorney CA, Ware JE, Jr., Raczek AE. The MOS 36-item short-form health survey (SF-36): II. Psychometric and clinical tests of validity in measuring physical and mental health constructs. *Med Care.* 1993;31:247-263.

Mendlowicz MV, Stein MB. Quality of life in individuals with anxiety disorders. *Am J Psychiatry.* 2000;157:669-682.

Mogotsi M, Kaminer D, Stein DJ. Quality of life in the anxiety disorders. *Harv Rev Psychiatry.* 2000;8:273-282.

Offord DR, Boyle MH, Campbell D, Goering P, Lin E, Wong M, Racine YA: One-year prevalence of psychiatric disorder in Ontarians 15 to 64 years of age. *Can J Psychiatry.* 1996;41:559-563

Patrick, D. L. and Erickson, P. Health Status and Health Policy: Quality of Life in Health Care Evaluation and Resource Allocation. Oxford University Press. 1993. New York.

Patterson TL, Kaplan RM, Grant I, Semple SJ, Moscona S, Koch WL, Harris MJ, Jeste DV. Quality of well-being in late-life psychosis. *Psychiatry Res.* 1996;63:169-181.

Patterson TL, Shaw W, Semple SJ, Moscona S, Harris MJ, Kaplan RM, Grant I, Jeste DV. Health-related quality of life in older patients with schizophrenia and other psychoses: relationships among psychosocial and psychiatric factors. *Int J Geriatr Psychiatry.* 1997;12:452-461.

Pyne JM, Patterson TL, Kaplan RM, Gillin JC, Koch WL, Grant I. Assessment of the quality of life of patients with major depression. *Psychiatr Serv.* 1997; 48:224-230.

Pyne JM, Patterson TL, Kaplan RM, Ho S, Gillin JC, Golshan S, Grant I. Preliminary longitudinal assessment of quality of life in patients with major depression. *Psychopharmacol Bull.* 1997;33:23-29.

Regier DA, Kaelber CT, Rae DS, Farmer ME, Knauper B, Kessler RC, Norquist GS. Limitations of Diagnostic Criteria and Assessment Instruments for Mental Disorders: Implications for Research and Policy. *Arch Gen Psychiatry.* 1998;55:109-115.

Reilly MC ZDE. The validity and reproducibility of a work productivity and impairment instrument. *PharmacoEconomics.* 1993;4:353-65.

Robb JC, Cooke RG, Devins GM, Young TL, Joffe RT. Quality of life and lifestyle in euthymic bipolar disorder. *J Psychiatr Res.* 1997;31:509-17.

Safren SA, Heimberg RG, Brown EJ, Holle C. Quality of life in social phobia. *Depression and Anxiety.* 1997;4:126-133.

Sareen J, Chartier M, Kjernisted KD, Stein MB. Comorbidity of Phobic Disorders with Alcoholism in a Canadian Community Sample. *Can J Psychiatry.* 2001;46:679-686.

Sareen J, Stein MB. A Review of Epidemiology and Approaches to the Treatment of Social Anxiety Disorder. *Drugs.* 2000;59:497-509.

Schneier FR, Heckelman LR, Campeas R, Fallon BA, Gitow A, Street L, Del Bene D, Liebowitz MR. Functional impairment in social phobia. *J Clin Psychiatry.* 1994;55:322-331.

Schneier FR, Heckelman LR, Garfinkel R, Campeas R, Fallon BA, Gitow A, Street L, Del Bene D, Liebowitz MR. Functional impairment in social phobia. *J Clin Psychiatry.* 1994;55:322-331.

Sheehan DV. The Anxiety Disease. 1983. New York: Charles Scribner's Sons. Stein MB How shy is too shy? *Lancet.* 1996;1131.

Stein MB, Fyer AJ, Davidson JRT, Pollack MH, Wiita B. Fluvoxamine in social phobia (social anxiety disorder): a double-blind, placebo-controlled clinical study. *Am J Psychiatry.* 1999;156:756-60.

Stein MB, Kean YM. Disability and Quality of Life in Social Phobia: Epidemiologic Findings. *Am J Psychiatry.* 2000;157:1606-1613.

Stein MB, McQuaid JR, Laffaye C, McCahill ME. Social Phobia in the Primary Care Medical Setting. *J Fam Pract*. 1999b;49:514-519.

Stein MB, Torgrud LJ, Walker JW. Social Phobia Symptoms, Subtypes, and Severity: Findings from a Community Survey. *Arch Gen Psychiatry*. 2000; 57:1046-1052.

Stein MB, Walker JR, Forde DR. Setting diagnostic thresholds for social phobia: Considerations from a community survey of social anxiety. *Am J of Psychiatry*. 1994;151:408-412.

Stewart AL, Hays RD, Ware JE. The MOS Short-Form General Health Survey: Reliability and validity in a patient population. *Med Care*. 1988;26:724-732.

Sullivan CM, Campbell R, Angelique H, Eby KK, Davidson WS. An advocacy intervention program for women with abusive partners. Six-month follow-up. *Am J Comm*. 1994;22(1), 101-122.

Ware JE, Jr., Kosinski M, Gandek B, Aaronson NK, Apolone G, Bech P, Brazier J, Bullinger M, Kaasa S, Lepiège A, Prieto L, Sullivan M. The factor structure of the SF-36 Health Survey in 10 countries: results from the IQOLA Project. *Med Care*. 1998;51:1159-65.

Ware JE, Jr., Sherbourne CD. The MOS 36-Item Short-Form Health Survey (SF-36), I: conceptual framework and item selection. *Med Care*. 1992; 30:473-483.

Weiller E, Bisserbe JC, Boyer P, Lepine JP, Lecrubier Y. Social phobia in general health care: an unrecognized undertreated disabling disorder. *Br J Psychiatry*. 1996;168:169-174.

Weissman MM, Bothwell S. Assessment of Social Adjustment by Patient Self-Report. *Arch Gen Psychiatry*. 1976;33:1111-5.

Weissman MM, Olfson M, Gameroff MJ, Feder A, Fuentes M. A comparison of three scales for assessing social functioning in primary care. *Am J Psychiatry*. 2001;158:460-466.

Weissman MM, Prusoff BA, Thompson WD, Harding PS, Myers JK. Social adjustment by self-report in a community sample and in psychiatric outpatients. *J Nerv Ment Dis.* 1978;166:317-326.

Wittchen H-U, Beloch E. The impact of social phobia on quality of life. *Int Clin Psychopharmacology.* 1996;11:15-23.

Wittchen H-U, Fuetsch M, Sonntag H, Muller N, Liebowitz M. Disability and quality of life in pure and comorbid social phobia. Findings from a controlled study. *Eur Psychiatry.* 2000;15:46-58.

Chapter 4
Cross-Cultural Aspects of Social Anxiety Disorder: The Influence of Culture on the Expression of Mental Distress

Umberto Albert, M.D., Giuseppe Maina, M.D., Filippo Bogetto, M.D., Mark H. Pollack, M.D.

This chapter will highlight the core concepts in the field of cross-cultural psychiatry, and will address how this is relevant for understanding the prevalence and phenomenology of social anxiety disorder (SAD) throughout the world. Cross-cultural psychiatry has as its goal the assessment of whether and to what degree that area of human experience which psychiatrists term "psychopathology" is universal or culturally specific (Littlewood, 1990). A cultural system, as defined by Geertz (1966) may be viewed as "the intersubjective world of common understandings into which all human individuals are born, in which they pursue their separate careers, and which they leave persisting behind them after they die." Cultural ideologies, institutions, and organizations provide the context and rules for interpersonal interactions. Family compositions and interactions, which are culturally influenced, prime and shape affect systems. Culture provides a lexicon for emotional experience, making some feelings salient and others more difficult to articulate. The level of tolerance for specific types and strength of emotional experience is also influenced by culture. Culture also influences the sources of distress, the interpretation and expression of illness, the strategies that individuals use to cope with distress including help-seeking behaviors, and the response of others to an individual's illness experience (Kirmayer, 2001).

The current approach of cross-cultural psychiatry is founded on the theoretical distinction between disease and illness (Kleinman, 1978). This distinction is derived from medical anthropology. The term disease, according to this model, refers to the biomedical aspects of a disorder. These biomedical aspects are thought to be uniform across different cultures. One way of verifying this assumption is to compare prevalence estimates obtained from large epidemiologic surveys conducted with the same methodology and standardized across different countries (cross-national data). Characteristics of the studied disorder, such as age at onset, sex ratio, and type of symptoms (eg, types of social situations avoided in SAD), may also be compared with this method. When we use the term disease we choose a clinical, positivistic approach: science describes universal laws. In using disease, then, we refer to psychobiological mechanisms that are thought to underlie a given disorder. The term illness, in medical anthropology, refers to the subjective perception and experience of a disorder and is postulated to differ across cultures. Disease mechanisms are universal but illnesses vary across time and culture. This approach considers psychiatric classification itself as a cultural product; Kleinman (1978) criticized as a "category fallacy" the assumption that Western diagnostic categories were themselves culture-free entities. Variations in the expression and perception of symptoms across cultures may influence the course and outcome of the disorder, as well as the recognition of the disorder by mental health care providers. An example would be the impact of cultural aspects on the course and outcome of schizophrenia. A series of studies performed in the 1980s and sponsored by the World Health Organization found that outcome of schizophrenia is superior in Third-World compared with Western countries, independent from the use of maintenance neuroleptic drugs (WHO, 1979; Sartorius et al, 1986; Leff et al, 1990). This result might be attributable, in part, to the greater tolerance by relatives of affected individuals in Third World countries for the illness and its associated disabilities, and to three other factors: a) a view of the problem as a serious, legitimate illness outside the patient's locus of control; b) styles of coping with troublesome behavior in a manner which avoids arguments or confrontations; and c) large kin-based households and networks in which the importance of family bonds induces relatives to assume responsibility for the patient's care and recovery (Leff et al, 1990). For mental disorders, the attention given to the illness perspective (ie, the perception and expression of the disorder by the patient) is of great importance in order to negotiate clinical interventions with the patient (Kirmayer, 2001). The understanding of the patient's explanatory model (ie understanding of the illness) apart from the understanding of the biomedical mechanisms that underlie a given disorder (ie, understanding of the disease) is crucial. For example, compliance with treatment is dependent on the patient's interpretation of their illness. Becoming attuned to this illness perspective is essential for the patient and psychiatrist to achieve a shared model of the disorder. Such a shared model forms the basis for discussion and planning for interventions (Kirmayer, 2001). Thus, combining these two perspectives (disease and illness) has immediate, practical implications for the clinician.

One reason for focusing on culture-bound syndromes or cross-cultural aspects of mental disorders is the increasing cultural diversity of persons referred to mental health facilities, both in the United States and in Europe. Knowledge of the cultural background of immigrants from countries with varying conceptions of mental disorders, as well as of their way of expressing distress or emotional problems, is essential in providing psychiatric care for them (Guarnaccia and Rogler, 1999).

With this cross-cultural framework, we will review the disease model and the illness model of social anxiety disorder. According to the first approach, we will address the following questions: is the prevalence of SAD similar in all countries studied to date? Are age at onset, sex ratio, and type of symptoms the same across the world? We will refer, when possible, to cross-national collaborative studies. According to the illness perspective, we will try to elucidate the potential variations of the perception of SAD in specific cultures and will review a culture-bound syndrome that, in its expression, could resemble SAD. The definition proposed by Prince and Tcheng-Laroche, (1987) of culture-bound syndromes refers to a collection of signs and symptoms (excluding notions of cause) that is restricted to a limited number of cultures primarily as a result of their psychosocial features. The essential feature of this definition is the concept that particular psychosocial features of a culture modulate the expression of the disorder in a way that is unique to that culture. Culture-bound syndromes are recognized by the current classification system in a glossary: the term culture-bound syndrome according to the DSM-IV-TR (APA, 2000) denotes 'recurrent, locality-specific patterns of aberrant behaviors and troubling experience that may or may not be linked to a particular DSM-IV diagnostic category'. DSM-IV itself distinguishes major categories that can be found throughout the world and whose "symptoms, course and social response are very often influenced by local cultural factors" from culture-bound syndromes, which 'are generally limited to specific societies or culture areas and are localized, folk, diagnostic categories that frame coherent meanings for certain repetitive, patterned, and troubling sets of experiences and observations.

The approach to culture-bound syndromes according to the disease model would be to reclassify them using "modern" nosologies; the anthropological view is that culture-bound syndromes reflect their particular time and culture, and thus it is not appropriate to reclassify these phenomena with diagnostic entities that refer to a Western culture-bound psychiatric nosological system.

Lifetime Prevalence of Social Anxiety Disorder

Cross-national data on the prevalence of SAD, in earlier DSM's labeled as "social phobia", come from epidemiologic surveys conducted mainly in Western countries with DSM-III, DSM-III R and DSM-IV criteria. Social phobia as a distinct diagnostic entity appeared in the 1980s with DSM-III. Prevalence rates of DSM-III defined social phobia have been gathered by using the Diagnostic Interview Schedule, although this instrument assesses social fears via only three criteria: fear of eating in front of people, of speaking in front of people, and of speaking to strangers or meeting new people. According to DSM-III criteria social phobia is prevalent in the Western world, with DSM-III prevalence rates ranging from 1.0% in Florence, Italy (Faravelli et al, 1989) to 4.1% in Paris, France (Lépine et al, 1993) (see table 1). The lower DSM-III lifetime rate found in Florence, Italy compared to other Western countries has been interpreted as biased by the hierarchical rule considered by the Italian team of researchers, while prevalence rates in other areas were calculated without considering hierarchical rules. If we exclude the Florence study, lifetime prevalence rates across the Western countries range from 1.6 to 4.1%. The prevalence of social phobia appeared significantly lower in Taiwan and South Korea, where lifetime prevalence rates were respectively 0.4-0.6% and 0.5% (Hwu et al, 1989; Lee et al, 1990). A possible explanation is that lifetime rates may actually not be low in Asia, but that the methodology used (derived from epidemiological studies performed in Western countries) is relatively insensitive in these countries (Lépine, 2001). The Cross-National Collaborative Study Group standardized prevalence rates of disorders in four countries with different historical, political and cultural profiles (the United States, Canada, Puerto Rico and Korea) to the age and sex distribution of the household population of the Epidemiologic Catchment Area study in order to allow more precise estimates and comparisons (Weissman et al, 1996). The resulting social phobia prevalence rates, frequency of comorbidity and suicide attempts, and age of onset, were comparable in the US, Canada and Puerto Rico (2.6%, 1.7% and 1.0% respectively). However, the Korean data, standardized to the ECA sample, differed; the social phobia prevalence rate was lower (0.5%), the

Table 1

Lifetime DSM-III Prevalence Rates of Social Anxiety Disorders Across Countries

Country	Prevalence (%)	Authors
Americas		
Puerto Rico	1.6	Canino et al, 1987
Edmonton, Alberta, Canada	1.7	Wells et al, 1989
United States (ECA Study)	2.7	Robins & Regier, 1991
North Carolina, US	3.8	Davidson et al, 1993
Europe		
Florence, Italy	1.0	Faravelli et al, 1989
Munich, Germany	2.5	Wittchen et al, 1992
Zurich, Switzerland	3.8	Degonda & Angst, 1993
Paris, France	4.1	Lepine et al, 1993
Iceland	3.5	Lindal & Stefansson, 1993
Asia		
Taiwan	0.4-0.6	Hwu et al, 1989
Seoul, Korea	0.5	Lee et al, 1990
Oceania		
Christchurch, New Zealand	3.5	Wells et al, 1989

female to male ratio was remarkably higher (10:1), and the mean age at onset was later (24.3 years) than in the three other countries. Moreover, the symptom profile differed by site; fear of speaking in front of a group was lower, and speaking to strangers was higher in Korea compared to other sites. The authors concluded that the development of social phobia in Asian samples was affected by cultural differences.

However, the relatively lower prevalence rates found in Korea and Taiwan, compared to Western countries raised the question of whether cultural bias in response to western-shaped questionnaires was responsible or whether the results represented true differences in psychopathology between the Asian and Western countries. One possible explanation, as formulated by Chapman et al (1995), is that there aren't true cross-cultural differences in prevalence rates, but rather cross-cultural differences in the context in which social fears are most commonly expressed. An example in support of this interpretation is the syndrome known in Japan and other East Asian countries as Taijin Kyofusho, which doesn't correspond exactly to the DSM description of SAD but resembles it. Thus, certain features of this syndrome might not be recognized as social anxiety symptoms by the currently used DSM-derived structured interview schedules. Taijin Kyofusho as well as the sociocultural factors that contribute to the specificity of this syndrome in Japan, is discussed later in this chapter.

Rates of social phobia using DSM-III-R criteria were examined with the CIDI (Composite International Diagnostic Interview) in three epidemiological studies performed in Europe (Basel, Switzerland; Wacker et al, 1992), the United States (National Comorbidity Survey; Kessler et al, 1994), and Ontario, Canada (Ontario Health Survey, Mental Health Supplement; Stein et al, 2000). These three studies reported higher prevalence rates of social phobia (16.0%, 13.3% and 13.0%, in Switzerland, the US and Canada respectively) compared to those gathered in studies utilizing DSM-III criteria. The use of the CIDI interview, which explores more abundant and diversified social situations, might explain these higher prevalence rates. Again, no large differences were found in prevalence rates among Western countries. Interestingly, in the National Comorbidity Study, performed in the United States, there were no differences in the prevalence of SAD between African-Americans and Caucasians, or between non-Hispanic Caucasians and Hispanics (Kessler et al, 1994).

Prevalence rates of SAD in the community, as defined by DSM-IV, have been evaluated in Europe and in Canada: Wittchen and colleagues (1999) found a prevalence of 7.3% in Munich, Germany; Lépine and Pélissolo (Pélissolo et al, 2000) in France reported a prevalence of moderate SAD of 7.3% and of severe SAD of 1.9%; Faravelli (Faravelli et al, 2000) reported a lifetime prevalence of 6.6% for social fears and for 4.0% of social fears and impairment (social anxiety disorder) in Florence, Italy. Finally, Stein et al

(2000) reported that the 12-month prevalence rate of SAD in Alberta and Manitoba, Canada, was 7.2%. No cross-national comparisons to date have been performed examining standardized prevalence rates of SAD in different countries utilizing DSM-III-R or DSM-IV criteria. However, the reported prevalence data from different studies suggest that rates of SAD as defined by DSM-III-R or DSM-IV are similar in Western countries.

However, cross-cultural differences may occur in the pattern of situations feared and avoided. Heimberg and colleagues (1997) performed a preliminary cross-cultural comparison of characteristics of social phobic samples (in treatment settings) in three culturally different countries: United States, Sweden (Europe), and Australia. Certain characteristics, such as index age and years since onset of social fears, were similar across countries; furthermore, when the authors compared fear ratings for eleven specific social situations, no group differences emerged for anxiety about parties, assertive interactions, use of public restrooms and maintaining conversations. Swedish social phobics were, however, significantly more fearful of eating/drinking in public, writing in public, participating in meetings and public speaking but less fearful of interacting with authority figures as compared to their US and Australian counterparts. Swedish subjects scored higher on measures of anxiety or avoidance of situations involving observation by others. The authors postulated that Swedish individuals associate many of these situations with participation in conversations during coffee breaks at work, a behavior that is strongly reinforced by their culture (Heimberg et al, 1997). Thus, results from this study, suggest cross-cultural differences in the expression of social phobic concerns. Also of interest, the Swedish sample was comprised primarily of females (80% of the sample), while the sex distribution in the other 2 groups was equal. The authors postulate that some aspects of Swedish culture may support treatment-seeking behaviors in women with social phobia more than in men.

Thus, although the overall prevalence of SAD in Western countries appears similar, it appears that expressions of the disorder may vary due to cultural influences consistent with the notion of SAD as an illness as well as a disease. Prevalence rates are similar in Western cultures (consistent with the disease model) but vary between West and East, which might reflect cultural differences. These cross-cultural differences have been proposed to exist in the context in which social fears are most commonly expressed in different parts of the world. Further, even within Western countries, the Heimberg (1997) study suggests that cultural differences may affect the expression of the disorder, consistent with the illness model.

An example of a cultural variation in the expression of SAD is Taijin Kyofusho, a syndrome found primarily in Japan that is generally considered a culture-bound syndrome.

Taijin Kyofusho

The syndrome of Taijin Kyofusho is an excellent example of how cultural factors (both for patients and psychiatrists) may influence the expression and perception of a mental disorder in a specific country. Taijin Kyofusho (TKS) is a well-described syndrome in Japan that is characterized by an individual's intense fear that his or her body, its parts or its functions (eg, appearance, odor, facial expressions, or movements) displease, embarrass, or are offensive to other people (DSM-IV-TR). It is classified by the DSM-IV-TR in the glossary for culture-bound syndromes. In Japanese, taijin means interpersonal, kyofu means fear and sho means disorder, and thus the term means fear of facing other people. In English, taijin kyofusho has also been termed anthropophobia.

TKS has a long history as a mental disorder in the Japanese psychiatric nosology. In contrast, SAD appeared in the Japanese psychiatric literature as a diagnostic entity only recently, perhaps contributing to its relatively low rate of diagnosis and the greater tendency by Japanese practitioners to use terms such as Taijin Kyofusho. Although we do not know the relative frequency of diagnosis of SAD compared to TKS in Japan, TKS was the subject of over 200 papers in the Japanese literature in 1999, according to Tajima (2001), demonstrating that it is widely recognized and written about in Japanese medical literature. TKS was first described in the 1920s by the Japanese psychiatrist Shoma Morita (Fujita, 1986). He considered TKS to be the result of a constitutional disposition termed shinkeishitsu, which can be translated in English as neurasthenia. According to Morita's description, shinkeishitsu, in particular conditions of stress, gives rise to disorders that, depending on the severity, manifest in three different syndromes: a neurasthenic state characterized by functional somatic symptoms, an obsessive-phobic state that can be termed Taijin Kyofusho, and an anxiety state with symptoms resembling panic disorder including hypochondriacal and phobic symptoms (Kirmayer, 1991). Following Morita's description , Japanese psychiatry devoted great attention to TKS. In the 1960s and 1970s TKS was considered a uniquely Japanese psychological disorder. Recently, however, there have been reports of TKS in Korea, although there appear to be no published papers in the English literature on the prevalence rate of TKS in countries other than Japan (Lee, 1987). Only two reports describe cases of TKS in the United States (McNally et al, 1990; Clarvit et al, 1996). The first is a description of an African-American woman with a fear of staring at the genitals of those surrounding her and offending them (McNally et al, 1990). This woman was referred for the treatment of obsessive-compulsive disorder (OCD); the authors believe that the diagnosis of OCD was initially made because TKS is an unfamiliar syndrome in the United States. Clarvit and colleagues (1996) reported on six subjects suffering from the so-called "offensive subtype of TKS" (in which the subject is afraid to embarrass, offend or displease others because of an imagined defect or a strange behavior); they concluded that features of the offensive type of TKS overlap with symptoms of SAD, and that it may not be as culture-bound as previously believed.

Prevalence studies of TKS in Japan confirm that this disorder is highly prevalent among psychiatric patients; reported rates range from 7.8% of outpatients with neuroses referred to a general university psychiatric clinic to 45.5% of outpatients with neuroses at a clinic offering Morita therapy, which is considered a specific treatment for TKS (Takahashi, 1989; Kirmayer, 1991). Kasahara (1987) found TKS in 18.6% of 430 students referred to the Kyoto University student health service for psychiatric problems, making it the third most common psychiatric disorder in frequency after depressive reactions and psychosomatic disorders (Kasahara, 1987).

No large-scale epidemiological study of the prevalence of TKS symptoms has been performed in the general population. The only community-based study of TKS in Japan is that by Ono and colleagues (Ono and Young, 2000): a total of 132 inhabitants in a small community in the city of Kofu were given questionnaires and were interviewed using a semi-structured interview aimed at eliciting the presence of TKS symptoms. Of the respondents, nine (6.8%) reported taijin kyofu symptoms; none of the TKS symptoms were serious enough to meet the criteria for a mental disorder. Seven of the nine subjects were females. The most common reported symptoms were the fear that their body could give off unpleasant odor, followed by fear of eye-to-eye contact and fear that an imagined defect in their bodies could embarrass or displease others. The authors concluded that taijin kyofu symptoms are common among Japanese people, mainly among females (although TKS is seen more frequently in clinical samples among males, which may be due to a greater difficulty for female patients in Japan to access treatment).

TKS has an age at onset between puberty and early adulthood (15-25 years); it is noteworthy that this age range is similar to that of SAD (Kirmayer, 1991; Weissman et al, 1996). It is considered to be more prevalent in males, with a male to female ratio ranging from 3:2 to 5:4 (Takahashi, 1989; Kirmayer, 1991), although as noted above this may reflect a bias in sample ascertainment in clinical settings. Similarly, studies in clinical settings suggest that males constitute a slightly higher proportion (up to 60%) of patients with SAD (Marks, 1970; Amies et al, 1983; Solyom et al, 1986; Weiller et al, 1996; Heimberg et al, 1997; Dingenmans et al, 2001; Perugi et al, 2001), despite epidemiologic studies suggest a higher prevalence in women (Weissman, et al 1996).

Clinical descriptions of TKS highlight that the most frequent symptoms are the fear that eye-to-eye contact or blushing may offend or displease others. Interestingly, these symptoms do not appear to be frequent in SAD. This particular expression of symptoms differentiates the two disorders and raises the question of whether the variations in symptoms displayed by patients with TKS as compared to social phobics are superficial differences in content due to cultural influences.

Taijin Kyofusho has been considered by some to be the Asian version of social anxiety disorder. Some authors postulate that the low prevalence rates of SAD found in epidemiological studies performed in East Asian countries, like Seoul, Korea (0.5%; Lee et al, 1990) and Taiwan (0.4-0.6; Hwu et al, 1989), could be explained by such a differential expression resulting in a failure to detect the disorder in the general population when utilizing currently available instruments (validated mainly in European and North American samples) (Chapman et al, 1995). TKS could thus be viewed, in a disease perspective, as a form of SAD.

Although both syndromes are characterized by excessive fear in social situations, what differentiates SAD from Taijin Kyofusho, is the object of the embarrassment (see table 2). In SAD, the person feels that he may be humiliated or embarrassed by his behavior in situations of social scrutiny. In

Taijin Kyofusho the object of the irrational fears is external: the person is afraid that his or her body, or perceived rude behavior, will displease, embarrass or offend other people. In other words, SAD is self-oriented or egocentric while TKS is other-oriented or allocentric. Both disorders may include anxiety symptoms, panic attacks, and phobic avoidance of social interactions. However, anxiety and phobic avoidance are not the only symptoms manifested by people suffering from TKS. TKS, in fact, does not constitute a single coherent syndrome. According to Kasahara (1987; cited by Kirmayer, 1991; Takahashi, 1989) there are four different types of TKS: 1) a transient mild type, that usually emerges in adolescence and disappears in early adulthood; 2) a neurotic or simple type, without delusions, in which TKS constitutes the pathological expression of a nervous temperament (shinkeishitsu); 3) a severe type, with ideas of reference and other delusions, such as that the patient is emitting something that adversely effects others, and/or the belief that others avoid the individual; 4) a secondary type, with symptoms arising as a prodrome of schizophrenia or as a postpsychotic syndrome during remission. Japanese psychiatry considers all these subtypes as manifestations of the same underlying disorder. In contrast, if we attempt to fit these types into DSM-IV diagnostic entities, we have to split TKS into different disorders. Only the simple type of TKS, according to the classification by Kasahara above, would fit to some degree within DSM-IV SAD, including its comparable age at onset. The transient type has overlap with DSM avoidant disorder of childhood or adolescence. The severe form of the disorder, with overvalued ideas or delusions could meet criteria for, depending on the degree of delusionality, as body dysmorphic disorder (or monosymptomatic hypochondriasis) or a delusional disorder, somatic type (eg, the old Munro's monosymptomatic hypochondriacal psychosis)(Munro, 1999). The secondary type would be viewed as part of schizophrenia or other psychotic disorders. Taijin Kyofusho, then, overlaps with DSM-IV social anxiety disorder, but also with somatoform disorders (hypochondriasis or body dysmorphic disorder), avoidant disorder or, in very severe cases, delusional disorder; moreover, some forms of TKS overlap also with obsessive-compulsive disorder (Russell, 1989; Kirmayer, 1991; Kirmayer, 1995; Phillips et al, 1993; Ono et al, 1996; Maeda et al, 1999). TKS, as described by Japanese psychiatry, is always egodystonic and this characteristic permits its distinction from Schizoidal Personality Disorder, which is egosyntonic. In TKS, as in SAD, the patient desires social contact, is distressed by his/her fears, and symptoms strongly interfere with his/her social, occupational and familial functioning.

Table 2

Comparison of Features of Social Phobia and Taijin Kyofusho

Social Phobia	Irrational fear	Results from being in social situations	The person feels that he or she may be humiliated or embarrassed by his/her actions
Taijin Kyofusho	Irrational fear	Results from being in social situations	The person is afraid that his or her body or rude behavior will displease, offend, or embarrass other people

As a disease, some types of TKS might then be considered the Asian version of SAD. Moreover, preliminary data show that TKS responds to serotonin reuptake inhibitors or phenelzine, both of which have proved effective in the treatment of SAD (Clarvit et al, 1996; Matsunaga et al, 2001). Matsunaga and colleagues (2001) reported that 16 (48%) of 33 patients treated for at least 6 months with clomipramine or fluvoxamine in Japan achieved responder status on the basis of a CGI improvement score of 1 or 2, with no differences between the two compounds. Although further research is needed to conclusively demonstrate that TKS responds to the same pharmacotherapies effective in social anxiety disorder; these preliminary results support the notion that TKS could be viewed, in a disease perspective, as an Asian form of SAD.

From the illness perspective (ie, the expression and perception of the disorder by patients), a difference between social anxiety disorder and Taijin Kyofusho emerges: the object of the fear is to be humiliated or embarrassed in situations of social scrutiny in SAD and to displease, embarrass or offend other people in TKS. These differences may reflect the true cultural-bound aspect of TKS, and can be understood by examining the sociocultural factors in the social presentation of self and its relation to the social order that characterize the Japanese culture.

Kirmayer (1991) described several cultural predisposing factors that help in understanding the specific fears of TKS sufferers. The mother-child relationship, model for the conduct of interpersonal relationships in adult life, is characterized in Japan by a high degree of physical contact and efforts to prevent distress by anticipation of the baby's need. Mothers gratify dependency in their children and transmit to them a view of the world outside the family as threatening. Thus, Japanese children tend to be more fearful of strangers and shy when entering school. Moreover, the school system in Japan, reflecting society's values, inculcates a strong sense of interdependence and responsibility for the feeling of others. The child is told to be sunao, which means obedient, docile, and passive, with the goal to build a harmonious social life in which the self is realized through identification with the group. In Japan a distinctive emphasis is devoted to the group over and above the individual, which leads to a greater awareness of how one is perceived by the other members of the group. Moreover, direct or explicit communication of needs is considered insensitive in the Japanese culture: the socially adept person is thought to understand others' needs without verbal communication. The cultural norm for Japan is then implicit communication. Social interaction in the United States and other Western cultures are characterized by a great emphasis on the open expression of interpersonal conflict and confrontation in everyday life (Kirmayer, 2001). In that sense, the self is defined as independent in Western culture versus interdependent in Japan. This cultural difference might help in explain why anxiety about social interactions in SAD is expressed with a focus on the subject and his/her behavior or appearance, whereas in TKS the focus is on the feelings of the other people whom the subject is afraid of hurting (Kleinknecht et al, 1997). Another cultural difference regards the role of gaze in nonverbal communication; in Japan people who make too much eye contact are likely to be considered aggressive or insensitive. Moreover, gaze as well as other nonverbal communication gestures are strictly governed in Japan by implicit laws of reciprocal obligations within a hierarchical frame: each individual participates and is defined by a multitude of hierarchical relationships. The Japanese subject is then constantly aware of such relationships and is taught to act appropriately according to his/her hierarchical status. Social interactions in Japan might then be more anxiety-provoking than in the West.

Ono and Young (2000) refer to another aspect of the dynamics of Japanese families that might be a contributing factor to the development of TKS: the structure of the traditional Japanese house. Doors made of paper instead of wood divide the rooms. People may then easily perceive what is happening in the next room and then are usually very sensitive to how they behave within the house.

In conclusion, Japanese cultural values, socialization practices, and sense of appropriate interpersonal relations are significant factors in the recognition and construction of TKS as a particular illness experience (Ono and Young, 2000). Chang suggests that the allocentric nature of TKS reflects those elements of Japanese culture that are common to East Asian societies as seen in their pattern of child-rearing practices, language, and social ideals. Thus, "TKS is an East Asian cultural patterning of social anxiety (phobia)" (Chang, 1997).

Thus, SAD as a disease appears to be highly prevalent and characterized by similar features across most countries in the world. In the absence of definitive data, we might hypothesize that the same biological correlates underlie its phenomenological expression. SAD as an illness varies across cultures. Taijin Kyofusho has been reviewed here as an example of how cultural values, socialization practices, and sense of appropriate interpersonal relations might be significant factors in the recognition and construction of SAD as a particular illness experience.

Conclusions

Medical anthropology provided psychiatry with a model of disease versus illness. Disease refers to the biomedical aspects of a disorder, which are thought to be uniform across different cultures. Illness refers to the expression and perception of a disorder, and it is considered to vary according to the cultural setting in which patient and psychiatrist meet.

This approach may be applied to anxiety disorders, and specifically to SAD. Social anxiety disorder may be considered a disease within this model, as it has a similar symptom profile and prevalence across countries in which epidemiological studies have been performed and shares similar characteristics across countries (eg, age of onset, sex ratio, associated comorbidities). It seems likely, though unproven to date, that the underlying neurobiology of SAD does not differ in different countries. However, as an illness, SAD varies across cultures: preliminary cross-cultural comparisons have shown differences in the social situations feared and avoided by North American, European and Australian patients. Moreover, treatment-seeking behaviors might also differ across countries. Further research is needed to fully understand the differences in the expression of SAD across countries. Elucidating differences in treatment-seeking behavior is also needed to improve the recognition of the disorder in different settings, an issue of critical importance for SAD, which is still often under-recognized and under-treated.

Taijin Kyofusho is an example of an anxiety disorder in which sociocultural factors, specific to a country, contribute to its expression. Taijin Kyofusho appears to be a true culture-bound syndrome. It might be considered as an equivalent of SAD in Japan and other East Asian countries, but represents a broader construct, including disorders other than SAD. Preliminary reports suggest that, like SAD, some cases of TKS may be SSRI-responsive (Matsunaga et al, 2001), However, the term TKS in Japan maintains a clinical utility as a) in its current description, it is a broader diagnostic construct than DSM Social Phobia; b) it is very well accepted by patients as a diagnosis; TKS is viewed as a more severe form of a normal anxiety state related to interpersonal interactions (taijin kyofu); and, c) TKS is well recognized as a nosological entity by clinicians, who apply specific culture-bound interventions such as Morita therapy for its treatment.

This example of cultural influences on the expression of SAD highlights the importance of considering cultural factors in clinical practice. In practice, patients should always be asked about their explanation and understanding of their anxiety in order to make these factors explicit. The addition of an illness perspective to the usual disease model of the anxiety disorders will enable clinicians to build a shared language and conceptual model of the disorder with their patients, which will increase the acceptability of, compliance with, and ultimately the effectiveness of therapeutic interventions.

References

American Psychiatric Association. Diagnostic and Statistical Manual of Mental Disorders, Fourth Edition, Text Revision, 2000. Washington, DC, American Psychiatric Association.

Amies PL, Gelder MG, Shaw PM. Social phobia: a comparative clinical study. *Br J Psychiatry*. 1983;142:174-179.

Canino GJ, Bird HR, Shrout PE, Rubio-Stipec M, Bravo M, Martinez R, Sesman M, Guevara LM. The prevalence of specific psychiatric disorders in Puerto Rico. *Arch Gen Psychiatry*. 1987;44:727-735.

Chang SC. Social anxiety (phobia) and East Asian culture. *Depress Anxiety* 1997;5(3):115-120.

Chapman TF, Mannuzza S, Fyer AJ. Epidemiology and family studies of social phobia. In: Heimberg RG, Liebowitz MR, Hope DA, Schneier FR (eds). Social phobia: Diagnostic assessment and treatment. New York, Guilford Press. 1995;21-40.

Clarvit SR, Schneier FR, Liebowitz MR. The offensive subtype of taijin-kyofu-sho in New York City: the phenomenology and treatment of a social anxiety disorder. *J Clin Psychiatry.* 1996;57:523-527.

Davidson JRT, Hughes DL, George LK, Blazer DG. The epidemiology of social phobia: findings from the Duke Epidemiological Catchment Area Study. *Psychol Med.* 1993;23:709-718.

Degonda M, Angst J. The Zurich Study. XX. Social phobia and agoraphobia. *Eur Arch Psychiatry Clin Neurosci.* 1993;243:95-102.

Dingenmans AE, van Vliet IM, Couvee J, Westenberg HG. Characteristics of patients with social phobia and their treatment in specialized clinics for anxiety disorders in the Netherlands. *J Affect Disord.* 2001;65:123-129.

Faravelli C, Degl'Innocenti BG, Aiazzi L, Incerpi G, Pallanti S. Epidemiology of anxiety disorders in Florence. *J Affect Disord.* 1989;19:1-5.

Faravelli C, Zucchi T, Viviani B, Salmoria R, Perone A, Paionni A, Scarpato A, Vigliaturo D, Rosi S, D'Adamo D, Bartolozzi D, Cecchi C, Abrardi L. Epidemiology of social phobia: a clinical approach. *Eur Psychiatry.* 2000; 15(1):17-24.

Fujita C. Morita therapy: a psychotherapeutic system for neurosis. 1986, Tokyo, New York: Igaku-shoin.

Geertz C. Religion as a cultural system. In: Banton M (editor). Anthropological approaches to religion. 1966, London: Tavistock.

Guarnaccia PJ, Rogler LH. Research on culture-bound syndromes: new directions. *Am J Psychiatry.* 1999;156:1322-1327.

Heimberg RG, Makris GS, Juster HR, Ost LG, Rapee RM. Social phobia: a preliminary cross-national comparison. *Depress Anxiety*. 1997;5(3):130-133.

Hwu HG, Yeh EK, Chang LY. Prevalence of psychiatric disorders in Taiwan defined by the Chinese Diagnostic Interview Schedule. *Acta Psychiatrica Scandinavica*. 1989;79:136-147.

Kasahara Y. Social phobia in Japan. Paper presented at the First Cultural Psychiatry Symposium between Japan and Korea, Seoul, South Korea, 13-14 February 1987.

Kessler RC, McGonagle KA, Zhao S, Nelson CB, Hughes M, Eshleman S, Wittchen HU, Kendler KS. Lifetime and 12-month prevalence of DSM-III-R psychiatric disorders in the United States. Results from the National Comorbidity Survey. *Arch Gen Psychiatry*. 1994;51:8-19.

Kirmayer LJ. The place of culture in psychiatric nosology: Taijin Kyofusho and DSM-III-R. *J Nerv Ment Dis*. 1991;179:19-28.

Kirmayer LJ. The cultural context of anxiety disorders. Psychiatric Clinics of North America 1995;18:503-521.

Kirmayer LJ. Cultural variations in the clinical presentation of depression and anxiety: implications for diagnosis and treatment. *J Clin Psychiatry*. 2001;62(suppl 13):22-28.

Kleinknecht RA, Dinnel DL, Kleinknecht EE, Hiruma N, Harada N. Cultural factors in social anxiety: a comparison of social phobia symptoms and Taijin kyofusho. *J Anxiety Disord*. 1997;11(2):157-177.

Kleinman A. Concepts and a model for the comparison of medical systems as cultural systems. *Social Science and Medicine*. 1978;12:85-93.

Lee SH. Social phobia in Korea. Paper presented at the First Cultural Psychiatry Symposium between Japan and Korea, Seoul, South Korea, 13-14 February 1987.

Lee CK, Kwak YS, Yamamoto J, Rhee H, Kim YS, Han JH, Choi JO, Lee YH. Psychiatric epidemiology in Korea. Part I: gender and age differences in Seoul. *Journal of Mental and Nervous Disease*. 1990;178:242-246.

Leff J, Wig NN, Bedi H, et al. Relatives' expressed emotion and the course of schizophrenia in Chandigarh. A two-year follow-up of first-contact sample. *Br J Psychiatry*. 1990;156:351-356.

Lépine JP, Lellouch J, Lovell A, Téhérani M, Pariente P. L'épidémiologie des troubles anxieux et dépressifs dans une population générale française. *Confrontations psychiatriques*. 1993;35:1-23.

Lépine JP, Wittchen HU, Essau CA. Lifetime and current comorbidity of anxiety and affective disorders:results from the international WHO/ADAMHA CIDI field trials. *International Journal of Methods in Psychiatric Research*. 1993;3:67-77.

Lépine JP. Epidemiology, burden, and disability in depression and anxiety. *J Clin Psychiatry*. 2001;62(suppl 13):4-10.

Lindal E, Stefansson JG. The lifetime prevalence of anxiety disorders in Iceland as estimated by the US national Institute of Mental Health Diagnostic Interview Schedule. *Acta Psychiatr Scand*. 1993;88:29-34.

Littlewood R. From categories to contexts: a decade of the 'new cross-cultural psychiatry'. *Br J Psychiatry*. 1990;156: 308-327.

Maeda F, Shirahase J, Asai M. Somatization in different cultures (I) – Taijin Kyofusho as one aspect of somatoform disorder in Japan. In: Somatoform disorders – a worldwide perspective. Ono Y, Janca A, Asai M, Sartorius N (Editors). Tokyo: Springer Verlag 1999;146-152.

Marks IM. The classification of phobic disorders. *Br J Psychiatry*. 1970;116: 377-386.

Matsunaga H, Kiriike N, Matsui T, Iwasaki Y, Stein DJ. Taijin kyofusho: a form of social anxiety disorder that responds to serotonin reuptake inhibitors? *Int J Neuropsychopharmacol*. 2001;4(3):231-237.

McNally R, Cassiday KL, Calamari JE. Taijin-kyofu-sho in a black American woman: behavioral treatment of a "culture-bound" anxiety disorder. *J Anxiety Disorders*. 1990;4:83-87.

Munro A. Delusional disorder. Paranoia and related illnesses. Cambridge University Press, Cambridge, UK: 1999.

Ono Y, Yoshimura K, Sueoka R, Yamauchi K, Mizushima H, Momose T, Nakamura K, Okonogi K, Asai M. Avoidant personality disorder and taijin kyofu: sociocultural implications of the WHO/ADAMHA International Study of Personality Disorders in Japan. *Acta Psychiat Scand.* 1996;93:172-176.

Ono Y, Young J. Taijin Kyofusho in Japan: social phobia or culture-bound syndrome? *Psychiatric Networks.* 2000;3:47-58.

Pélissolo A, Andre C, Moutard-Martin F, Wittchen HU, Lepine JP. Social phobia in the community: relationship between diagnostic threshold and prevalence. *Eur Psychiatry.* 2000;15(1):25-28.

Perugi G, Nassini S, Maremmani I, Madaro D, Toni C, Simonini E, Akiskal HS. Putative clinical subtypes of social phobia: a factor-analytical study. *Acta Psychiatr Scand.* 2001;104:280-288.

Phillips KA, McElroy SL, Keck PE Jr., Pope HG Jr., Hudson JI. Body Dysmorphic Disorder: 30 cases of imagined ugliness. *Am J Psychiatry.* 1993; 150:302-308.

Prince R, Tcheng-Laroche F. Culture-bound syndromes and international disease classification. *Cult Med Psychiatry.* 1987;11:3-19.

Robins LN, Regier DA, eds. Psychiatric disorders in America: the Epidemiologic Catchment Area Study. New York, NY: Free Press, 1991.

Russell JG. Anxiety disorders in Japan: a review of the Japanese literature on shinkeishitsu and taijinkyofusho. *Cult Med Psychiatry.* 1989;13(4):391-403.

Sartorius N, Jabensky A, Korten G, et al. Early manifestations and first-contact incidence of schizophrenia in different cultures. *Psychol Med.* 1986;16: 909-928.

Solyom L, Ledwidge B, Solyom C. Delineating social phobia. *Br J Psychiatry.* 1986;149:377-386.

Stein MB, Torgrud LJ, Walker JR. Social phobia symptoms, subtypes, and severity. Findings from a community survey. *Arch Gen Psychiatry.* 2000;57: 1046-1052.

Tajima O. Mental health care in Japan: recognition and treatment of depression and anxiety disorders. *J Clin Psychiatry.* 2001;62(suppl 13):39-44.

Takahashi T. Social phobia syndrome in Japan. *Compr Psychiatry* 1989;30: 45-52.

Wacker HR, Mullejans R, Klein KH, Battegay R. Identification of cases of anxiety disorders and affective disorders in the community according to ICD-10 and DSM-III-R by using the Composite International Diagnostic Interview (CIDI). *Int J Meth Psychiat Res.* 1992;2:91-100.

Weiller E, Bisserbe JC, Boyer P, Lepine JP, Lecrubier Y. Social phobia in general health care. An unrecognized undertreated disabling disorder. *Br J Psychiatry.* 1996;168:169-174.

Weissman MM, Bland RC, Canino GJ, Greenwald S, Lee CK, Newman SC, Rubio-Stipec M, Wickramatne PJ. The cross-national epidemiology of social phobia: a preliminary report. *Int Clin Psychopharmacol.* 1996;11(suppl 3):9-14.

Wells JE, Bushnell JA, Hornblow AR, Joyce PR, Oakley-Browne MA. Christchurch Psychiatric Epidemiologic Study, I: methodology and lifetime prevalence for specific psychiatric disorders. *Aust N Z J Psychiatry.* 1989; 23:315-326.

Wittchen HU, Essau CA, von Zerssen D, Krieg JC, Zaudig M. Lifetime and six-month prevalence of mental disorders in the Munich Follow-up Study. *Eur Arch Psychiatry Clin Neurosci.* 1992;241:247-258.

Wittchen HU, Stein M, Kessler RC. Social fears and social phobia in a community sample of adolescents and young adults: prevalence, risk factors and comorbidity. *Psychol Med.* 1999;29:309-323.

World Health Organization. Schizophrenia: an international follow-up study. Chichester: John Wiley & Sons, 1979.

Chapter 5
The Neurobiology of Social Anxiety Disorder

Justine M. Kent, M.D., Sanjay J. Mathew, M.D., Jack M. Gorman, M.D.

Introduction

Interest in the study of the neurobiology of social anxiety disorder, while persistently lagging behind the other anxiety disorders, has recently been reinvigorated, primarily through neuroimaging techniques. Social anxiety disorder is now chiefly conceptualized as a neurodevelopmental illness, tending to be chronic in nature, which involves aberrant functioning in several neurobiological systems. In this chapter, we review our current state of understanding of developmental, genetic, neurobiological, and neuroanatomical contributions to social anxiety. A review of preclinical models of social interaction and attachment, while critically important in informing clinical work in this area, is beyond the scope of this chapter and the reader is referred to Mathew and colleagues for review (Mathew et al, 2001).

Current neuroanatomic and neurochemical hypotheses of social anxiety have been informed by preclinical research involving models of fear and stress. Although the model of fear conditioning is commonly invoked as important in the etiology of phobias, evidence suggests that social phobia principally develops in the absence of an initial, threatening exposure. Another potential explanation is that modeling of fearful responding by others underlies the appearance of social anxiety in the absence of direct experience. Yet another possibility is that social phobia manifests itself as a result of dysfunction within an evolved neural network specifically designed to assess social cues for threatening content. Currently, neuroanatomically based models for the phobias remain in the early stages of development (see Fyer, 1998; Li et al, 2001; Mathew et al, 2001; Stein, 1998). The development of any comprehensive neurobiological model of social anxiety disorder requires the integration of information from genetic, preclinical, and clinical studies, with neuroimaging studies of the type described below informing such models.

Developmental Issues

Of the adult anxiety disorders, social anxiety disorder is the one most frequently identified as having its onset in childhood, suggesting that developmental antecedents may be particularly important in this disorder. Much of the work describing the appearance of fearful and anxious behaviors across the early stages of development comes from the laboratory of Kagan and colleagues. Kagan first noted that infants at four months of age who had low tolerance for novelty and changes in their environment, as evidenced by autonomic activation and outward signs of distress, were more likely to become fearful or "behaviorally inhibited" at 21 months of age (Kagan, 1997). Likewise, higher rates of anxiety disorders were identified at follow-up visits at ages 4, 5-1/2, and 7-1/2 in those children categorized as behaviorally inhibited at 21 months (Hirshfeld et al, 1992). Behavioral inhibition has also been associated specifically with increased risk of developing social anxiety disorder in adolescence, and is believed by many to be the developmental precursor to adult social anxiety (Kagan, 1997; Rosenbaum et al, 1993). Pine and colleagues have identified a more specific link, reporting an association between adolescent social anxiety disorder and adult social anxiety disorder: odds ratio=3.37 (Pine et al, 1998). Thus, several lines of evidence support a developmental continuum from childhood behavioral inhibition to adolescent social anxiety disorder to adult social anxiety disorder. Why not all children identified as behaviorally inhibited go on to develop significant problems with social anxiety is likely explained by a complex interaction of environmental, cognitive, and biologic factors which require further investigation.

Genetic Studies in Social Anxiety Disorder

Genetic studies of social anxiety disorder are limited, but indicate that genetic transmission of this disorder, like many psychiatric disorders, is complex. Results from an early study by Kendler and colleagues (1992) examining concordance rates for social anxiety in monozygotic female twins suggest that genetic factors have a modest, but significant effect on the development of social anxiety. They reported concordance rates for social phobia of 44.4% in monozygotic twins and 15.3% in dizygotic twins. Extending these findings by improving diagnostic reliability, Kendler and colleagues (Kendler et al, 1999) interviewed 854 pairs of female twins at two visits, eight years apart. The estimated heritability within this sample rose to 51%, consistent with a moderate effect. In a later study involving over 700 pairs of monozygotic male twins and almost 500 pairs of dizygotic male twins, Kendler et al (2001) reported on rates of five different phobias.

The investigators concluded that genetic factors increased risk for all phobia subtypes, while individual-specific environmental/experiential factors increased risk in a phobia-subtype specific manner.

Family studies also suggest that behavioral inhibition has a familial aggregation, especially for the generalized subtype of social anxiety disorder (Mannuzza et al, 1995; Stein et al, 1998). Fyer and colleagues (1995) reported a 16% rate of social anxiety disorder in first-degree relatives of probands with the disorder (relative risk 3.12). In a direct interview study, Stein and colleagues reported that the generalized subtype of social phobia occurred at nearly a 10-fold greater rate in first-degree relatives of social phobic probands than in the general population (Stein et al, 1998). In addition, children of patients with social anxiety disorder have been shown to be at increased risk for developing both social anxiety and other anxiety disorders. In a study of the offspring of 26 patients with social phobia, Mancini and colleagues reported that 23% met criteria for social phobia, while an additional 30% met criteria for overanxious disorder (Mancini et al, 1996). Lieb and colleagues (2000) quantified this risk, reporting an odds ratio of 4.7 for social phobia among parents and children. In addition, children at high risk for anxiety disorders have been shown to demonstrate increased physiological responsivity, consistent with a temperamental and probably biological predisposition for the development of anxiety disorders (Merikangas et al, 1999).

As much as these data from genetic and familial aggregation studies suggest some genetic predisposition to the development of social anxiety disorder, to our knowledge, there are no published results of genomic scans suggesting candidate genes for social anxiety. Progress in understanding the genetic contribution to the development of social anxiety disorder will undoubtedly expand in concert with our understanding of the human genome.

Neurobiological Studies Employing Pharmacological Probes

Limited evidence implicates several major neurotransmitter systems in the pathophysiology of social anxiety disorder, including serotonin, norepinephrine, dopamine, and corticotrophin releasing hormone (CRH). In general, patients with adult social anxiety respond to general anxiogenic probes, such as carbon dioxide inhalation and pentagastrin infusion, with psychological and physiological markers intermediate between those of patients with panic disorder and healthy, non-psychiatric controls (McCann et al, 1997; Papp et al, 1993). However, in a study conducted in children with social anxiety disorder, Pine and colleagues found no association between respiratory sensitivity to carbon dioxide inhalation and symptomatology (Pine et al, 1998).

Among studies utilizing serotonergic probes, Tancer and colleagues (1994-1995) have reported elevated cortisol levels, but normal prolactin levels, in response to the indirect serotonin agonist fenfluramine in social anxiety patients compared to normal controls, consistent with that observed in panic disorder. Likewise, Hollander et al (1998) reported a significantly elevated cortisol response and normal prolactin response to the mixed serotonergic agonist-antagonist m-chlorophenyl-piperazine (m-CPP) in female subjects with social phobia. Overall, these results suggest that post-synaptic 5-HT2 receptors may be supersensitized in social phobia, while 5-HT1 receptor activity, which regulates prolactin responding, may be normal. Although these results indicate that serotonin plays some role in social anxiety disorder, it is unclear how and through which pathways serotonin may regulate social behavior. Stein has suggested that deficiencies in integrating social information appropriately may result from dysfunction within the mesolimbic reward pathways involving the ventral tegmental area, resulting in a lack of reinforcement of normally rewarding social interactions (Stein, 1998). Because serotonergic projections from the dorsal raphe nuclei to the ventral tegmental area modulate dopaminergic transmission in this region, this is one potential pathway by which serotonin may influence social reward. In fact, SSRIs, medications which have been demonstrated to successfully treat symptoms of social anxiety disorder in numerous controlled trials, have also been shown to increase dopaminergic transmission in the ventral tegmental area in preclinical studies (Herve et al, 1987).

Studies investigating the role of noradrenaline and the phenomenon of autonomic hyperarousal in social anxiety have employed varied methods. In challenge studies with the alpha-2 adrenergic antagonist yohimbine, which acutely increases norepinephrine levels via interruption of the presynaptic negative feedback mechanism, patients with social anxiety disorder have demonstrated increased symptomatology associated with increased plasma 3-methoxy-4-hydroxyphenylglycol (MHPG) concentrations (Potts et al, 1996). However, direct infusion of epinephrine did not cause significant elevations in anxiety, making the role of this neurotransmitter in social anxiety somewhat unclear (Papp, 1988). Response to the alpha-2 adrenergic agonist, clonidine, differed depending on whether it was given orally or intravenously, with only the intravenous infusion resulting in a blunted growth hormone response (Tancer et al, 1993). Blunting of the growth hormone response to clonidine has been reported in depression and other anxiety disorders such as panic and generalized anxiety disorder, and is believed to be a result of desensitization or downregulation of post-synaptic alpha-2 adrenergic receptors resulting from excess noradrenergic activity. Another possibility is that the blunted growth hormone response to clonidine reflects increased activity of corticotrophin releasing factor, a critical neuropeptide in fear responding (Coplan et al, 1997; Coplan et al, 2000).

Investigation of the dopamine system in social anxiety disorder using pharmacological probes is limited, to our knowledge, to a single study using L-dopa. In this study, no abnormalities in dopaminergic function were reported (Tancer et al, 1994-1995). In a study of 29 patients with panic disorder and comorbid social phobia, significantly lower levels of homovanillic acid (HVA), the major metabolite of dopamine, were found in the cerebrospinal fluid of patients versus controls (Johnson et al,1994). Despite these limited findings involving the dopamine system, recent results from neuroimaging studies, described below, suggest a potentially significant role for dopamine in the pathogenesis of social anxiety.

Neuroanatomical models of social information processing
Recent work in non-human primates and in humans has utilized neuroimaging techniques to define neural systems that are activated in the processing of social information. Through this work, it is now clear that specific neural networks exist for assessing threatening content in social cues. These include cues conveyed via facial expressions, eye gaze, vocal intonation, and body gestures. Successful and adaptive social behavior rests on the ability to perceive and then flexibly process and react to social signals, which are constantly shifting in meaning. Amaral and colleagues have demonstrated that bilateral, axon-sparing lesions of the amygdala in rhesus monkeys result in social "disinhibition:" that is, the monkeys interact more with strangers and are more socially gregarious (Amaral, 2002). In humans, the amygdala has been shown to be important in assigning emotional valence to facial expressions. Haxby and colleagues (2002) have proposed a neuroanatomical model for processing of facial expressions, beginning with a "core system" comprised of interconnected regions within the occipitotemporal extrastriate visual cortex. Information from these areas is then

conveyed for further processing to several structures, which Haxby has described as the "extended system," which are involved in biographical recognition, discrimination of speech via mouth movements, spatially-directed attention, and affective assignment and emotional processing. Within this extended system, the amygdala is activated during affective assignment and emotional processing, particularly during the perception of negative, and in particular, fearful faces (Breiter et al, 1996; Morris et al, 1998; Morris et al, 1996; Whalen et al, 1998) and during direct eye contact (Kawashima et al, 1999). Thus, the amygdala is an area of interest in social anxiety, and, as discussed below, there is now evidence from neuroimaging studies of patients with social anxiety disorder supporting a model of exaggerated activity within this highly evolutionarily conserved neuroanatomical circuit for facial perception.

Neuroimaging Studies in Social Anxiety Disorder

Despite the high prevalence of social anxiety disorder, there is only a single volumetric study reported in social phobia. Potts and colleagues (1996) used morphometric MRI to measure total cerebrum, caudate, putamen and thalamus in 22 subjects with social phobia and 20 matched healthy control subjects. No significant between-group differences were found in any of the brain regions examined.

Functional imaging studies in social phobia have been conducted in neutral/resting states, and during cognitive activation tasks and symptom provocation paradigms. In a neutral state imaging study employing single photon emission tomography (SPECT) of patients with social phobia versus healthy control subjects, no significant between-group differences in rCBF were reported (Stein & Leslie, 1996). Symptom provocation and exposure studies have, however, proven more fruitful. Using fMRI to measure brain activity, Birbaumer and colleagues (1998) studied seven patients with social phobia compared with five healthy control subjects while exposing them to slides of neutral human faces or aversive odors. Social phobics demonstrated greater amygdalar activation in response to the human face stimuli versus the healthy comparison group. In a later study, Schneider et al (1999) used fMRI to measure brain activity during a classical conditioning paradigm. Twelve subjects with social phobia and an equal number of healthy control subjects underwent conditioning, with neutral face stimuli serving as the conditioned stimuli and odors (aversive odor, odorless air) serving as the unconditioned stimuli. When neutral faces were linked with the negative odor, subjects with social phobia exhibited increased rCBF in the amygdala and hippocampus, while healthy comparison subjects had signal decreases in these same regions. Thus, aversive conditioning with human face stimuli suggests that social phobics incorrectly assign threat to human faces, even when depicting neutral expressions.

Symptom provocation studies have also provided important information regarding the neuroanatomy underlying social anxiety. Tillfors and colleagues (2001) studied the rCBF response of 18 subjects with social phobia and six non-anxious, healthy comparison subjects using PET while subjects spoke in front of an audience (public speaking task) or alone (private speaking task). In response to the greater anxiety-generating public (versus private) speaking task, patients with social phobia demonstrated a significantly greater rCBF response in the right amygdala and periamygdaloid cortex compared to control subjects. Interestingly, rCBF decreased in subjects with social phobia in cortical regions, including the orbitofrontal and insular cortices and the temporal pole, while healthy comparison subjects demonstrated increases in rCBF in these same cortical areas. This response pattern in social phobic subjects, relatively consistent across studies, suggests that increased subcortical/limbic activity is accompanied by relatively decreased frontal cortical activity. This shift in brain activity is consistent with a failure of cortical processing and a shift to the phylogenetically older subcortical fear circuitry. Thus, in response to exposure to either human face stimuli or the stress of public speaking, patients with social phobia display exaggerated activity within key structures in fear responding, such as the amygdala and medial temporal areas.

There are now two reported imaging studies examining the effects of treatment on regional brain activity in social phobia. Van der Linden and colleagues (Van der Linden et al, 2000) studied the effect of pharmacotherapy with the SSRI citalopram on rCBF with SPECT in 15 subjects with social phobia, who underwent scanning before and after eight weeks of treatment. Reductions in rCBF were noted in the anterolateral left temporal cortex, left cingulate, and left midfrontal cortex in response to SSRI treatment. Those subjects judged as non-responders to treatment had greater rCBF at baseline in the anterolateral left temporal cortex and the lateral left mid-frontal cortex when compared to responders. Limitations of this study include the fact that several subjects had other comorbid anxiety disorders and two patients were on additional psychotropic medications at the time of scanning.

A more recent study examined the effects of two different anxiety treatments, pharmacotherapy with a SSRI and cognitive behavioral therapy (CBT), on rCBF in patients with social anxiety disorder. In a randomized design, 18 patients were scanned using PET techniques during a public speaking task (Fumark et al, 2002). Subjects were divided into three groups: citalopram treatment, CBT, or waiting list (control group). Regional CBF was measured before, and then after nine weeks of treatment or nine weeks on the waiting list. Results demonstrated similar changes in rCBF in responders of both treatment groups in response to public speaking: decreases bilaterally in rCBF in the amygdala, hippocampus, and related periamygdaloid, perihippocampal, and rhinal cortices, while no significant changes in rCBF were observed in the wait list control group. These findings suggest that both pharmacotherapy with a SSRI and CBT, when effective in reducing social anxiety symptoms, attenuate activity in brain regions associated with the neural network identified as underlying danger perception and fear responding. Change in rCBF followed improvement, and was not specific to treatment modality.

Several imaging studies examining neurochemistry and neuroreceptor abnormalities in social phobia have recently been reported. Magnetic resonance spectroscopy studies suggest abnormalities in brain metabolite ratios, consistent with increased choline and myo-inositol in both cortical and subcortical gray areas (Davidson et al, 1993; Tupler et al, 1997). Two neuroreceptor studies have focused on the dopamine system in social anxiety. Tiihonen et al (1997) used the radiotracer I-123-labelled-beta CIT with SPECT to measure the density of dopamine reuptake sites in 11 generalized social phobia subjects and 28 healthy comparison subjects. In the social phobia versus comparison group, significant reductions in striatal dopamine reuptake binding site density were found. In a later study, Schneier et al (2000) measured dopamine D2 receptor binding in the striatum of ten subjects with social anxiety and an equal number of matched healthy comparison subjects using the radiotracer [123I] iodobenzamide with SPECT. Subjects with social phobia demonstrated significantly decreased D2 receptor binding when compared with controls, with a trend ($p<0.07$) toward a negative correlation of binding potential and score on the Liebowitz Social Anxiety Scale. In a related study, decreased D2 receptor binding has also been reported in healthy subjects scoring high on the personality trait of detachment (Breier et al, 1998). In a recent PET study by our group, we measured binding potential for the serotonin reuptake transporter (SERT) using the [11C] McN 5652 radioligand in seven patients with social anxiety disorder versus an equal number of matched controls and found no difference in binding potential (Kent et al, unpublished data). Though this data should be interpreted cautiously given the small number of subjects, the results suggest that there is no major abnormality in SERT density in social anxiety disorder, although this does not preclude abnormalities in other aspects of the serotonergic system.

Summary

Both twin and family studies provide evidence for a significant genetic component in the transmission of social anxiety disorder. Familial aggregation studies also suggest that there are genetic differences in transmission between the generalized and discrete subtypes of social anxiety disorder. The sum of neurobiological studies utilizing pharmacological probes suggest potential dysfunction in central dopamine, serotonin, and norepinephrine systems in social anxiety disorder; however, more recent neuroimaging studies examining the neurochemistry of social anxiety support a central role for dopamine. Evidence supporting deficits in dopamine function in social phobia have now been reported in two studies, consistent with theories implicating the dopamine system in social reward (Stein, 1998b).

Although the body of functional imaging data in social anxiety has expanded in the last few years, it remains insufficient to establish a complete neuroanatomical model. Certain preliminary hypotheses regarding the underlying neural networks can be drawn, however, due to a convergence of findings in the social phobia literature. In response to exposure to either human face stimuli or to the stress of public speaking, subjects with social phobia demonstrate exaggerated activity in the amygdala and related medial temporal lobe areas. Subjects with social phobia also show abnormal activity within medial temporal lobe structures during aversive conditioning with human face stimuli. Cortical restraint over subcortical fear structures appears to be deficient, as evidenced by a shift in brain activity from cortical areas, normally activated during higher level processing of social/emotional stimuli, to the amygdala, hippocampus, and related subcortical structures. Thus, hyperreactivity within fear neural pathways centered on the amygdala may result in incorrect assignment of threat to social cues, such as facial expressions, and functional deficiencies in the striatal dopamine reward system may account for a lack of positive reinforcement/reward for engaging in social interaction. As preclinical, genetic, neuroendocrine, neurotransmitter, and neuroimaging studies continue to improve our understanding of normal and pathological social anxiety, neural circuitry models will continue to evolve, aiding our understanding of this complex disorder.

References

Amaral D. The primate amygdala and the neurobiology of social behavior: Implications for understanding social anxiety. *Biol Psychiatry.* 2002;51, 11-17.

Birbaume N, Grodd W, Diedrich O, Klose U, Erb M, Lotze M, Schneider F, Weiss U, Fior H. fMRI reveals amygdala activation to human faces in social phobics. *NeuroReport.* 1998;9(6):1223-1226.

Breier A, Kestler L, Adler C, Elman I, Wiesenfeld N, Malhotra A, Pickar D. Dopamine D2 receptor density and personal detachment in healthy subjects. *Am J Psychiatry.* 1998;155:1440-1442.

Breiter H, Etcoff N, Whalen P, Kennedy W, Rauch S, Buckner R, Strauss M, Human S, Rosen B. Response and habituation of the human amygdala during visual processing of facial expression. *Neuron.* 1996;17:875-887.

Coplan J, Pine D, Papp L, Gorman J. A view on noradrenergic, hypothalamic-pituitary-adrenal axis and extrahypothalamic corticotrophin-releasing factor function in anxiety and affective disorders: the reduced growth hormone response to clonidine. *Psychopharmacol Bull.* 1997;33:193-204.

Coplan J, Smith E, Trost R, Scharf B, Altemus M, Bjornson L, Owens M, Gorman J, Nemeroff C, Rosenblum L. Growth hormone response to clonidine in adversely reared young adult primates: relationship to serial cerebrospinal fluid corticotropin-releasing factor concentrations. *Psychiatry Res.* 2000;95:3-12.

Davidson J, Krishnan K, Charles H, Boyko O, Potts N, Ford S, Patterson L. Magnetic resonance spectroscopy in social phobia: preliminary findings. *J Clin Psychiatry.* 1993;54:19-25.

Fumark T, Tillfors M, Marteinsdottir I, Fischer H, Pissiota A, Langstrom B, Fredrikson M. Common changes in cerebral blood flow in patients with social phobia treated with citalopram or cognitive-behavioral therapy. *Arch Gen Psychiatry.* 2002;59:425-433.

Fyer A. Current approaches to etiology and pathophysiology of specific phobia. *Biol Psychiatry.* 1998;44:1295-1304.

Fyer A, Mannuzza S, Chapman T, Martin L, Klein D. Specificity in familial aggregation of phobic disorders. *Arch Gen Psychiatry.* 1995;52:564-573.

Haxby J, Hoffman E, Gobbini M. Human neural systems for face recognition and social communication. *Biol Psychiatry.* 2002;51:59-67.

Herve D, Pickel V, Joh T, Beaudet A. Serotonin axon terminals in the ventral tegmental area of the rat: fine structure and synaptic input to dopaminergic neurons. *Brain Res.* 1987;435:71-83.

Hirshfeld D, Rosenbaum J, Biederman J, Bolduc E, Faraone S, Snidman N, Reznick J, Kagan J. Stable behavioral inhibition and its association with anxiety disorder. *J Am Acad Child Adolesc Psychiatry.* 1992;31:103-111.

Hollander E, Kwon J, Weiller F, Cohen L, Stein D, DeCaria C, Liebowitz M, Simeon D. Serotonergic function in social phobia: comparison to normal control and obsessive-compulsive disorder subjects. *Psychiatry Re*s. 1998; 79:213-217.

Johnson M, Lydiard R, Zealber, J, Fossey M, Ballenger J. Plasma and CSF HVA levels in panic patients with comorbid social phobia. *Biol Psychiatry.* 1994;36:425-427.

Kagan J. Temperament and the reactions to unfamiliarity. *Child Dev.* 1997; 68:139-143.

Kawashima R, Sugiura M, Kato T, Nakamura A, Hatano K, Ito K. The human amygdala plays an important role in gaze monitoring. A PET study. *Brain.* 1999;122:779-783.

Kendler K, Karkowski L, Prescott C. Fears and phobias: reliability and heritability. *Psychol Med.* 1999;29:539-553.

Kendler K, Myers J, Prescott C, Neale M. The genetic epidemiology of irrational fears and phobias in men. *Arch Gen Psychiatry.* 2001;58:257-265.

Kendler K, Neale M, Kessler R, Heath A, Eaves L. The genetic epidemiology of phobias in women: the interrelationship of agoraphobia, social phobia, situational phobia, and simple phobia. *Arch Gen Psychiatry.* 1992;49:273-281.

Li D, Chokka P, Tibbo P. Toward an integrative understanding of social phobia. *J Psychiatry Neurosci.* 2001;26:190-202.

Lieb R, Wittchen HU, Hofler M, Fuetsch M, Stein M, Merikangas K. Parental psychopathology, parenting styles, and the risk of social phobia in offspring. *Arch Gen Psychiatry.* 2000;57:(859-866).

Mancini C, van Ameringen M, Szatmari P, Fugere C, Boyle M. A high-risk pilot study of the children of adults with social phobia. *J Am Acad Child Adolesc Psychiatry.* 1996;35:1511-1517.

Mannuzza S, Schneier F, Chapman T, Liebowitz M, Klein D, Fyer A. Generalized social phobia: reliability and validity. *Arch Gen Psychiatry.* 1995;52:(230-237).

Mathew S, Coplan J, Gorman J. Neurobiological mechanisms of social anxiety disorder. *Am J Psychiatry.* 2001;158:1558-1567.

McCann U, Slate S, Geraci M, Roscow-Terrill D, Uhde T. A comparison of the effects of intravenous pentagastrin on patients with social phobia, panic disorder and healthy controls. *Neuropsychopharmacology.* 1997; 16:229-237.

Merikangas K, Avenevoli S, Dierker L, Grillon C. Vulnerability factors among children at risk for anxiety disorders. *Biol Psychiatry.* 1999; 46:(1523-1535).

Morris J, Friston K, Buchel C, Frith C, Young A, Calder A, Dolan R. A neuromodulatory role for the human amygdala in processing emotional facial expressions. *Brain.* 1998;121:47-57.

Morris J, Frith C, Perrett D, Rowland D, Young A, Calder A, Dolan R. A differential neural response in the human amygdala to fearful and happy facial expressions. *Nature.* 1996;383:812-815.

Papp LS, Gorman JM, Liebowitz MR, Fyer AJ, Cohen B, Klein DF. Epinephrine infusions in patients with social phobia. *Am J Psychiatry*. 1988; 145:733-736.

Papp LS, Klein D, Martinez J, Schneier F, Cole R, Liebowitz M, Hollander E, Fyer A, Jordan F, Gorman J. Diagnostic and substance specificity of carbon-dioxide-induced panic. *Am J Psychiatry*.1993;150:250-257.

Pine D, Cohen P, Gurley D, Brook J, Ma Y. The risk for early adulthood anxiety and depressive disorders in adolescents with anxiety and depressive disorders. *Arch Gen Psychiatry*.1998;55:56-64.

Pine D, Klein R, Coplan J, Papp L, Hoven C, Martinez J, Kovalenko P, Mandell D, Moreau D, Klein D, Gorman J. Differential carbon dioxide sensitivity in childhood anxiety disorders and non-ill comparison group. *Arch Gen Psychiatry*. 2000;57:960-967.

Potts N, Book S, Davidson J. The neurobiology of social phobia. *Int Clin Psychopharmacol*. 1996;11(suppl 3):43-48.

Rosenbaum J, Biederman J, Bolduc-Murphy E, Faraone S, Chaloff J, Hirschfeld D, Kagan J. Behavioral inhibition in childhood: a risk factor for anxiety disorders. *Harvard Rev Psychiatry*. 1993;1:2-16.

Schneider F, Weiss U, Kessler C, Muller-Gartner HW, Posse S, Salloum JB, Grodd W, Himmelmann F, Gabel W, Birbaumer N. Subcortical correlates of differential classical conditioning of aversive emotional reactions in social phobia. *Biol Psychiatry*. 1999;45:863-871.

Schneier F, Liebowitz M, Abi-Dargham A, Zea-Ponce Y, Shu-Hsing L, Laruelle M. Low dopamine D2 receptor binding potential in social phobia. *Am J Psychiatry*. 2000;157:457-459.

Stein M. Neurobiological perspectives on social phobia: from affiliation to zoology. *Biol Psychiatry*. 1998;44:1277-1285.

Stein M, Chartier M, Hazen A, Kozak M, Tancer M, Lander S, Furer P, Chubaty D, Walker J. A direct-interview family study of generalized social phobia. *Am J Psychiatry*. 1998;155:(90-97).

Stein M, Leslie W. A brain SPECT study of generalized social phobia. *Biol Psychiatry*. 1996;39:825-828.

Tancer M, Mailman R, Stein M, Mason G, Carson S, Golden R. Neuroendocrine responsivity to monoaminergic system probes in generalized social phobia. *Anxiety*. 1994-1995;1:216-223.

Tancer M, Stein M, Uhde T. Growth hormone response to intravenous clonidine in social phobia: comparison to patients with panic disorder and healthy volunteers. *Biol Psychiatry*. 1993;34:591-595.

Tiihonen J, Kuikka J, Bergstrom K, Lepola U, Koponen H, Leinonen E. Dopamine reuptake site densities in patients with social phobia. *Am J Psychiatry*. 1997;154:239-242.

Tillfors M, Furmark T, Marteinsdottir I, Fischer H, Pissiota A, Langstrom B, & Fredrikson M. Cerebral blood flow in subjects with social phobia during stressful speaking tasks: a PET study. *Am J Psychiatry*. 2001;158:1220-1226.

Tupler L, Davidson J, Smith R, Lazeyras F, Charles H, Krishnan K. A repeat proton magnetic resonance spectroscopy study in social phobia. *Biol Psychiatry*. 1997;42:419-424.

Van der Linden G, van Heerden B, Warwick J, Wessels C, van Kradenburg, J, Zungu-Dirwayi N, Stein D. Functional brain imaging and pharmacotherapy in social phobia: single photon emission computed tomography before and after treatment with the selective serotonin reuptake inhibitor citalopram. *Prog Neuro-Psychopharmacol Biol Psychiat*. 2000;24:419-438.

Whalen P, Rauch S, Etcoff N, McInerney S, Lee M, Jenike M. Masked presentations of emotional facial expressions modulate amygdala activity without explicit knowledge. *J Neurosci*. 1998;18:411-418.

Chapter 6

Considering Mechanisms of Action in the Treatment of Social Anxiety Disorder

Michael W. Otto, Ph.D., Steven A. Safren, Ph.D.,
Despina C. Nicolaou, M.S., and Mark H. Pollack, M.D.

As detailed in Chapters 7 and 8 of this volume, there is a wealth of evidence supporting both pharmacologic and cognitive-behavioral interventions for social anxiety disorder (SAD). Comparison treatment studies (eg, Heimberg et al, 1998; Otto et al, 2000) and a meta-analytic review of the treatment outcome literature (Gould et al, 1997) suggest that these treatment modalities provide approximately equivalent outcome. There is also evidence that cognitive-behavioral and pharmacologic interventions are equally tolerable to patients (at least as assessed by drop-out rates in clinical trials) and there appears to be little evidence for differential predictors of response for these two modalities of treatment (R. Gould et al, 1997; Otto et al, 2000). Among cognitive-behavioral treatments, exposure-based and combined cognitive-restructuring and exposure treatments appear to have a subtle edge over cognitive interventions alone, and these treatments appear to be more reliably powerful than relaxation-based treatment and social-skills training alone (for reviews see R. Gould et al, 1997; Feske & Chambless, 1995; Juster & Heimberg, 1995; Taylor, 1996; Heimberg & Barlow, 1991). Among pharmacologic treatments, the monoamine oxidase inhibitors (MAOIs), serotonin selective reuptake inhibitors (SSRIs), and benzodiazepines have the highest estimates of efficacy (R. Gould et al, 1997). The fact that different modalities and strategies of treatment have similar rates of efficacy and similar predictors of outcome presents an interesting challenge for the identification of mechanisms of action for these treatments.

In this chapter, we consider both biological and psychosocial perspectives on treatment mechanism, and seek to provide a unified accounting of how CBT and pharmacotherapy can interrupt the cycle of apprehension, anxiety, and avoidance that characterizes SAD. We also discuss some of the implications of this perspective for combination-treatment strategies.

Biological Considerations   Specification of potential biological mechanisms in the treatment of SAD is limited by an incomplete model of the underlying neurobiology of this and other anxiety disorders. Nonetheless, it is relevant to review of some of the current hypotheses based on studies of laboratory animals, non-human primates, and humans.

In studies of social subordination in non-human primates, the non-dominant animals spend more time alone and fearfully attending to their social environment; thus, in terms of their overt behavior they may share some similarities with socially-phobic humans. These subordinate animals have a number of neuroendocrine abnormalities including impaired serotonergic and dopaminergic function. For example, in a challenge study in subordinate primates, prolactin release in response to a dopaminergic antagonist was decreased, suggesting decreased sensitivity of post-synaptic dopamine receptors (Shively, 1998). Neuroimaging studies also point to an association of decreased central dopaminergic function and social anxiety; a PET study in primates demonstrated decreased striatal dopamine D2 binding in animals with subordinate social status (Grant et al, 1998). A SPECT study in humans with generalized SAD reported evidence of decreased striatal D2 dopamine receptor binding (Schneier et al, 2000). Similarly, another SPECT study of patients with SAD demonstrated decreased striatal dopamine reuptake sites, perhaps reflecting a decrease in the overall number of dopaminergic synapses and neurons in the striatum of individuals with SAD (Tiihonen et al, 1997). Consistent with this evidence of dopaminergic dysregulation is the observation that monoamine oxidase inhibitors (MAOIs), which have dopaminergic properties, are effective for SAD whereas tricyclic antidepressants, which are devoid of dopaminergic effects, are not (Liebowitz et al, 1992; Simpson et al, 1998).

Regarding serotonergic functioning, there are associations between social withdrawal in non-human primates and lower levels of central serotonergic activity (Shively, 1998). Similarly, low levels in cerebrospinal fluid (CSF) of the serotonin metabolite 5-HIAA in free ranging primates were associated with decreased social competence (Mehlman et al, 1995). However, evidence of serotonergic dysregulation from challenge studies in humans with SAD is less clear (Tancer et al, 1994) and the degree to which serotonergic pathways may regulate social interaction and anxiety remains uncertain. Stein (1998) has hypothesized that some of the difficulties experienced by individuals with SAD in social settings may be secondary to dysfunction in dopaminergic mesolimbic reward pathways, such that these individuals do not experience the normal incentives of social interactions. Serotonergic projections from the dorsal raphe nuclei to the ventral tegmental area modulate these dopaminergic reward pathways; it may be that serotonin plays a role in social interaction through these pathways. Consistent with this hypothesis is the observation that SSRIs, which are effective for social anxiety disorder, increase dopamine transmission in the ventral tegmental area (Herve et al, 1987). Further, in one study of non-human primates, enhancement of serotonergic activity led to increased social interactiveness, whereas low serotonin levels were associated with increased avoidance (Raleigh et al, 1983).

Taken together, these lines of research support both dopaminergic and serotonergic regulation of aspects of social stress and avoidance, but with less evidence linking these pathways specifically to SAD. As noted, attention to these pathways is encouraged by the success of dopaminergic or serotonergic agents: MAOIs and SSRIs, respectively. However, these agents have broad efficacy across the anxiety disorders, and other agents, such as benzodiazepines, are also effective for SAD. Accordingly, it is important to consider the role of these agents and dopaminergic and serotonergic pathways in relation to a broader accounting of systems underlying anxiety, apprehension, and avoidance. For this goal, consideration of Gray's (1982a, 1982b) neuropsychological theory of anxiety is useful. According to this early and influential account, both dopamine and serotonin play a central role in the signaling of the Behavioral Inhibition System (BIS). This system consists of the septohippocampal system, the Papez circuit, the prefrontal cortex, and several ascending monoaminergic pathways, which enervate the cortex. The BIS is thought to mediate potentially anxious experiences, such as novel encounters or stimuli linked to punishment, by increasing attention and arousal, and inhibiting current behaviors.

Gray hypothesized that during anxious pathologic states such as SAD, the BIS is overstimulated due to either conditioning experiences or inappropriate dopaminergic or serotonergic stimulation of the septohippocampal system. Although it is difficult to delineate the specific serotonergic and noradrenergic influences on this regulatory system, serotonergic inputs have been associated with the aversive labeling of stimuli as well as motor inhibition. Consequently, antidepressant treatment is thought to target these serotonergic and noradrenergic afferents by reducing their stimulation of the septohippocampal system. Similarly, benzodiazepine treatments moderate the BIS by promoting the effects of gamma-aminobutyric acid (GABA), an inhibitory neurotransmitter that employs a number of mechanisms that influence the BIS (Gray, 1982a, 1982b).

This provides one perspective on the mechanism of action of pharmacotherapy for SAD; successful agents may exert their effects on the BIS, reducing anxiety and behavioral inhibition, in accordance with their broader efficacy across the anxiety disorders. However, this accounting is incomplete without consideration of the role that anxiolysis, or modulation of tendencies toward behavioral inhibition, plays in helping patients recover from SAD. Accordingly, a broader perspective on mechanism of action can be achieved by considering the interplay between anxiolysis and behavioral inhibition and some of the information processing, affective, and behavioral patterns characterizing SAD (Otto & Safren, 2000).

The Impact of Anxiolysis on SAD

Chapter 8 in this volume provides a brief accounting of some of the common cognitive, behavioral, and affective patterns observed in patients with SAD and in socially anxious analogue populations (see also Clark & McManus, 2002; Roth & Heimberg, 2001; Otto & Safren, 2000). Specifically, individuals with SAD are particularly vigilant to negative social cues and are prone to negative interpretations of social interactions (eg, Foa et al, 2000; Stopa & Clark, 2000). This "one-two punch" of negative interpretations of ambiguous events and vigilance to negative outcomes has the natural result of helping ensure that individuals with SAD are confronted with anxiety-provoking social cues. Furthermore, any resulting anxiety is likely to further enhance feelings of social failure and anxious apprehension. For example, individuals with SAD have increased self-focused attention when in social situations, and overestimate the degree to which their anxiety is perceptible to others (for review see Clark & McManus, 2002). The result is an amplification of anxiety in social situations; anxiety itself becomes a signal of social failure, cueing additional anxiety and avoidance (see Chapter 8 for further detail). These chains of negative expectations, anxious apprehension, and vigilance to and overinterpretation of negative social and symptom cues is complemented by selective recall and negative interpretation of social performance after social events, including beliefs that there are greater social costs of poor performance (for review see Clark & McManus, 2002). The result of such negative post-event processing is enhanced negative expectations for subsequent social events (Mellings & Alden, 2000). Subsequent avoidance of social situations helps lock in the memories of social failure and disallows acquisition of information that would help disconfirm existing beliefs and negative expectations.

Given these patterns, one of the effects of anxiolysis brought by pharmacotherapy is diminution of one of the perceived cues of social failure – the anxiety response itself. With fewer symptoms of anxiety in social situations, individuals with SAD may be more likely to attend to other relevant social cues. Indeed, there is evidence that when self-focused attention is reduced, SAD patients improve more from social exposure (Wells & Papageorgiou, 1998). The degree of negative affect also appears to influence the adoption of negative thoughts and beliefs (for review see Otto & Safren, 2000), including fears of negative evaluations from others (Ball et al, 1995). Accordingly, pharmacologic modulation of anxious and depressed mood may have important effects on reducing the impact of negative expectations and vigilance to negative outcomes. This is further supported by evidence that pharmacotherapy ameliorates negative social expectations at least as well as cognitive-behavioral strategies (Otto et al, 2000). Similar evidence exists for the ability for successful pharmacotherapy to reduce information-processing biases toward social threat cues (Mattia et al, 1993). Finally, pharmacologically-mediated reductions in behavioral inhibition (eg, via modulation of serotonergic systems) may play a role in enhancing the willingness of SAD patients to participate In feared social interactions. With reductions in anxiety and negative expectations, patients may achieve greater (perceived) social success in these interactions. Accordingly, after pharmacotherapy, each successive interaction allows a patient to begin to garner a sense of ensuing confidence in their social abilities as well as further reductions in anticipatory anxiety and negative expectations prior to forthcoming social contact.

Of particular note in this accounting of the translation of pharmacologic effects on anxiety into improved social confidence is the presumption that social exposure plays an important role. This presumption is consistent with recommendations from expert pharmacotherapists for the routine application of exposure assignments in the context of pharmacotherapy (Sutherland & Davidson, 1995). It is also consistent with evidence in other anxiety disorders of the crucial role that exposure-based experience plays in translating pharmacological actions into clinical success. For example, in their study of panic disorder, Telch et al (1985) showed that when exposure was discouraged by clinicians, the beneficial effects of imipramine were diminished.

As we have discussed elsewhere (Otto & Safren, 2000), some of these hypothesized actions of pharmacotherapy are open to empirical testing. For example, the time course of changes in fears of anxiety in social situations relative to other social fears, can provide insight into the degree to which pharmacotherapy has initial, specific effects on catastrophic interpretations of anxiety sensations, and whether other changes in negative cognitions change more slowly over time. Likewise, examination of the effects of anti-exposure instruction during the early phase of medication treatment may help elucidate which cognitive changes are a more direct effect of medications, and which are dependent on successful exposure to social situations for change. Finally, examination of residual levels of fears of negative evaluation, relative to residual anxious distress or avoidance, offers the potential of clarifying which changes are most important for maintenance of treatment gains from medication.

Medication treatment may also offer other beneficial effects that are not reliant on the primarily anxiolytic mechanisms discussed above. For example, there is some evidence for pharmacotherapy to reduce the negative impact of stressors (in this case, stress from feared social interactions) on neurogensis. More specifically, E. Gould et al (1997), examining a group of subordinate tree shrews in a laboratory setting, reported that stressful experiences were associated with a rapid decrease in the number of new cells produced in the dentate gyrus. Inhibition of granule cell proliferation in hippocampus and other brain regions following stressful experiences may be secondary to production of increased levels of circulating glucocorticoids and stimulation of glutamate release. Mathews and colleagues (2001) have hypothesized that excessive glutaminergic transmission in hippocampus as well as cortical regions, might be a critical component in the underlying pathophysiology of stress-related anxiety conditions such as SAD, and that treatment may prevent inhibition of neurogenesis by stimulating neurogenic factors and modifying glutaminergic neurotransmission. Thus, one potential mechanism through which effective treatments may exert their effect is by modulating neurotropic factors in the brain that are inhibited by stressors — serotonin selective reuptake inhibitors (SSRIs), for instance, which are effective for the treatment of social anxiety disorder (see Chapter 7), increase the expression of BDNF (brain derived neurotropic factor) in the hippocampus (Nibuya et al, 1996; Duman et al, 1997).

Finally, recent research has also expanded consideration of the ways in which pharmacotherapy may enhance beneficial learning from successful exposure experiences. For example, Davis and Myers (2002) detail the role of glutamate and GABA in fear extinction, and introduce the possibility that modulation of glutamatergic systems (with specific attention on D-cycloserine) during programmed exposure may increase the speed and durability of fear reduction.

Mechanisms of Action of CBT

As detailed in Chapter 8 of this volume, CBT brings to bear a variety of informational, cognitive-restructuring, and exposure interventions to successfully treat SAD. Relative to a cognitive-behavioral model of the disorder, informational and cognitive interventions are used to: 1) correct the dysfunctional thoughts that evoke apprehension and anxiety; 2) eliminate failure-focused attention and enhance the development of adaptive cognitive skills; 3) eliminate situational avoidance as well as subtle avoidance strategies (safety behaviors); 4) enhance accurate evaluation of performance in social situations, and 5) provide corrective social experiences via structured exposure exercises. Research indicates that therapeutic benefit from CBT is not dependent on non-specific treatment effects such as group support and time with a caring therapist (Heimberg et al, 1990; Heimberg & Juster, 1994), nor is it explained simply by expectations of improvement, although positive expectancies are nonetheless correlated with treatment benefit (Safren et al, 1997).

The combined learning brought by cognitive and exposure interventions are designed to change the meaning and processing of social cues, so that anxiety and avoidance are no longer elicited. From a cognitive perspective, any of a number of changes in the patient's evaluation of social cues and her or his competence may serve as a mediator of therapeutic benefit. Specifically, Hofmann (2000) reviewed the role of three related cognitive processes in relation to benefits achieved in CBT: 1) changes in negative cognitive appraisals, particularly reductions in the perceived costs (negative outcomes) of social interactions; 2) changes in self efficacy, particularly, the perceived ability to effectively confront and negotiate social situations, and 3) perceived emotional control, specifically the perception of improved control over the magnitude or consequences of anxiety in social situations. Given the difficulties differentiating the specific scientific predictions (and resulting support) for these accounts (Hofmann, 2000), these perspectives on the change process may serve a more heuristic rather than scientific purpose.

More specific guidance around potentially important aspects of the change process for CBT is provided by Wells and associates. Specifically, Wells et al (1995) noted that social contact alone does not ensure that successful fear-extinction strategies are being put into play. Wells and associates observed that while some patients were exposing themselves to social situations, their SAD was nevertheless maintained. Wells et al (1995) used the phrase "safety behaviors" to describe subtle avoidance strategies often employed by these individuals (eg, averting one's eyes while talking) to provide a sense of security in social situations. Safety behaviors may also include cognitive strategies such as "acting" the part of another during social interactions. Use of these behaviors is associated with lower anxiety reduction from exposure procedures, perhaps because they prevent unambiguous learning that negative outcomes do not occur without the use of these safety strategies.

Accordingly, Wells et al (1995; p. 160) suggested guidelines for maximizing the effectiveness of exposure by attending to safety behaviors and cognitive biases that may insulate patients from successful learning:

1. Patients' feared catastrophes and their perceived likelihood should be assessed.
2. Safety behaviors that are rationally linked to these feared catastrophes should be identified.
3. A cognitive set focusing on active disconfirmation of negative beliefs should be established.
4. Safety behaviors should be eliminated or reversed during exposure.
5. The outcome of the assignment should be discussed in information-processing terms.

Post-exposure processing should specifically include inquiries whether feared outcomes occurred, with elicitation of the patient's explanation why they did not. In particular, the therapist should assess whether nonoccurrence of feared outcomes is attributed to residual safety behavior or whether the exposure exercise produced important changes in beliefs.

Inherent within this approach is the assumption that exposure is an active process that must take into account information processing biases, and that the goal of exposure is more than the simple loosening of fear associations. Instead, it is the active relearning of safety in a once-phobic situation. Accordingly, to maximize this learning therapists need to be vigilant that this learning is not conditional (eg, "I will be OK only if I do not sweat") by providing unambiguous opportunities for learning during social exposure.

These considerations from an information-processing perspective are fully consistent with principles of extinction learning that have been consolidated over the last decade (for review, see Bouton, 2002). Rather than representing a weakening of fear associations, exposure-based extinction can be characterized as an alteration of the meaning of the fear cue (eg, with successful exposure, social situations no longer cue danger-based interpretations and anxiety). After extinction training, memories of the original fear learning and the extinction (safety) learning are in competition, with the subsequent meaning of the fear cue (safety or danger) determined in part by which memory is evoked by the context in which it appears. Research suggests that the second association learned (extinction) is particularly dependent on context for retrieval, and with the wrong context, fear associations may re-emerge (see Bouton, 2002). Conditional learning of safety (ie, only in the context of safety behaviors) accordingly leave individuals at risk for relapse should they be exposed to social cues in a different context (when safety behaviors are not present). Accordingly, to maximize extinction of fear cues, therapists need to maximize the number of context cues for safety learning. In humans, some of the context effects may be represented by cognitive shifts, where patients learn to actively approach social situations differently, without relying on specific safety behaviors to "make it through" the social encounter.

In summary, cognitive-behavioral treatments combining exposure with cognitive restructuring provide a format for correcting dysfunctional thoughts, redirecting failure-focused attention, and eliminating safety behaviors, while promoting the learning of safety in relation to social cues. During initial exposure practice, patients learn that they tend to meet objective performance goals despite their subjective experience of anxiety. With subsequent exposures, confidence rises and negative expectations and evocation of anxiety in social situations is attenuated further. Successful exposure leads to more positive memories and more adaptive expectations for future performance. Over time, fear memories are replaced by alternative, more-adaptive associations and beliefs.

Issues in Combination Treatment Strategies

So far in our discussion of treatment mechanisms, pharmacologic and cognitive-behavioral treatment strategies have been considered separately. This is true even though we have tried to map some of the known benefits of pharmacotherapy onto a model of SAD that is more traditionally associated with psychosocial accounts of the disorder. We also could have done the opposite: asserting that the biological effects of CBT are likely to normalize aberrant CNS circuits much in the same way as has been demonstrated for CBT for the circuits involved in obsessive-compulsive disorder (Schwartz et al, 1996). Indeed, it seems likely that changes in temperament-related social inhibition (eg, Rapee, 2002) will lead to changes in serotonergic activity, in the same way this activity appears to change following alterations in social dominance in primates (Raleigh et al, 1984). However, such considerations have to remain speculative given the limited development of the biological literature for SAD. Nonetheless, it is important to note that understanding biological treatment from a psychosocial perspective, or psychosocial treatment from a biological perspective, is not the same as asserting similar mechanisms of change for these treatment modalities.

In contrast, to oversimplify our discussions thus far, we have asserted that pharmacologic treatments alter the anxiety signal thereby changing core cognitive and behavioral aspects of the disorder, whereas CBT intervenes with core cognitive and behavioral (including affective-regulation) aspects of the disorder, thereby changing the anxiety response to social cues. A central question is whether these mechanisms of action are complementary or, to address the question at a less theoretical level, whether combined treatment is better than either modality of treatment alone?

We have already discussed the potential importance of routine encouragement of social exposure practice as part of standard pharmacotherapy; at this point we will address the nature of the benefits of adding medications to CBT. As discussed briefly in Chapter 8, across the anxiety disorders it appears that such combination treatment tends to offer only subtle advantages over CBT alone (Foa et al, 2002), and the small body of research to date suggests this trend may extend to SAD as well. Moreover, there is evidence from studies of panic disorder that combination treatment may sap some of the durability of treatment gains from CBT, at least when medications are later discontinued (cf., Barlow et al, 2000; Marks et al, 1993). Why would pharmacotherapy and its discontinuation disrupt the maintenance of treatment gains commonly observed for CBT? A potential answer is provided by further examination of the extinction literature. As detailed by Bouton (2002), extinction effects are often context dependent, and contexts can include the physical environment, time of day, and internal events such as drug or affective state. As demonstrated in animal studies, changes in internal state (eg, anxiety reduction from a benzodiazepine) may be a powerful enough context so that adequate safety learning is achieved only in that context. When the drug state is withdrawn, so is the learned safety, a finding consistent with the loss of CBT efficacy following medication discontinuation.

An additional source of potential negative interactions between CBT and medications concerns the blockade of anxiety cues by medication (for review see Otto, 2002). The learning that negative outcomes do not occur, despite the presence of initial anxiety, may lead to safety learning that is more resistant to relapse. Again using animal research as a model (see Bouton, 2002), inclusion of occasional aversive events during exposure (extinction trials) may lead to greater resistance to relapse, presumably because the anxiety becomes part of the context for extinction. Accordingly, when anxiety is encountered in the future, learned safety may persist as the primary association. For this reason, completion of CBT in the absence of medication-related anxiolysis may provide patients with more complete learning of safety, especially in relation to emotional cues of anxiety. This hypothesized mechanism is consistent with information processing accounts of fear associations, where elicitation of anxiety during exposure is thought to lead to more complete safety learning (Foa & Kozak, 1986).

It is important to note that these concerns about combined treatment may be specific to the timing of combination-treatment onset and offset (Foa et al, 2002). A variety of studies indicate that deleterious effects of combination treatment are not evident when CBT is offered during and after medication discontinuation, presumably because patients are able to extend their extinction learning when the contextual cues of medication (and anxiety suppression) are no longer present (Otto, 2002). Accordingly, our concerns about combination treatments will need to be evaluated relative to the range of ways medications and CBT can be combined, particularly relative to strategies to maintain treatment gains over the long term. For example, short-term use of medications as a prelude to CBT, with continuation of CBT beyond medication discontinuation, may be one way to combine these strategies more successfully. However, our concerns do raise the issue that there may be good reasons not to assume that combination strategies are more effective or cost-effective for the average patient when longer-term outcome is considered.

Concluding Comments

In this chapter, we reviewed evidence for some of the neuroanatomic circuits and information processing characteristics associated with SAD. We then devoted attention to the way in which pharmacologic and cognitive-behavioral treatments achieve their outcomes by interrupting ongoing cycles of the negative social expectations, vigilance to negative outcomes, anxiety symptoms, negative interpretations of symptoms and outcomes, and avoidance and escape responses that characterize this disorder. Pharmacologic and cognitive-behavioral interventions were hypothesized to intervene at different points in this chain of symptoms. Although both treatments provide beneficial outcome, different mechanisms of action may lead to difficulties following medication discontinuation in combination treatment, at least relative to the longer-term maintenance of treatment gains associated with CBT monotherapy. However, these cautions were drawn from work in other anxiety disorders; the treatment literature for SAD is still in the early phase in considering the benefits of combined treatment relative to monotherapy with pharmacotherapy or CBT, particularly in relation to longer-term outcomes.

References

Ball SG, Otto MW, Pollack MH, Uccello R, Rosenbaum JF. Differentiating social phobia and panic disorder: A test of core beliefs. *Cognitive Therapy and Research*. 1995;19:473-482.

Barlow DH, Gorman JM, Shear MK, Woods SW:.Cognitive-behavioral therapy, imipramine, or their combination for panic disorder: A randomized controlled trial. *Journal of the American Medical Association*. 2000;283: 2529-2536.

Bouton ME. Context, ambiguity, and unlearning: Sources of relapse after behavioral extinction. *Biological Psychiatry*. 2002;52:976-986.

Bruch MA, Mattia JI, Heimberg RG, Holt CS. Cognitive specificity in social anxiety and depression: Supporting evidence and qualifications due to affective confounding. *Cognitive Therapy and Research*. 1993;17:1-21.

Clark DM, McManus F. Information processing in social phobia. *Biological Psychiatry*. 2002;51:92-100.

Clark DM, Wells A. A cognitive model of social phobia. In RG Heimberg, MR Liebowitz, DA Hope, FR Schneier (Eds.) *Social phobia: Diagnosis, assessment, and treatment* (pp. 69-93). 1995; New York: Guilford Press.

Davidson JRT, Tupler LA, Potts NLS. Treatment of social phobia with benzodiazepines. *Journal of Clinical Psychiatry*. 1994;55 (Suppl 6):28-32.

Davis M, Myers KM. The role of glutamate and GABA in fear extinction: Clinical implications for exposure therapy. *Biological Psychiatry*. 2002; 52:998-1007.

Duman RS, Heninger GR, Nestler EJ. A molecular and cellular theory of depression. *Archives of General Psychiatry*. 1997;54:597-606.

Feske U, Chambless DL. Cognitive behavioral verses exposure only treatment for social phobia: A meta-analysis. *Behavior Therapy*.1995; 26:695-720.

Foa EB, Franklin ME, Moser J. Context in the clinic: How well do CBT and medications work in combination. *Biological Psychiatry*. 2002;52:987-997.

Foa EB, Kozak MJ. Emotional processing of fear: Exposure to corrective information. *Psychological Bulletin*. 1986;99:20-35.

Foa EB, Gilboa-Schechtman E, Amir N, Freshman M. Memory bias in generalized social phobia: Remembering negative emotional expressions. *Journal of Anxiety Disorders*. 2000;14:501-519.

Gould E, McEwen BS, Tanapat P, Galea LAM, Fuchs E. Neurogenesis in the dentate gyrus of the adult tree shrew is regulated by psychosocial stress and NMDA receptor activation. *Journal of Neuroscience*. 1997;17:2492-2498.

Gould RA, Buckminster S, Pollack MH, Otto MW, Yap L. Cognitive-behavioral and pharmacological treatment for social phobia: A meta-analysis. *Clinical Psychology: Science and Practice*. 1997;4:291-306.

Grant KA, Shively CA, Nader MA, Ehrenkaufer RL, Line SW, Morton TE, Gage HD, Mach RH. Effect of social status on striatal dopamine D2 receptor binding characteristics in cynomolgus monkeys assessed with positron emission tomography. *Synapse*. 1998;29:80-83.

Gray JA. Precis of the neuropsychology of anxiety: An enquiry into the functions of the septo-hippocampal system. *Behavioral and Brain Sciences*. 1982a;5:469-534.

Gray JA. The neuropsychology of anxiety: An enquiry into the functions of the septo-hippocampal system. 1982b;Oxford: Oxford University Press.

Heimberg RG, Liebowitz MR, Hope DA, Schneier FR, Holt CS, Welkowitz LA, Juster HR, Campeas R, Bruch MA, Cloitre M, Fallon B, Klein DF. Cognitive behavioral group therapy vs phenelzine therapy for social phobia: 12-week outcome. *Archives of General Psychiatry*. 1998;55:1133-1141.

Heimberg RG, Barlow DH. New developments in cognitive-behavioral therapy for social phobia. *Journal of Clinical Psychiatry*. 1991;52:(suppl), 21-30.

Heimberg RG, Juster HR. Treatment of social phobia in cognitive-behavioral groups. *Journal of Clinical Psychiatry*. 1994;55 (Suppl 6):38-46.

Heimberg RG, Dodge CS, Hope DA, Kennedy CR, Zollo LJ, Becker RJ. Cognitive behavioral group treatment of social phobia: Comparison with a credible placebo control. *Cognitive Therapy and Research*. 1990;14:1-23.

Herve D, Pickel V, Joh T, Beaudet A. Serotonin axon terminals in the ventral tegmental area of the rat: fine structure and synaptic input to dopaminergic neurons. *Brain Research*. 1987;435:71-83.

Hofmann SG. Treatment of social phobia: Potential mediators and moderators. *Clinical Psychology: Science and Practice*. 2000;7:3-16.

Juster HR, Heimberg RG. Social phobia. Longitudinal course and long-term outcome of cognitive-behavioral treatment. *Psychiatric Clinics of North America*. 1995;18:821-42.

Liebowitz MR, Campeas R, Hollander E. Possible dopamine dysregulation in social phobia and atypical depression. *Psychiatry Research*. 1987;22:89-90.

Liebowitz MR, Schneier F, Campeas R, Hollander E, Hatterer J, Fyer A, Gorman J, Papp L, Davies S, Gully R. Phenelzine vs atenolol in social phobia: a placebo-controlled comparison. *Archives of General Psychiatry*. 1992; 49:290-300.

Marks IM, Swinson RP, Basoglu M, Kuch K, Noshirvani H, O'Sullivan G, Lelliott PT, Kirby M, McNamee G, Sengun S, and Wickwire K. Alprazolam and exposure alone and combined in panic disorder with agoraphobia: A controlled study in London and Toronto. *British Journal of Psychiatry*. 1993;162:776-787.

Mathews SJ, Coplan, JD; Gorman, JM. Neurobiological mechanisms of Social Anxiety Disorder. *American Journal of Psychiatry*. 2001;158:1558-1567.

Mattia JI, Heimberg RG, Hope DA. The revised stroop color-naming task in social phobics. *Behaviour Research and Therapy*. 1993;31:305-313.

Mattick RP, Peters L, Clark JC. Exposure and cognitive restructuring for social phobia: A controlled study. *Behavior Therapy*. 1989;20:3-23.

McEwan KL, Devins GM. Is increased arousal in social anxiety noticed by others? *Journal of Abnormal Psychology*. 1993;92:417-421.

Mellings TM, Alden LE. Cognitive processes in social anxiety: the effects of self-focus, rumination andanticipatory processing.*Behavior. Research and Therapy,* 2000;38:243-257.

Mehlman PT, Higley JD, Faucher I, Lilly AA, Taub DM, Vickers J, Suomi SJ, Linnoila M. Correlation of CSF 5-HIAA concentration with sociality and the timing of emigration in free-ranging primates. *American Journal of Psychiatry*. 1995;152:907-913.

Mersch PP, Emmelkamp PMG, Lips C. Social phobia: Individual response patterns and the effects of behavioral and cognitive interventions. A follow-up study. *Behaviour Research and Therapy*. 1991;29:357-362.

Newman MG, Hofmann SG, Trabert W, Roth WT, Taylor CB. Does behavioral treatment of social phobia lead to cognitive changes? *Behavior Therapy*. 1994;25:503-517.

Nibuya M, Nestler EJ, Duman RS. Chronic antidepressant administration increases the expression of cAMP response element binding protein (CREB) in rat hippocampus. *Journal of Neuroscience*. 1996;16:2365-2372.

Otto MW. Learning and "unlearning" fears: Preparedness, neural pathways, and patients. *Biological Psychiatry*. 2002;52:917-920.

Otto MW. Cognitive-behavioral therapy for social anxiety disorder: Model, methods, and outcome. *Journal of Clinical Psychiatry*. 1999;60 (suppl 9):14-19.

Otto MW, Pollack MH, Gould RA, Worthington JJ, Heimberg RG, McArdle E T, Rosenbaum JF. A comparison of the efficacy of clonazepam and cognitive-behavioral group therapy for the treatment of social phobia. *Journal of Anxiety Disorder*s. 2000;14:345-358.

Otto MW, Safren SA. Mechanisms of action in the treatment of social phobia. In Hofmann SG, DiBartolo PM (Eds.) *Social phobia and social anxiety: An integration* (pp. 391-407). 2000;Needham Heights, MA: Allyn & Bacon.

Potts NLS, Davidson JRT. Pharmacological treatments: Literature review. In Heimberg RG, Liebowitz MR, Hope DA, Schneier FR (Eds.), Social phobia: Diagnosis, assessment, and treatment (pp. 334-365). 1995;New York: Guilford.

Raleigh MJ, Brammer GL, McGuire MT. Male dominance, serotonergic systems, and the behavioral and physiological effects of drugs in vervet monkeys (Cercopithecus aethiops sabaeus). *Prog Clin Biol Res*. 1983; 131:185-197.

Raleigh MJ, McGuire MT, Brammer GL, Yuwiler A. Social and environmental influences on blood serotonin concentrations in monkeys. *Archives of General Psychiatry*. 1984;41:405-410.

Rapee RM. The development and modification of temperamental risk for anxiety disorders: Prevention of a lifetime of anxiety? *Biological Psychiatry*. 2002;52:947-957.

Rapee RM, Heimberg RG. A cognitive-behavioral model of anxiety in social phobia. *Behaviour Research and Therapy*. 1997;35:741-756.

Roth DA, Heimberg RG. Cognitive-behavioral models of social anxiety disorder. *Psychiatric Clinics of North America*. 2001;24:753-771.

Safren SA, Heimberg RG, Juster HR. The relationship of patient expectancies to initial severity and treatment outcome in Cognitive-Behavioral Group Treatment of Social Phobia. *Journal of Consulting and Clinical Psychology*. 1997;65:694-698.

Safren SA, Heimberg RG, Turk C. Factor structure of the Social Phobia Scale and the Social Interaction Anxiety Scale. *Behaviour Research and Therapy*. 1998;36:443-453.

Schneier FR, Liebowitz MR, Abi-Dargham A, Zea-Ponce Y, Lin S-H, Laruelle M. Low dopamine D2 receptor binding potential in social phobia. *American Journal of Psychiatry*. 2000;157:457-459.

Schwartz JM, Stoessel PW, Baxter LR, Jr., Martin KM, Phelps ME. Systematic changes in cerebral glucose metabolic rate after successful behavior modification treatment of obsessive-compulsive disorder. *Archives of General Psychiatry*. 1996;53:109-114.

Shively CA. Social subordination stress, behavior, and central monoaminergic function in female cynomolgus monkeys. *Biological Psychiatry*. 1998; 44:882-891.

Simpson HB, Schneier F, Campeas R, Marshall RD, Fallon BA, Davies S, Klein DF, Liebowitz MR. Imipramine in the treatment of social phobia. *Journal of Clinical Psychopharmacology*. 1998;18:132-135.

Stein MB. Neurobiological perspectives on social phobia: from affiliation to zoology. *Biological Psychiatry*. 1998;44:1277-1285.

Stopa L, Clark DM. Social Phobia and interpretation of social events. *Behavior, Research, and Therapy*. 2000;38:273-283.

Sutherland SM, Davidson JRT. b-Blockers and benzodiazepines in pharmacotherapy. In MB Stein (Ed.) Social phobia: Clinical and research perspectives. 1995; Washington, DC: American Psychiatric Press (pp. 323-326).

Sutherland SM, Tupler LA, Colket JT, Davidson JRT. A 2-year follow-up of social phobia: Status after a brief medication trial. *Journal of Nervous and Mental Disease*. 1996;184:731-738.

Tancer ME, Mailman RB, Stein MB, Mason GA, Carson SW, Golden RN. Neuroendocrine responsivity to monoaminergic system probes in generalized social phobia. *Anxiety*. 1994-1995;1:216-223.

Tancer ME, Lewis MH, Stein MB. Biological aspects. In: MB Stein (Ed.) *Social Phobia: Clinical and Research Perspectives* (pp. 323-326). 1995; Washington, DC: American Psychiatric Press.

Taylor S. Meta-analysis of cognitive-behavioral treatments for social phobia. *Journal of Behaviour Therapy and Experimental Psychiatry*. 1996;27:1-9.

Telch MJ, Agras WS, Taylor CB, Roth WT, Gallen C. Combined pharmacological and behavioral treatment for agoraphobia. *Behaviour Research and Therapy*. 1985;23:325-335.

Tiihonen J, Kuikka J, Bergstrom K, Lepola U, Koponen H, Leinonen E. Dopamine reuptake site densities in patients with social phobia. *American Journal of Psychiatry.* 1997;154:239-242.

Wells A, Clark DM, Salkovskis P, Ludgate J, Hackmann A, Gelder M. Social phobia: The role of in-situation safety behaviors in maintaining anxiety and negative beliefs. *Behavior Therapy.* 1995;26:153-161.

Wells A, Papageorgiou C. Social phobia: Effects of external attention on anxiety, negative beliefs, and perspective taking. *Behavior Therapy.* 1998;29:357-370.

Westra H, Stewart SH. Cognitive behavioral therapy and pharmacotherapy: Complimentary or contradictory approaches to the treatment of anxiety? *Clinical Psychology Review.* 1998;18:307-340.

Chapter 7
Pharmacotherapy of Social Anxiety Disorder: Current Practice and Future Promise

Elizabeth A. Hoge, M.D. and Mark H. Pollack, M.D.

Introduction

Social phobia, also known as social anxiety disorder, is a relatively common psychiatric disorder, associated with significant adverse impact on educational, occupational, and social functioning. Generalized social anxiety disorder is associated with a higher rate of lifetime suicide attempts, lower wages, decreased likelihood of earning a college degree or achieving a professional occupation, and increased utilization of health care resources (Katzelnick et al, 2001). As the high prevalence and detrimental impact of social phobia has been increasingly recognized, so has interest in the development of effective and practical pharmacological treatment options. In this chapter we will review the pharmacological agents that have demonstrated efficacy for social phobia and discuss potential augmentation strategies for improving outcome in affected adults and children.

Beta Blockers

Beta-blockers, such as propranolol (Inderal) and atenolol (Tenormin) have been used successfully in individuals with non-generalized social anxiety, such as those with "performance anxiety" about public speaking or other performance situations, including significant test-taking anxiety. For instance, in a double blind study of 29 musicians with performance anxiety, the administration of propranolol before a recital led to reductions in symptoms of stage fright and improvement in the quality of the musical performance as judged by music critics (Brantigan et al, 1982). In one survey, 13% of participants at an international cardiology meeting, reported using beta-blockers to reduce performance anxiety before their presentation (Gossard et al, 1984). In a study of 32 high school students with test taking anxiety that impaired their performance on exams, including a first attempt at the Scholastic Aptitude Test (SAT), administration of 40 mg of propranolol one hour before repeating the SAT resulted in an average increase of 130 points (Faigel, 1991).

The direct effects of beta-blockers are limited to a blunting of symptoms of physiological arousal associated with anxiety or fear, such as tachycardia and tremor. As discussed in greater detail by Rayburn and colleagues in this volume (see Chapter 8), it is the individual's attention and concern about these symptoms, eg, "my hands are shaking and my voice is quavering," in social situations that often leads to an escalating cycle of arousal, agitation, and further elevations in social anxiety. Beta-blockers are presumed to be effective in reducing performance anxiety by interrupting this escalating fear cycle; they block the physiologic symptoms of arousal and thus mitigate the individual's escalating concern and focus on their anxiety.

However, beta-blockers are generally not as effective at reducing the emotional and cognitive aspects of social anxiety as they are the physiologic symptoms, and thus have not been considered first-line agents for generalized social anxiety disorder. In a double-blind, placebo-controlled study (Liebowitz et al, 1992) of the beta-blocker atenolol and the monoamine oxidase inhibitor phenelzine for the treatment of social phobia, the effect of atenolol was not significantly different than placebo (see table 1). In that study, response was defined as a Clinical Global Impression of Improvement (CGI-I) score of 1 ("very much improved") or 2 ("much improved") (Guy, 1976); only 30% of atenolol treated patients met response criteria, compared to 64% of patients on phenelzine and 23% on placebo. Of note, the response rate with atenolol for patients with non-generalized (performance-related) social anxiety (40%) was greater than for generalized social anxiety (28%) consistent with its presumed effectiveness for performance anxiety; however, the study was not adequately powered to examine differences in response for the subtypes of social phobia by treatment, and this difference did not achieve statistical significance.

Beta-blockers such as propranolol (10-80mg/day) or atenolol (50-150 mg/day) are typically administered on an "as needed" basis 1-2 hours before a performance situation, although some patients facing frequent performance challenges take them on a more routine basis. Typical side effects of the beta-blockers include lightheadedness, bradycardia, sedation, and nausea. In practice, since atenolol is less lipophilic (Conant et al, 1989) and thus less centrally active, it is often less sedating than propranolol. It is important that patients first test the effects of the beta-blocker prior to use in an actual performance-related event. This will help establish the tolerability of an effective dose and avoid the occurrence of side effects, such as marked lightheadedness, that could be disruptive on the day of the event and serve to further increase performance anxiety.

Monoamine Oxidase Inhibitors (MAOIs)

The MAOIs were the "gold standard" pharmacologic treatment for social phobia in the period before the widespread use of the serotonin selective reuptake inhibitors (SSRIs). A number of investigators, including Liebowitz and others at Columbia, noted that MAOIs were particularly effective for the atypical subtype of depression, which is characterized in part by "rejection sensitivity" (Welkowitz & Liebowitz, 1990). This "interpersonal hypersensitivity" was evocative of the focus of concern in social phobia, leading these clinical researchers to examine and subsequently demonstrate the effectiveness of the MAOIs for patients with social phobia. The efficacy of MAOIs (as compared to tricyclics for instance) in social phobia has been in part attributed to their effects on enhancing dopaminergic neurotransmission, given the accruing data suggesting potential dysregulation in central dopaminergic systems in social phobia (Welkowitz & Liebowitz, 1990).

Although clearly effective, the MAOIs have been supplanted as first line pharmacotherapy for social anxiety disorder by the SSRIs, because of the troubling side effects associated with the older agents including orthostatic hypotension, paresthesias, weight gain and sexual dysfunction. In addition, MAOI therapy is complicated by the need for careful attention to diet and use of concomitant medication because of the risk of potentially fatal hypertensive reactions and serotonin syndrome if the proscriptions are violated.

Phenelzine has been the most well studied of the MAOIs for the treatment of social anxiety, although tranylcypromine has also proven effective (Versiani et al, 1988). In a double blind randomized study by Liebowitz and colleagues (1992) comparing atenolol and phenelzine (Liebowitz et al, 1992), 64% of patients responded to phenelzine, compared to only 23% responding to placebo (p=0.003). Another double-blind, randomized, placebo-controlled study of 78 patients treated with phenelzine or the reversible MAOI, moclobemide, also demonstrated the significant efficacy of phenelzine over placebo (Versiani et al, 1992). After 16 weeks of treatment in that study, patients who had responded to phenelzine were randomized to either continue or switch to placebo. Patients discontinuing

Table 1

Drug	Study	N	Design	Daily Dose, or Mean Dose at End of Trial	Duration
atenolol	Liebowitz 1992	74	RCT	Flex dose, mean=97.6 mg	8 weeks
phenelzine	Liebowitz 1992	74	RCT	Flex dose, mean=75.7 mg	8 weeks
	Versiani 1992	78	RCT	Flex dose, mean=68 mg	8 weeks
	Heimberg 1998	133	RCT	Flex dose, mean=59.6 mg	12 weeks
brofaromine	Lott 1997	102	RCT	50 to 150 mg	10 weeks
moclobemide	Noyes 1997	506	RCT	5 assigned doses from 75-900 mg	12 weeks
clonazepam	Davidson 1993	75	RCT	Flex dose, mean=2.4 mg	10 weeks
	Otto 2000	45	Drug vs CBGT	Flex dose, mean=0.5 to 4 mg	12 weeks

Response: CGI-I of 1 or 2	Other Outcome Measures	Response: LSAS		Baseline Score:	Endpoint Score:	Treatment Difference (change in drug − change in placebo)
30% responded (23% placebo) p=NS		Drug: PBO:		67.4 58.7	57.0 51.9 p=NS	3.6
64% responded (23% placebo) p=0.003		Drug: PBO:		75.3 58.7	41.2 51.9 p<0.001	27.3
		Drug: PBO:		68.5 65.2	14.0 56.2 p<0.001	45.5
	77% responded (41% placebo) measured by SPDSCF (p<0.005)	Drug: PBO:		67.4 65.1	31.9 50.8 (p<0.01)	21.2
50% responded (19% placebo) p=0.001		Drug: PBO:		81.8 79.8	62.6 70.7 (p<0.016)	10.1
No difference from placebo		Actual values not reported; p=NS				
78% responded (20% placebo) p=0.0001		Drug: PBO:		78.3 77.5	38.1 61.7 p<0.0001	24.4
	20% remission (CGI-S<2) in drug group, vs 25% in CBGT	Drug: CBGT		69.5 65.2	29.1 40.2 NS	N/A (no placebo group)

Table 1 (continued)

Drug	Study	N	Design	Daily Dose, or Mean Dose at End of Trial	Duration
fluvoxamine	Van Vliet 1994	30	RCT	Flex dose, mean=150 mg	12 weeks
	Stein 1999	92	RCT	Flex dose, mean=202 mg	12 weeks
fluvoxamine-controlled-release	Sheehan 2002 (poster)	300	RCT	Flex dose mean=212 mg	12 weeks
paroxetine	Stein 1996	36	Open-label, then randomized	Forced-escalation, mean dose 47.9 mg	11 weeks, then 12 weeks discontinuation
	Baldwin 1999	290	RCT	Flex dose, mean=34.7 mg	12 weeks
	Allgulander 2001	92	Placebo controlled	NR	12 weeks
	Stein 1998	187	RCT, 1wk PBO run-in	Flex dose, mean=36.6 mg	12 weeks
	Liebowitz 2002	384	RCT PC, 1-wk PBO run-in	Fixed doses: 20, 40, and 60 mg	12 weeks
	Randall, 2001 SAD + alcohol 1995	15	RCT	Flex dose	8 weeks
sertraline	Katzelnick 1995	10	RCT Crossover	Flex dose, mean=133.5 mg	10 weeks tx, then 10 weeks crossover

Response: CGI-I of 1 or 2	Other Outcome Measures	Response: LSAS		
		Baseline Score:	**Endpoint Score:**	**Treatment Difference**
46% responded (7% placebo)				
42.9% responded (22.7% placebo)		NR	NR	14.2 (95% CI, -23.5 to -4.9)
		Drug: 97.4 PBO: 95.8	61.3 68.5 (p=0.02)	7.2
76.7% responded	During discontinuation, 5/8 of placebo relapsed, 1/8 of drug group	Drug: 75.1	37.2 p<0.0005	
65.7% responded (32.4% placebo) p<0.001		Drug: 87.6 PBO: 86.1	58.2 70.5 (p<0.001)	13.8
NR		Drug: 70.9 PBO: 78.4	36.9 71.4 p=NS	27
55.0% (23.9% placebo) p=0.001		Drug: 78.0 PBO: 83.5	47.5 69.0 (95%CI)	21.5
40 mg: 46.6% (placebo 28.3%) p=0.012 (20 mg and 60 mg not sig)		Drug: 20 mg 79.8 40 mg 77.5 60 mg 76.9 PBO: 73.3	48.4 53.0 51.7 58.3	16.4 9.5 (ns) 10.2 (ns)
67% (22% placebo p≤0.05)		Drug: 79.7 PBO: 73.2	44.6 63.0 p=0.001	18.5
NR	50% responded (9% placebo) on the Liebowotz Social Phobic Disorders Rating Form. (p=0.03)	Drug: 65.5 PBO: 72.3	38.6 64.5 (p<0.05)	19.2

Table 1 *(continued)*

Drug	Study	N	Design	Daily Dose, or Mean Dose at End of Trial	Duration
	Van Ameringen 2001	204	RCT after 1 week placebo lead-in	Flex dose, mean=146.7 mg	20 weeks
	Liebowitz 2002 (poster)	211	RCT after 1 week placebo lead-in	Flex dose, mean=144 mg	12 weeks
fluoxetine	Van Ameringen 1993	16	Open-label	Flex dose, mean=36.9 mg	12 weeks
	Kobak 2002	60	RCT, 1 wk placebo run-in	Flex dose, mean=50 mg	14 weeks
cilatopram	Simon 2001	9	case series	Flex dose, mean=46.7 mg	12 weeks
	Bouwer	22	Open, uncontrolled	Flex dose, 20-40 mg	12 weeks
escitalopram	Kasper 2002 (poster)	358	RCT, 1 wk placebo run-in	NR	12 weeks
venlafaxine	Liebowitz 2002 (poster) two studies:	279	RCT, 1 wk placebo run-in	Flex dose, mean= 146.6 mg	12 weeks
		272	RCT, 1 wk placebo run-in	Flex dose, 160.3 mg	12 weeks
bupropion SR	Emmanuel 2000	18	Open-label	Flex dose, mean=366 mg	12 weeks

Response: CGI-I of 1 or 2	Other Outcome Measures	Response: LSAS		
		Baseline Score:	Endpoint Score:	Treatment Difference
53% (placebo 29%) p<0.01	Brief Social Phobia scale decreased 34.3% (18.6% on placebo) p<0.01	Not used		
56% responded (placebo 29%) p=0.001		Drug: 91.3 PBO: 93.9	60.3 72.2 (p=0.001)	9.3
	77% responded by global improvement scale	Not used		
40% responded (placebo 30%) p=NS		Drug: 81.9 PBO: 81.6	59.3 81.6 p=NS	
78%		Drug: 74.4	34.7	N/A
86%		Drug: 136.2	45.5	N/A
54% responded (placebo=39%) p≤0.001		Drug: 96.3 PBO: 95.4	61.9 68.2	7.3 (p<0.01)
50% (34%, placebo) *		Drug: 91.1 PBO: 86.7	60.9 68.9	12.1 p=0.001
44% (30% placebo) *		Drug: 90.8 PBO: 87.4	57.7 66.0	11.7 p=0.003
60%		Drug: 70.8	45.1 (p<0.01)	N/A

Table 1 *(continued)*

Drug	Study	N	Design	Daily Dose, or Mean Dose at End of Trial	Duration
gabapentin	Pande 1999	69	RCT, 1 wk placebo run-in	Flex dose, 900-3600 mg	14 weeks
valproic acid	Kinrys 2002 (in press)	17	Open trial	Flex dose, mean=1985 mg	12 weeks
buspirone	Clark, 1991	94	RCT	Flex dose, mean=32 mg	6 weeks
	Van Ameringen 1996	10	Open label, augment-ation study	Flex dose, mean=45 mg	8 weeks
	Van Vliet	30	RCT	30 mg	12 weeks
imipramine	Simpson 1998	15	Open label	Flex dose, mean=222 mg	8 week
	Emmanuel 1997	41	RCT	Flex dose, mean=149 mg	8 week

NS= not significant   N/A=not applicable   NR=not reported   SPDSCF=Social Phobic Disorders Severity and Change Form

Note: number in chart for LSAS endpoint and treatment difference were calculated from data given, when they were not reported.
*approximate values from Figure when actual numbers not reported

Response: CGI-I of 1 or 2	Other Outcome Measures		Response: LSAS		
			Baseline Score:	**Endpoint Score:**	**Treatment Difference**
38% responded (17% placebo)		**Drug**: **PBO**:	87.4 83.4	60.3 71.8 (p=0.008)	15.5
		Drug:	62.8	43.6 p<0.0001	
	Self-Statement Quest: placebo improvement >drug		Not used		
70%			Not used		
	27% improved (13% placebo) on the social Phobia Scale, anxiety subscale, but not stat. significant		Not used		
No significant improvement					
	No significant difference from placebo on any measure				

phenelzine experienced a significant return of their anxiety; the Liebowitz Social Anxiety Scale (LSAS) score increased from a mean of 10.1 at week 16 to 40.6 by week 24 (8 weeks after treatment discontinuation). Another double-blind placebo-controlled trial compared phenelzine, alprazolam and cognitive-behavioral group therapy; patients improved on phenelzine, though the change was not significantly greater than for placebo. However, the study had a number of methodological limitations, constraining the interpretation of its findings, including a relatively small sample size. In addition, all patients received self-directed exposure instructions, and thus some active treatment elements, such that all treatment groups, including placebo, improved and differences in efficacy between interventions could not be detected (Gelernter et al, 1991). More recently, Heimberg and colleagues conducted a study comparing cognitive behavioral group therapy (CBGT), phenelzine, an educational-supportive group and placebo for the treatment of social phobia (n=133) (Heimberg et al, 1998). At 12 weeks, 77% of patients taking phenelzine were considered responders based on the Social Phobic Disorders Severity and Change Form (SPDSCF), compared to 41% of those in the placebo group (p<0.005); 75% of those receiving the CBGT intervention and 35% of those in the educational-supportive group also responded.

Concerns about the safety of the irreversible MAOIs such as phenelzine have stimulated considerable interest in a related group of compounds, the reversible inhibitors of monoamine oxidase A (RIMAs). The RIMAs can be displaced off the monoamine oxidase enzyme when a substrate such as tyramine is presented, and therefore do not carry with them the need for strict dietary prohibitions and risk of hypertensive crises associated with the irreversible MAOIs such as phenelzine. While some clinical trials have reported positive results with RIMAs such as moclobemide and brofaromine for social phobia, other studies have not. In a study comparing phenelzine and moclobemide (Versiani et al, 1992), 82% of patients taking moclobemide and 91% of those taking phenelzine were considered improved, with moclobemide much better tolerated by patients. In a double-blind placebo-controlled trial of brofaromine (Lott et al, 1997), 50% of patients responded to treatment compared to 19% of the placebo group (p=0.001) after 10 weeks. However, a large clinical trial program with moclobemide in the United States failed to demonstrate robust efficacy for the agent (Noyes et al, 1997) and plans to bring it to market in this country were dropped. Brofaromine is now off patent and is also not likely to be developed for release. As a result, whereas moclobemide is now available in Canada, there are no RIMAs currently available in the United States, nor any likely to be imminently available.

Phenelzine may be initiated at 15 mg po bid, and titrated up to a typical therapeutic dose of 60 to 90 mg / day, with some refractory patients requiring higher doses in order to respond. As with any MAOI, patients should be instructed to adhere to a diet free of tyramine-containing foods and to avoid sympathomimetic drugs, in order to avoid the risk of hypertensive crisis. To avoid drug-drug interactions, it is best to wait 2 weeks after discontinuing a non-MAOI (4 to 5 weeks for fluoxetine) before starting therapy with an MAOI, and also to wait 2 weeks after discontinuing an MAOI before starting another antidepressant.

Benzodiazepines

Although benzodiazepines are widely used for many anxiety disorders, there is relatively little data systematically investigating their use in social phobia. In the study by Gelernter and colleagues (1991), which as noted above should be understood in the context of its methodological limitations, patients taking alprazolam improved, though not significantly more than placebo. Nonetheless, in that study alprazolam was associated with a high incidence of relapse within 2 months of discontinuing treatment. In a double-blind placebo-controlled trial of 75 patients, 78% treated with clonazepam and 20% of patients taking placebo responded, as measured by the Clinical Global Impression of Improvement rating (CGI-I; p=0.0001) (Davidson et al, 1993). Furthermore, this response was noted as early as the second week, which is sooner than typically seen with antidepressant therapy. More recently, Otto et al compared clonazepam with cognitive-behavioral group therapy (Otto et al, 2000). After 12 weeks, 20% of patients treated with clonazepam met criteria for remission (defined as CGI-severity < 2) compared to 25% of those treated with CBGT.

Benzodiazepines have the advantage of a relatively rapid onset of effect, favorable side effect profile and ability to be administered on an as-needed basis. However, their use may be associated with treatment emergent adverse effects including sedation, ataxia, and cognitive and psychomotor impairment. Regular use is associated with physiologic dependence although abuse liability is generally limited to those with a predisposing diathesis or history of alcohol or substance abuse, for whom alternative therapeutic interventions should be employed when possible. In addition, benzodiazepines are not generally effective for, and may sometimes worsen, the comorbid depression that frequently presents comorbidly with social anxiety disorder. Benzodiazepines are initiated at low dose (eg, clonazepam 0.25-0.5 mg qhs) to minimize emergent adverse effects and titrated up as tolerated to therapeutic doses (eg, clonazepam 1-4 mg / d or its equivalent). Use of a longer-acting benzodiazepine such as clonazepam can minimize interdose rebound anxiety when continuous anxiolytic effect is desired, whereas a shorter-acting agent with a more rapid onset of effect such as alprazolam or lorazepam can be used on an as-needed basis for performance situations. However, similar to beta-blockers, benzodiazepines should be first tried by the patient before the day of a performance situation, in order to assess side effects, such as sedation, which could impair function for some. Further, concurrent alcohol use should be minimized or avoided with benzodiazepine administration.

Serotonin Selective Reuptake Inhibitors (SSRIs)

Serotonin selective reuptake inhibitors have become first line pharmacotherapy for the treatment of social anxiety disorder because of their demonstrated efficacy, favorable side effect profile, and safety (including lack of abuse liability or risk of hypertensive reactions). Furthermore, the SSRI's are broad-spectrum agents, treating a number of the common disorders that present comorbidly with social anxiety disorder including depression, panic and other anxiety disorders. Many of the SSRIs, including paroxetine, fluvoxamine, sertraline, and escitalopram have demonstrated efficacy for the treatment of social anxiety in placebo controlled studies. Several studies have reported fluvoxamine (Luvox) efficacious for social anxiety disorder. One double-blind, placebo-controlled trial studied 30 patients for 12 weeks and found improvement in 46% of subjects treated with fluvoxamine compared to 7% of those treated with placebo (van Vliet et al, 1994). Another study examined 92 patients and reported that 43% of subjects treated with fluvoxamine and 23% treated with placebo improved (p=0.04) (Stein et al, 1999). A recent study of 300 subjects with generalized social anxiety disorder treated over 12 weeks with a controlled-release formulation of fluvoxamine (Sheehan et al, 2002) noted a 37% reduction of symptoms as measured by the LSAS for the active drug, compared with a 28% reduction in the placebo treated group (p=0.02).

Paroxetine (Paxil) was the first drug to receive an FDA-approval for the social anxiety disorder indication. In a forced-escalation open-label study of paroxetine, 77% of 36 treated patients responded to paroxetine after 11 weeks (Stein et al, 1996). Responders were then randomized in double blind fashion to either continue at the same dose or switch to placebo for an additional 12 weeks, and relapse rates were measured. Although the results were not statistically significant, perhaps due to the small sample size, only 1 out of 8 of the continued treatment group relapsed (defined as returning to original scores or worse) compared to 5 out of 8 of the placebo treated group. Stein and colleagues reported a double-blind, placebo-controlled 12 week trial of paroxetine (N=187), (Stein et al, 1998) in which 55% of patients responded, compared to 23.9% of the placebo group (p=0.001).

Baldwin and colleagues (1999) reported on results from a double-blind placebo-controlled multicenter study of paroxetine performed in several European countries and South Africa (Baldwin et al, 1999). Two thirds (65.7%) of the 290 patients with social phobia responded to paroxetine as measured by the CGI-I, compared with 32.4% of the placebo group. The treatment difference, (ie, change in mean LSAS scores between the treatment and placebo groups) of 13.8 points was significant (p<0.02). In a long-term prospective study done in Sweden, 92 patients were randomized to treatment with paroxetine or placebo for 12 weeks and re-evaluated at 32 months (Allgulander & Nilsson, 2001). At 12 weeks, the LSAS scores of the paroxetine-treated group dropped 34 points, while those of the placebo treated group decreased by only seven. Patients who continued treatment after the acute study had a better outcome at the 32-month follow-up. Of note, 24 patients at follow-up were still symptomatic but had not sought further treatment. Many of these subjects said that they "did not want to bother," getting further treatment and had settled for a lower level of functioning, as evidenced by remaining in a relatively lower job level than would be expected given their educational background and other job opportunities. This observation underscores the need for additional education for patients, clinicians and the general public regarding the negative impact of social anxiety disorder and the availability of effective treatments.

A recent double-blind, randomized, controlled, fixed dose trial examined the effectiveness of paroxetine in 384 patients assigned to either 20, 40 or 60 mg/d of paroxetine or placebo (Liebowitz, 2002). Responder rates were greater for the paroxetine 40 mg/d compared to placebo treated patients (46.6% vs 28.3%) while the drop in LSAS was significant for the 20 mg / d group compared to placebo. Improvement on both these measures approached significance for all of the doses of active medication.

The proportion of patients who were "very much improved" was more than twice as high for the paroxetine treated patients compared to those on placebo (20 mg: 19.1%; 40 mg: 20.5%; 60 mg: 22%; placebo: 7.6%).

Comorbid alcohol abuse or dependence is relatively common, occurring in 19-28% of patients with social anxiety disorder, and may in some cases reflect an attempt at "self-medication." In a small, randomized controlled study (Randall et al, 2001), 15 subjects with social anxiety and active alcohol use disorders were randomized to receive either paroxetine or placebo. At the end of 8 weeks, 67% of the subjects in the paroxetine group improved in terms of their social anxiety, compared to 22% of the placebo group. Although group means for reduction in alcohol use tended to improve in the paroxetine but not placebo treated patients, the study was underpowered to demonstrate a statistically significant effect. However, there was a significant effect of paroxetine compared to placebo in CGI-Improvement ratings for alcohol use (p=0.05). This study did suggest the potential salutary effects of treatment on both social anxiety and alcohol use in this comorbid population, although further research in this area is clearly warranted.

There is also growing evidence demonstrating the efficacy of sertraline (Zoloft) for the treatment of social anxiety disorder which recently received FDA approval for this indication. In a small crossover study of 12 patients with social phobia, 50% of sertraline treated patients experienced moderate to marked improvement compared with 9% of the group receiving placebo (p=0.03) (Katzelnick et al, 1995). More recent studies have yielded similar findings. A large Canadian trial assessed 204 patients with generalized social phobia, for 20 weeks; 53% of patients receiving sertraline were considered responders, while 29% of the placebo group responded (p < 0.01) (Van Ameringen et al, 2001). Later, 50 of the patients who responded during the initial treatment period entered a relapse prevention continuation trial for an additional 24 weeks. Half of these patients were randomly assigned to continue on sertraline and half were switched to placebo. Only 4% of the sertraline-continuation group relapsed, whereas 36% of the placebo group relapsed by the end of the study (p=0.01) (Walker et al, 2000). Another large multicenter trial, recruiting patients with moderate-to-severe levels of social phobia (baseline LSAS score of >68), reported significantly greater response rates as assessed on the CGI-I among sertraline treated patients (56%) compared to those on placebo (29%) (Liebowitz et al, 2002).

Fluoxetine (Prozac), has been subject to somewhat less systematic testing than other SSRIs for the treatment of social phobia. A 1993 open clinical trial with fluoxetine in social phobia reported that 10 out of the 16 patients (63%) entering the study were responders (Van Ameringen et al,1993). More recently, fluoxetine was demonstrated to be no more effective than placebo in a double-blind placebo-controlled 14 week study of 60 patients with social phobia (Kobak et al, 2002). This is of interest, though should be interpreted in light of the relatively small sample size in the trial, and the lack of compelling theoretical or research support to date for differential efficacy within the SSRI class in the anxiety disorders. In an interesting case series report, adjunctive fluoxetine was reported effective in reducing increased social anxiety thought to be a result of serotonergic effects of clozapine administration in 8 of 12 schizophrenic patients (Pallanti et al, 1999). One study attempted to correlate brain fluoxetine levels as measured with magnetic resonance spectroscopy, with therapeutic response in a small group (N=8) of patients being treated for social phobia (Miner et al, 1995). Intriguingly, responders did indeed have higher brain fluoxetine levels than non-responders, though the difference in this study did not achieve statistical significance.

A number of case series have reported on the efficacy of citalopram (Celexa) for the treatment of social phobia, including one that described 9 patients receiving a mean dose of 46.7 mg. At week 12, seven of the nine patients responded to citalopram, with a mean decrease in LSAS of 34.7 points (Simon et al, 2001). Another open, uncontrolled study of 22 patients receiving citalopram reported an 86% response rate on the CGI-I (Bouwer & Stein, 1998). Escitalopram (Lexapro), an isomer of citalopram, recently released on the market for depression, has also demonstrated efficacy for social phobia. In a multi-center, double-blind, placebo-controlled, randomized study in patients with social anxiety disorder, response rates for those receiving escitalopram were significantly greater than for those on placebo (54% versus 39% respectively, p≤0.001) (Kasper et al, 2002).

Treatment with the SSRIs for social phobia is typically initiated at low doses (eg, paroxetine 10 mg/d, sertraline 25 mg/d) and titrated up against therapeutic response and tolerability (eg, paroxetine 20-60 mg/d; sertraline 50-200 mg/d). SSRI therapy is characteristically associated with a therapeutic lag in efficacy of 2-3 weeks, although full response may not occur for months. Typical treatment emergent adverse effects include nausea, headache, dizziness, sedation, increased anxiety, and sexual dysfunction.

Serotonin-Norepinephrine Reuptake Inhibitors (SNRIs)

Venlafaxine (Effexor) is a reuptake inhibitor of both serotonin and norepinephrine, which has also demonstrated efficacy for social anxiety disorder. A small open-label trial of the immediate release formulation of venlafaxine noted marked improvement in 8 of 9 patients who had not responded to previous trials with SSRIs (Kelsey, 1995). Recently, two double-blind, placebo-controlled 12-week studies with 279 and 272 patients respectively examined the efficacy of the extended release formulation of venlafaxine (Effexor-XR) for the treatment of generalized social anxiety disorder (Liebowitz & Mangano, 2002). At endpoint, the mean LSAS scores decreased by 30.2 points in one study (p<0.001) and 33.1 points in the other (p<0.003). As a result of these positive outcomes, venlafaxine-XR recently received FDA approval for the treatment of social phobia. Venlafaxine XR can be initiated at 37.5-75 mg/d in patients with social phobia and titrated up against improvement and tolerability to a therapeutic dose range (typically 150-225 mg/d). Treatment emergent adverse effects are similar to those of the SSRIs, with a small proportion of patients experiencing hypertension at higher doses.

Other Medications

Bupropion (Wellbutrin SR), a norepinephrine and dopamine reuptake inhibitor, has been studied in a small open-label trial for social anxiety. After 12 weeks, six out of ten subjects responded to treatment as measured by a CGI-I of 1 or 2 ("much improved" or "very much improved"), suggesting this drug's possible usefulness for social anxiety, although randomized, controlled studies are required to confirm this preliminary finding (Emmanuel et al, 2000). Bupropion-SR can be initiated at 100 mg/day and titrated up to 400 mg/day, administered in a bid dose; side effects include dizziness, headache, insomnia, nausea, tremor, tachycardia, and sedation, with a small increased risk of seizures at doses above recommended levels.

Buspirone (Buspar) is a serotonin-1A receptor partial agonist used primarily for the treatment of generalized anxiety symptoms, although impressions of its effectiveness in clinical practice vary widely. Results from studies of its efficacy for the treatment of social anxiety disorder are mixed. One study (Clark & Agras, 1991) of performance-related social anxiety compared buspirone with cognitive-behavioral therapy. In this study, subjects gave performances in a laboratory setting during which heart rate was monitored. Buspirone failed to show significant effect on reducing anxiety or heart rate; in fact, there was a statistically significant reduction in anxiety ratings as assessed by the "Self-Statement Questionnaire" (Steptoe & Fidler,

1987) that favored placebo. In a double-blind placebo-controlled 12-week trial of buspirone in 30 patients with social phobia, (van Vliet et al, 1997) no significant differences in efficacy were found between the medication and placebo treated groups. However, one report suggests that buspirone may be useful as an adjunct for social phobic patients incompletely responsive to SSRI therapy (Van Ameringen et al, 1996). Van Ameringen and colleagues (1996) reported, that in an open trial of ten patients with social anxiety disorder persistently symptomatic despite SSRI therapy, seven of ten achieved responder status after the addition of buspirone (mean dose 45 mg/d).

Gabapentin, a GABA (gamma aminobutyric acid) analogue, with an unclear mechanism of action that may involve interaction with the GABA transporter leading to increased levels of this inhibitory neurotransmitter (Stahl, 2000), has been reported effective in the treatment of a number of anxiety disorders, including panic disorder and PTSD (Brannon et al, 2000; Pande et al, 2000). Pande and colleagues (1999) reported results of a double-blind, placebo-controlled, parallel-group trial with 69 patients with social anxiety disorder, treated with doses of gabapentin ranging from 900 to 3600 mg daily, with most patients receiving greater than 2100 mg / d (Pande et al, 1999). Gabapentin treated subjects experienced a significantly greater reduction in mean LSAS scores, compared to those receiving placebo (27.3 points versus 11.9 respectively (P<0.008)).

Valproic acid, an anticonvulsant mood stabilizer with reported efficacy in small trials of panic disorder (Keck et al, 1993) and PTSD (Clark et al, 1999) has recently been tested in social anxiety disorder. In an open trial, 17 patients with social phobia were given a flexible dose of valproate between 500-2500 mg/d; after 12 weeks, there were significant improvements on the CGI-I and LSAS. The drug was reasonably well tolerated, with only one subject dropping out due to adverse events (Kinrys et al, 2002).

Tricyclic antidepressants (TCAs) have been useful for a broad array of anxiety disorders including panic disorder, post-traumatic stress disorder, generalized anxiety disorder and, in the case of clomipramine, obsessive-compulsive disorder. TCAs have been evaluated for the treatment of social anxiety disorder as well. In an open 8-week trial in 15 patients, imipramine did not demonstrate significant efficacy as assessed by the CGI-I (Simpson et al, 1998). In a double-blind, placebo-controlled trial of imipramine at a mean dose of 149 mg/day, no significant difference in outcome was detected between the imipramine and placebo treated group (Emmanuel et al, 1997). Thus, based on the evidence to date, TCAs are generally not considered effective for the treatment of social anxiety disorder.

Augmentation Strategies for Incomplete or Non-Responders

There has been very little research done to date on strategies (including augmentation) for patients with social anxiety disorder who remain symptomatic despite initial treatment. Benzodiazepines such as clonazepam are commonly added to antidepressant therapy to boost response, though this intervention has not been systematically studied to date. As noted above, 7 of 10 patients responded to the open addition of buspirone 45 mg/d to an ongoing trial with an SSRI.(Van Ameringen et al, 1996). Another study examined adjunctive pindolol, an agent with 5HT-1A autoreceptor antagonist properties (Blier et al, 1997) which in some but not all studies has been demonstrated to accelerate or augment response to antidepressants for depression (Martinez et al, 2000). In this placebo-controlled study, 5 mg tid of pindolol was given to 14 patients with generalized social phobia who remained symptomatic despite treatment with paroxetine for at least 10 weeks; however, no significant improvement was found for pindolol compared to placebo (Stein et al, 2001). Nonetheless, other beta-blockers such as atenolol and propranolol have demonstrated efficacy for the treatment of the performance anxiety subtype of social phobia. Other medications such as clonidine (Goldstein, 1987) and ondansetron (Bell & De Vaugh-Giess, 1994), have been reported helpful for social anxiety in case reports, but there is little systematic data following up on these observations.

Treatment in Children

There are a number of studies underway examining the treatment of social anxiety disorder in children, with published data slowly emerging. Case reports and open series have suggested that agents like fluoxetine, paroxetine, sertraline and nefazadone may be useful for social anxiety disorder in children (Birmaher et al, 1994; Black et al, 1992; Mancini et al, 1999). In an open 12 week trial of citalopram (maximum dose 40 mg/d) administered in conjunction with 8 brief psychoeducational and behavioral counseling sessions (which included parents), 10 of 12 (83%) children improved, suggesting the potential efficacy of combined pharmacologic and psychosocial interventions for the treatment of social anxiety disorder in children (Chavira & Stein, 2002). The efficacy of fluvoxamine at a maximum dose of 300 mg/d was examined in a placebo controlled study of a group of children between the ages of 6 and 17 with anxiety disorders, including social anxiety, separation anxiety, and generalized anxiety disorder, who remained symptomatic after 3 weeks of a supportive psychoeducational intervention (The Research Unit on Pediatric Psycopharmacology Anxiety Study Group, 2001). Seventy-six percent of children in the fluvoxamine group responded to the treatment, compared with 29% in the placebo treated group (p<.001).The active medication was generally well tolerated with fewer than 10% of the children discontinuing treatment because of side effects.

Emerging data from treatment studies in children and adolescents with social anxiety disorder will increase our understanding of the acute and long-term risks and benefits of pharmacotherapy in younger individuals. These studies should help shed light on optimal strategies for sequencing and combining psychosocial interventions with medications for children. A critical issue to be addressed with longitudinal study is the impact of therapeutic interventions for social anxiety not just during childhood, but on manifestations of anxiety and the development of comorbidity as these children enter adulthood and over the course of their lifetime.

Remission

Most of the studies examining pharmacotherapy trials for social phobia report outcome in terms of improvement in symptoms or rates of response. However, sometimes this improvement, though statistically significant, may not be clinically dramatic, and many patients, albeit improved with treatment, remain notably symptomatic and distressed. In clinical practice, most of these persistently symptomatic individuals require additional therapeutic intervention in order to achieve a satisfactory and meaningful outcome. The concept of targeting remission as the goal of treatment in the anxiety disorders has only recently emerged as a major issue of discussion in the clinical and research literature. A series of consensus conferences proposed guidelines for the definition of remission in a variety of anxiety disorders including social phobia (Ballenger et al, 1998). Proposed criteria for remission include an LSAS score of <30 based in part on work by Mennin and colleagues (Mennin et al, 2002) who examined LSAS ratings of 364 patients with social anxiety and 34 normal controls. In that study, a total score of <30 on the LSAS separated normal controls from patients with generalized social phobia with a good combination of sensitivity and specificity. In addition, the consensus guidelines suggest that fully remitted patients should have minimal or no residual anticipatory anxiety, functional impairment or associated depressive symptoms.

Some studies report rates of remission as an outcome measure, although none to date have utilized a comprehensive multiaxial definition as suggested above. For instance, in a 12 week study by Otto and colleagues (Otto et al, 2000) comparing clonazepam with cognitive-behavioral group therapy, the authors defined remission as a CGI-severity rating of < 2 (ie, "normal") and reported rates of 20% and 25% respectively. An analysis of a 12-week, fixed-dose placebo-controlled study of paroxetine reported rates of remission (ie, CGI-S of 1) of 11.2%, 8% and 6.6% for paroxetine 20, 40 and 60 mg/day respectively, compared to 3.3% for placebo (Liebowitz et al, 2002).

Conclusion and Future Directions

The increased recognition of the prevalence, early onset, chronicity and morbid impact of social phobia has spurred development efforts to find more effective and better tolerated pharmacotherapies for this condition. The MAOIs, though long the "gold standard" pharmacotherapy for social phobia, have been supplanted as first-line agents by newer antidepressants such as the SSRIs and SNRIs that have demonstrated efficacy in large scale randomized controlled trials, and have a more favorable side effect profile. A variety of other pharmacologic agents with novel mechanisms of actions including corticotropin releasing factor (CRF) antagonists, neurokinin (NK)-substance P antagonists, metabotropic glutamate receptor agonists, GABAergic agents and receptor modulators, and compounds with effects on a variety of serotonin, noradrenergic and dopaminergic receptors and their subtypes are in various stages of development. It is hoped that these agents will provide us with more effective and well-tolerated agents for the therapeutic armamentarium in the future. However, at present, many issues remain to be addressed in the treatment of social phobia with currently available interventions. These include: 1) the development of pharmacologic and non-pharmacologic strategies and their combination to optimize outcome for partial or non-responders to initial treatment, 2) the impact of early intervention on the lifetime course of the disorder, 3) the comparative effects of a variety of pharmacologic and psychosocial interventions as assessed in direct head to head trials, and 4) determination of the optimal duration of treatment. What is also needed for the latter is the identification of patient and illness predictors that allow for the accurate differentiation of those individuals who require ongoing maintenance therapy and those who may be safely discontinued, as well as a better understanding of the optimal time period for treatment discontinuation.

References

Allgulander C, Nilsson B. A prospective study of 86 new patients with social anxiety disorder. *Acta Psychiatr Scand.* 2001;103(6):447-452.

Baldwin D, Bobes J, Stein DJ, Scharwachter I, Faure M. Paroxetine in social phobia/social anxiety disorder. Randomised, double-blind, placebo-controlled study. Paroxetine Study Group. *Br J Psychiatry.* 1999;175:120-126.

Ballenger JC, Davidson JR, Lecrubier Y, Nutt DJ, Bobes J, Beidel DC, Ono Y, Westenberg HG. Consensus statement on social anxiety disorder from the International Consensus Group on Depression and Anxiety. *J Clin Psychiatry.* 1998;59(Suppl 17):54-60.

Bell J, De Vaugh-Geiss J. Multi-center trial of a 5-HT3 antagonist, ondansetron, in social phobia. Paper presented at the 33rd Annual Meeting of the American College of Neuropsychopharmacology, San Juan, Puerto Rico, 1994.

Birmaher B, Waterman GS, Ryan N, Cully M, Balach L, Ingram J, Brodsky M. Fluoxetine for childhood anxiety disorders. *J Am Acad Child Adolesc Psychiatry.* 1994;33(7):993-999.

Black B, Uhde TW, Tancer ME. Fluoxetine for the treatment of social phobia. *J Clin Psychopharmacol.* 1992;12(4):293-295.

Blier P, Bergeron R, de Montigny C. Selective activation of postsynaptic 5-HT1A receptors induces rapid antidepressant response. *Neuropsychopharmacology.* 1997;16(5):333-338.

Bouwer C, Stein DJ. Use of the selective serotonin reuptake inhibitor citalopram in the treatment of generalized social phobia. *J Affect Disord.* 1998;49(1):79-82.

Brannon N, Labbate L, Huber M. Gabapentin treatment for posttraumatic stress disorder. *Can J Psychiatry.* 2000;45(1):84.

Brantigan CO, Brantigan TA, Joseph, N. Effect of beta blockade and beta stimulation on stage fright. *Am J Med.* 1982;72(1):88-94.

Chavira DA, Stein MB. Combined psychoeducation and treatment with selective serotonin reuptake inhibitors for youth with generalized social anxiety disorder. *J Child Adolesc Psychopharmacol*. 2002;12(1):47-54.

Clark DB, Agras WS. The assessment and treatment of performance anxiety in musicians. *Am J Psychiatry*. 1991;148(5):598-605.

Clark RD, Canive JM, Calais LA, Qualls CR, Tuason VB. Divalproex in post-traumatic stress disorder: an open-label clinical trial. *J Trauma Stress*. 1999;12(2):395-401.

Conant J, Engler R, Janowsky D, Maisel A, Gilpin E, LeWinter M. Central nervous system side effects of beta-adrenergic blocking agents with high and low lipid solubility. *J Cardiovasc Pharmacol*. 1989;13(4):656-661.

Davidson J R, Potts N, Richichi E, Krishnan R, Ford SM, Smith R, Wilson WH. Treatment of social phobia with clonazepam and placebo. *J Clin Psychopharmacol*. 1993;13(6):423-428.

Emmanuel NP, Brawman-Mintzer O, Morton WA, Book SW, Johnson MR, Lorberbaum JP, Ballenger JC, Lydiard RB. Bupropion-SR in treatment of social phobia. *Depress Anxiety*. 2000;12(2):111-113.

Emmanuel NP, Johnson M, Villareal G. Imipramine in the treatment of social phobia: a double-blind study. American College of Neuropsychopharmacology 36th meeting; Waikoloa, HI, 1997.

Faigel HC. The effect of beta blockade on stress-induced cognitive dysfunction in adolescents. *Clin Pediatr*. 1991 (Phila); 30(7):441-445.

Gelernter CS, Uhde TW, Cimbolic P, Arnkoff DB, Vittone BJ, Tancer ME, Bartko JJ. Cognitive-behavioral and pharmacological treatments of social phobia. A controlled study. *Arch Gen Psychiatry*. 1991; 48(10):938-945.

Goldstein S. Treatment of social phobia with clonidine. *Biol Psychiatry*. 1987;22(3):369-372.

Gossard D, Dennis C, DeBusk RF. Use of beta-blocking agents to reduce the stress of presentation at an international cardiology meeting: results of a survey. *Am J Cardiol*. 1984;54(1):240-241.

Guy W. ECDEU Assessment Manual for Psychopharmacology. 1976; Rockville, MD: US Department of Health, Education and Welfare.

Heimberg RG, Liebowitz MR, Hope DA, Schneier FR, Holt CS, Welkowitz LA, Juster HR, Campeas R, Bruch MA, Cloitre M, Fallon B, Klein DF. Cognitive behavioral group therapy vs phenelzine therapy for social phobia: 12-week outcome. *Arch Gen Psychiatry*. 1998;55(12):1133-1141.

Kasper S, Loft H, Smith JR. Escitalopram is efficacious and well-tolerated in the treatment of social anxiety disorder (poster). ADAA National Conference; Austin, TX, 2002.

Katzelnick DJ, Kobak KA, DeLeire T, Henk HJ, Greist JH, Davidson JR, Schneier FR, Stein MB, Helstad CP. Impact of generalized social anxiety disorder in managed care. *Am J Psychiatry*. 2001;158(12):1999-2007.

Katzelnick DJ, Kobak KA, Greist JH, Jefferson JW, Mantle JM, Serlin RC. Sertraline for social phobia: a double-blind, placebo-controlled crossover study. *Am J Psychiatry*. 1995;152(9):1368-1371.

Keck PE, Jr., Taylor VE, Tugrul KC, McElroy SL, Bennett JA. Valproate treatment of panic disorder and lactate-induced panic attacks. *Biol Psychiatry*. 1993;33(7):542-546.

Kelsey JE. Venlafaxine in social phobia. *Psychopharmacol Bull*. 1995;31 (4):767-771.

Kinrys G, Pollack MH, Simon NM, Worthington JJ, Nardi AE, Versiani M. Valproic acid for the treatment of social anxiety disorder. *Int Clin Psychopharmacol*. 2003;18(3):169-172

Kobak KA, Greist JH, Jefferson JW, Katzelnick DJ. Fluoxetine in social phobia: a double-blind, placebo-controlled pilot study. *J Clin Psychopharmacol*. 2002;22(3):257-262.

Liebowitz MR, DeMartinis N, Weihs KL, Chung H, Clary CM. Results from a randomized, double-blind, multicenter trial of sertraline in the treatment of moderate-to-severe social phobia (Social Anxiety Disorder). Paper presented at the NCDEU 42nd annual meeting, Boca Raton, FL, 2002.

Liebowitz MR, Mangano RM. Venlafaxine XR in Generalized Social Anxiety Disorder (Poster). 2002 NCDEU 42nd annual meeting, Boca Raton, FL.

Liebowitz MR, Schneier F, Campeas R, Hollander E, Hatterer J, Fyer A, Gorman J, Papp L, Davies S, Gully R. et al. Phenelzine vs atenolol in social phobia. A placebo-controlled comparison. *Arch Gen Psychiatry.* 1992;49(4):290-300.

Liebowitz MR, Stein MB, Tancer M, Carpenter D, Oakes R, Pitts CD. A randomized, double-blind, fixed-dose comparison of paroxetine and placebo in the treatment of generalized social anxiety disorder. *J Clin Psychiatry.* 2002;63(1):66-74.

Lott M, Greist JH, Jefferson JW, Kobak KA, Katzelnick DJ, Katz RJ, Schaettle SC. Brofaromine for social phobia: a multicenter, placebo-controlled, double-blind study. *J Clin Psychopharmacol.* 1997;17(4):255-260.

Mancini C, Van Ameringen M, Oakman JM, Farvolden P. Serotonergic agents in the treatment of social phobia in children and adolescents: a case series. *Depress Anxiety.* 1999; 10(1):33-39.

Martinez D, Broft A, Laruelle M. Pindolol augmentation of antidepressant treatment: recent contributions from brain imaging studies. *Biol Psychiatry.* 2000; 48(8):844-853.

Mennin DS, Fresco DM, Heimberg RG, Schneier FR, Davies SO, Liebowitz MR. Screening for social anxiety disorder in the clinical setting: using the Liebowitz Social Anxiety Scale. *J Anxiety Disord.* 2002;16(6): 661-673.

Miner CM, Davidson JR, Potts NL, Tupler LA, Charles HC, & Krishnan KR. Brain fluoxetine measurements using fluorine magnetic resonance spectroscopy in patients with social phobia. *Biol Psychiatry.* 1995;38(10):696-698.

Noyes R Jr., Moroz G, Davidson JR, Liebowitz MR, Davidson A, Siegel J, Bell J, Cain JW, Curlik SM, Kent TA, Lydiard RB, Mallinger AG, Pollack MH, Rapaport M, Rasmussen SA, Hedges D, Schweizer E, Uhlenhuth EH. Moclobemide in social phobia: a controlled dose-response trial. *J Clin Psychopharmacol*. 1997;17(4):247-254.

Otto MW, Pollack MH, Gould RA, Worthington JJ 3rd, McArdle ET, Rosenbaum JF. A comparison of the efficacy of clonazepam and cognitive-behavioral group therapy for the treatment of social phobia. *J Anxiety Disord*. 2000;14(4):345-358.

Pallanti S, Quercioli L, Rossi A, Pazzagli A. The emergence of social phobia during clozapine treatment and its response to fluoxetine augmentation. *J Clin Psychiatry*. 1999;60(12):819-823.

Pande AC, Davidson JR, Jefferson JW, Janney CA, Katzelnick DJ, Weisler RH, Greist JH, Sutherland SM. Treatment of social phobia with gabapentin: a placebo-controlled study. *J Clin Psychopharmacol*. 1999;19(4):341-348.

Pande AC, Pollack MH, Crockatt J, Greiner M, Chouinard G, Lydiard RB, Taylor CB, Dager SR, Shiovitz T. Placebo-controlled study of gabapentin treatment of panic disorder. *J Clin Psychopharmacol*. 2000;20(4):467-471.

Randall CL, Johnson MR, Thevos AK, Sonne SC, Thomas SE, Willard SL, Brady KT, Davidson JR. Paroxetine for social anxiety and alcohol use in dual-diagnosed patients. *Depress Anxiety*. 2001;14(4):255-262.

Research Unit on Pediatric Psychopharmacology Anxiety Study Group. Fluvoxamine for the treatment of anxiety disorders in children and adolescents. *N Engl J Med*. 2001;344(17):1279-1285.

Sheehan DV, Kalali AH, Yang H, Barbato LM, Li D, Gerritsen van der Hoop R. Efficacy and safety of a flexible-dose regimen of fluvoxamine controlled release for the treatment of generalized social anxiety disorder. New Clinical Drug Evaluation Unit. NCDEU 42nd annual meeting, Boca Raton, FL, 2002.

Simon NM, Sharma SG, Worthington JJ, Marzol PC, Pollack MH. Citalopram for social phobia: a clinical case series. *Prog Neuropsychopharmacol Biol Psychiatry.* 2001;25(7):1469-1474.

Simpson HB, Schneier FR, Campeas RB, Marshall RD, Fallon BA, Davies S, Klein DF, Liebowitz MR. Imipramine in the treatment of social phobia. *J Clin Psychopharmacol.* 1998;18(2):132-135.

Stahl SM. Essential Psychopharmacology; Neuroscientific Basis and Practical Applications (second edition ed.) 2000; Cambridge, UK: Cambridge University Press.

Stein MB, Chartier MJ, Hazen AL, Kroft CD, Chale RA, Cote D, Walker JR. Paroxetine in the treatment of generalized social phobia: open-label treatment and double-blind placebo-controlled discontinuation. *J Clin Psychopharmacol.* 1996;16(3):218-222.

Stein MB, Fye, AJ, Davidson JR, Pollack MH, Wiita B. Fluvoxamine treatment of social phobia (social anxiety disorder): a double-blind, placebo-controlled study. *Am J Psychiatry.* 1999;156(5):756-760.

Stein MB, Liebowitz MR, Lydiard RB, Pitts CD, Bushnell W, Gergel I. Paroxetine treatment of generalized social phobia (social anxiety disorder): a randomized controlled trial. *JAMA.* 1998;280(8):708-713.

Stein MB, Sareen J, Hami S, Chao J. Pindolol potentiation of paroxetine for generalized social phobia: a double-blind, placebo-controlled, crossover study. *Am J Psychiatry.* 2001;158(10):1725-1727.

Steptoe A, Fidler H. Stage fright in orchestral musicians: a study of cognitive and behavioural strategies in performance anxiety. *Br J Psychol.* 1987;78(Pt 2):241-249.

Van Ameringen M, Mancini C, Streiner DL. Fluoxetine efficacy in social phobia. *J Clin Psychiatry.* 1993;54(1):27-32.

Van Ameringen M, Mancini C, Wilson C. Buspirone augmentation of selective serotonin reuptake inhibitors (SSRIs) in social phobia. *J Affect Disord.* 1996;39(2):115-121.

Van Ameringen MA, Lane RM, Walker JR, Bowen RC, Chokka PR, Goldner EM, Johnston DG, Lavallee YJ, Nandy S, Pecknold JC, Hadrava V, Swinson RP. Sertraline treatment of generalized social phobia: a 20-week, double-blind, placebo-controlled study. *Am J Psychiatry*. 2001;158(2):275-281.

van Vliet IM, den Boer JA, Westenberg HG. Psychopharmacological treatment of social phobia; a double blind placebo controlled study with fluvoxamine. *Psychopharmacology*. (Berl), 1994;115(1-2):128-134.

van Vliet IM, den Boer JA, Westenberg HG, Pian KL. Clinical effects of buspirone in social phobia: a double-blind placebo-controlled study. *J Clin Psychiatry*. 1997;58(4):164-168.

Versiani M, Mundim FD, Nardi AE, Liebowitz MR. Tranylcypromine in social phobia. *J Clin Psychopharmacol*. 1988;8(4):279-283.

Versiani M, Nardi AE, Mundim FD, Alves AB, Liebowitz MR, Amrein R. Pharmacotherapy of social phobia. A controlled study with moclobemide and phenelzine. *Br J Psychiatry*. 1992;161:353-360.

Walker JR, Van Ameringen MA, Swinson R, Bowen RC, Chokka PR, Goldner E, Johnston DC, Lavallie YJ, Nandy S, Pecknold JC, Hadrava V, Lane RM. Prevention of relapse in generalized social phobia: results of a 24- week study in responders to 20 weeks of sertraline treatment. *J Clin Psychopharmacol*. 2000;20(6):636-644.

Welkowitz LA, Liebowitz MR. Pharmacologic treatment of social phobia and performance anxiety. In R Noyes Jr., M Roth, GD Burrows (Eds.) 1990; *Handbook of Anxiety* (Vol. 4, pp. 233-250): Elsevier Science Publishers.

Chapter 8

Cognitive-Behavioral Therapy for Social Anxiety Disorder

Nadine Recker Rayburn, M.A., Francisco J. Farach, B.A.,
Adam S. Radomsky, Ph.D., and Michael W. Otto, Ph.D.

Attempts to refine and validate treatment interventions for social anxiety disorder (SAD; also known as social phobia) over the last 10 years have produced a considerable treatment-outcome literature. Results from this literature consistently support the efficacy of two treatment modalities—cognitive-behavioral therapy (CBT) and pharmacotherapy—and suggest that they produce approximately equivalent acute outcome (Gould et al, 1997). In this chapter, we provide a conceptual model of SAD from a cognitive-behavioral perspective, a description of treatment elements, and a review of the outcome findings.

A Conceptual Model of Social Anxiety Disorder

Central to cognitive-behavioral conceptualizations of SAD is attention to the self-perpetuating chains of expectations of social failure, negative self-evaluations, increasing anxiety, and avoidance that characterize patients with SAD (Clark & Wells, 1995; Heimberg & Barlow, 1991; Rapee & Heimberg, 1997). Negative expectations about social situations include fears of intolerable or uncontrollable anxiety (eg, "I will be so nervous; I won't be able to continue"), expectations or fears of poor social performance (eg, "I'm going to blow it again," or "I'll never be able to have a normal conversation"), and expectations of negative evaluations by other people (eg, "People will think I'm stupid"). The natural consequence of these expectations is an increase in anxious apprehension about social situations.

Upon entering social situations, individuals with SAD are vigilant to cues that signal potentially negative outcomes. Studies have shown that SAD patients exhibit an attentional bias to social threat cues, including negative interpretations of ambiguous social situations (Amir et al, 1998; Stopa & Clark, 2000) and increased attention to social-threat words or negative facial expressions (Asmundson & Stein, 1994; Foa et al, 2000; Gilboa-Schechtman et al, 1999; Veljaca & Rapee, 1998). This combination of negative interpretations of ambiguous events and vigilance to negative outcomes has important consequences for enhancing or perpetuating anxiety. The narrowing of attention to negative social cues hampers the processing of information that contradicts negative expectations, and as a result, appropriate social performance is not given proper recognition. A perfectly adequate introduction to a group may be interpreted as a "disaster" because one audience member frowned, whereas the approving nods of others in the audience may escape awareness. Additionally, attention to and scanning for potential negative outcomes may hamper social performance by diverting attention from relevant social cues and behaviors, such as attending to the topic of a conversation. The result is that individuals with SAD may be performing social tasks under difficult "dual task" conditions that involve the cognitive demands of normal social processing plus the demands of maintaining vigilance to feared potential outcomes.

Furthermore, there is good evidence that individuals with SAD exhibit increased self-focused attention in anxiety-provoking social situations and overestimate the degree to which their anxiety is perceptible to others (for review see Clark & McManus, 2002). The result is an amplification of the perceived consequences of social anxiety. For example, whereas an individual without social anxiety may be unaware of or quickly dismiss a mild quaver in her or his voice, such a cue is unlikely to escape detection by a socially-anxious individual. Once noticed, it may well be interpreted as a sign of social failure (eg, "Everyone could tell that I was too nervous and thought I was incompetent"). Self-focused attention, vigilance to negative consequences, and the presence of negative or catastrophic interpretations of social anxiety help ensure that any minor errors or symptoms are "amplified" into signs of social failure (see Figure 1). In particular, Otto (1999) drew attention to three specific amplifying cognitions that help define minor events as social catastrophes: 1) even small errors mean that a person is defective; 2) being anxious in social situations is evidence that one is socially inept, and 3) any behavior that deviates from "normal" represents further evidence of dysfunction. Otto labels these cognitions "amplifying beliefs" because they magnify existing concerns and cause additional anxiety. In this context, it is important to remember that a high level of anxiety, including panic attacks, is not uncommon in SAD. SAD is differentiated

Figure 1

Consequences of negative expectations

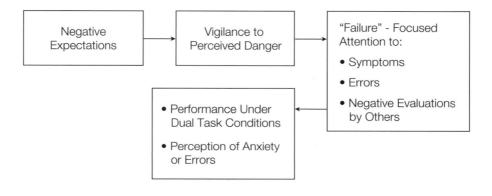

from panic disorder in part on the basis of the concern about embarrassment or humiliation in front of others that is central to the perceived consequences of panic in SAD (Ball et al, 1995; Mannuzza et al, 1990).

These tendencies to attend to and over-interpret negative social or symptom cues are complemented by selective recall and negative interpretation of social performance after the fact, including overestimation of the social cost of poor performance (Clark & McManus, 2002; McManus et al, 2000). Negative post-event processing of social situations also appears to enhance negative expectations for subsequent social events (Mellings & Alden, 2000).

One of the natural consequences of this cycle of negative expectations and anxiety is the urge to escape or avoid social situations. Avoidance can include actual behavioral avoidance, as well as more subtle avoidance strategies such as the incomplete processing of actual external social cues. For example, vigilance to negative facial expressions may be complemented by the rapid avoidance of these faces once they are detected (for review see Clark & McManus, 2002; Roth & Heimberg, 2001). The result of both kinds of avoidance is that individuals with SAD have fewer opportunities to learn that negative outcomes do not occur. Instead, social situations may become an endless series of perceived narrow escapes from expected social catastrophes. These behaviors lock in the memories of social failure and prohibit the acquisition of information that would disconfirm existing beliefs and negative expectations. Over time, the maintenance of avoidance behaviors interferes with the practice of social skills, which may result in even more performance limitations.

The nature of subtle avoidance in social situations may also help explain why individuals with SAD do not seem to benefit from the social exposures they do complete. Wells et al (1995) addressed this question by attending to the subtle avoidance behaviors (termed "safety behaviors" because of their presumed ability to provide social safety) used by socially anxious individuals. These behaviors include averting one's eyes while speaking (so as not to get overwhelmed by being looked at), speaking rapidly (so as not to freeze up mid-sentence), or clenching one's hands (to hide trembling). In a small study, Wells et al (1995) nicely demonstrated that the use of these safety behaviors was associated with less fear reduction from exposure. It appeared that by using safety behaviors to "play it safe" in social situations, socially anxious individuals learned only that it was possible to survive social situations, not that they could perform adequately without the use of safety behaviors.

Figure 2 summarizes the cascade of negative expectations, vigilance to negative outcomes, catastrophic interpretations of these outcomes (including the social costs of anxiety itself), avoidance, and enhanced negative social expectations that are thought to underlie and maintain SAD. Accordingly, the process of treatment of SAD can be translated into the task of eliminating these patterns. Specifically, following the model described above, cognitive-behavioral interventions should 1) correct maladaptive or dysfunctional cognitions that produce anxious apprehension; 2) adjust core amplifying cognitions; 3) reduce attention to failure cues; 4) reduce avoidance and safety behaviors, and 5) increase exposure to, and accurate appraisal of, social performance and outcome.

Elements of Cognitive-Behavioral Intervention

CBT for SAD has been validated for use in either individual or group therapy formats. Emphasis is placed on a collaborative effort that is aimed at helping patients identify and disrupt the entrenched, self-perpetuating cycles of anxiety and avoidance that foster and maintain social anxiety.

Figure 2

A cognitive-behavioral model of core patterns in social anxiety disorder

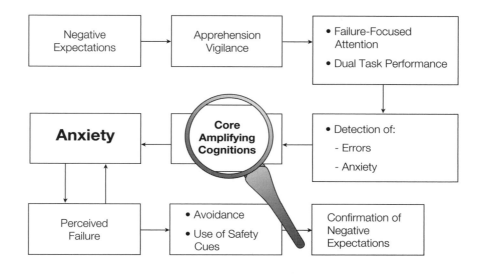

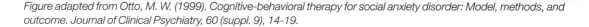

Figure adapted from Otto, M. W. (1999). Cognitive-behavioral therapy for social anxiety disorder: Model, methods, and outcome. Journal of Clinical Psychiatry, 60 (suppl. 9), 14-19.

Although available cognitive-behavioral treatment packages do not contain identical treatment elements, they usually include some combination of informational intervention, cognitive restructuring, and exposure elements (for review see Gould et al, 1997; Heimberg & Juster, 1995). Treatment packages may also include social skills training and relaxation training where appropriate.

Treatment typically begins with informational interventions that are designed to supply the patient with a cognitive-behavioral model of social anxiety. The patient is taught to use this model as a framework for understanding the role of cognitive restructuring and exposure elements in later sessions, and as an impetus to actively engage in a joint treatment effort. Radomsky and Otto (2001) characterize the therapist's roles in this stage of treatment as expert consultant and personal coach. The therapist provides information about the disorder within a specific framework, and assists the patient with the challenging tasks of summoning the motivation to change and disrupt entrenched patterns of fear and anxiety. In particular, informational discussion emphasizes the interrelated roles of self-perpetuating, dysfunctional cognitive cycles, anxiety, and avoidance. The patient is encouraged to imagine and conceptualize his or her experience of social anxiety within the framework of the model. This process benefits the patient by normalizing the anxiety experience, linking it to the conceptual elements of the cognitive-behavioral model, and in so doing, providing disorder-specific patterns to be targeted by treatment.

Informational interventions provide a natural bridge to cognitive interventions. Cognitive restructuring teaches patients to consider their thoughts as hypotheses that await either validation or disconfirmation, rather than as facts about the world or themselves. Patients learn about the anxiety-inducing effect of their thoughts on the anticipation of negative performance ("I'm going to screw up"), the negative interpretation of actual social performance (eg, "Here I go again, I have nothing interesting to say"), and the negative ruminations about past social encounters (eg, "I made a fool of myself"). Patients are taught to identify these thoughts and "catch" them when they occur in social situations. Monitoring thoughts during spontaneous or planned anxiety experiences (ie, exposures, see below) facilitates this process.

Through guided discussion and Socratic questioning by the therapist, patients then learn to logically evaluate their thoughts and thought patterns before, during, and after anxiety experiences. Therapists utilize a variety of strategies to aid in this process. First, the therapist may ask the patient to assess the accuracy of catastrophic cognitions by evaluating the objective evidence for and against their validity. For example, a patient who thinks "I made a fool of myself when I gave the speech" is asked to generate evidence regarding the veracity of this thought. In other words, what evidence does the patient have that this thought is true or not true? Here it is important to instruct patients in the generation of appropriate types of evidence. Patients frequently state that they failed a social situation "because they felt anxious." As discussed previously, patients tend to hold the assumption that the way they feel about themselves is the way that they are perceived by others. In addition, in their view, experiencing anxiety is a negative outcome in itself. Consequently, patients need to be taught that their feelings of anxiety are inappropriate measures of social performance. Therapist and patient need to discuss and agree upon what constitutes an objective assessment of social competence.

In this context, it is also important to teach patients about the concept of cognitive distortions—ie, logical errors in thinking. In Heimberg and associates' (Heimberg et al, 1990; Heimberg et al, 1995b) manualized cognitive-behavioral group treatment (CBGT) for SAD, patients learn about cognitive errors that individuals with SAD frequently commit. One common error is "all-or-nothing thinking," which is the tendency to perceive the world in a polarized fashion where only two categories of outcomes are possible. Thus, socially anxious people believe that if their performance in a social situation falls short of perfect (eg, if they lose their train of thought for a brief moment during a conversation), it means that they are a complete failure. Another common thinking error is "mind reading," which is the tendency to assume that one knows what other people are thinking. Frequently, socially anxious patients claim "they just know" that other people are evaluating them negatively in the absence of any objective evidence.

In addition to gathering evidence about a thought's validity and investigating the presence of cognitive errors, patients are also taught to directly challenge their thoughts. When they become aware of a negative thought in a social situation, patients learn to ask themselves, "Do I know for certain that … will occur? What is the worst that could happen? And how could I cope with this outcome if it occurred?" These logical challenges enhance patients' own monitoring in actual situations and help them learn that predicted negative outcomes do not necessarily follow. For example, they realize that a brief period of silence in a conversation does not mean they are incompetent, or they realize that blushing in a social situation is not a catastrophe.

Ultimately, the goal of cognitive interventions is for patients to develop more adaptive self-talk before, during, and after social situations. The emphasis on accurate and logical thinking is one of the mechanisms by which patients learn to appreciate the fact that their social fears are unfounded. They realize that there are no valid reasons to regard social situations as threatening. Hence, cognitive restructuring represents an important stepping stone in the process of relearning safety in social situations. The efficacy of these interventions alone for treating SAD is supported in outcome studies; however, there is evidence that exposure interventions represent the most potent ingredient in CBT for SAD (for meta-analytic reviews see Feske & Chambless, 1995; Gould et al, 1997; Taylor, 1996).

Exposure interventions guide the patient to systematically confront the feared stimuli (ie, social situations). Exposure interventions are designed to help patients enter social situations, and then allow fear to dissipate naturally by remaining in the situation, interpreting it accurately, and performing adequately. Patients gain the opportunity to relearn a sense of safety through the process of not prematurely escaping from, or avoiding, social situations.

Exposure interventions are typically implemented in conjunction with the cognitive interventions described in previous sections. Ideally, patients should learn to challenge negative thoughts whenever they occur during exposure exercises. Hence, exposures provide an excellent opportunity to develop cognitive skills in situations in which these skills are needed most. For example, in Heimberg's group treatment program (Heimberg et al, 1990; 1995), exposure is conducted in the context of the group setting, during weekly 2.5-hour sessions. Group treatment of social phobia offers the advantage of having a ready-made setting (ie, the presence of other group members) for constructing simulated exposure exercises. For example, group members often role-play an audience in order for one group member to practice giving a speech. Hence, even situations that may occur relatively infrequently, but are nevertheless highly relevant for some group members (eg, attending a formal cocktail party), can be incorporated and rehearsed in the therapy session.

Exposure proceeds along a hierarchy of personalized, increasingly difficult exposure tasks. Before each role-played exposure rehearsal in session, the patient's dysfunctional thoughts and expectations are identified and reviewed, and more adaptive cognitive responses are generated. Then, during and after the exposure, these alternative and more rational cognitions are rehearsed. Exposure in session is then complemented by exposure assignments between sessions. As the patient becomes increasingly comfortable in the initial exposure situations, he or she progresses to more challenging tasks.

Exposure also provides a tool to help patients break some of the biased attentional processes that help maintain the disorder. In particular, instruction to shift from self-focused attention to what actually occurs (ie, the behaviors of others) during social exposures appears to enhance outcome (Wells & Papageorgiou, 1998). Indeed, to improve the outcome of exposure, Wells et al (1995) recommend ensuring that dysfunctional thoughts and maladaptive attentional bias are adequately targeted by: 1) assessing patients' beliefs about the likelihood of their feared catastrophes; 2) identifying the subtle avoidance behaviors ("safety behaviors") linked to these feared catastrophes; 3) outlining specific tests to disconfirm expected negative outcomes; 4) eliminating safety behaviors during the exposure exercise, and 5) reviewing and processing the exposure in terms of what was learned (relative to expectations of catastrophic outcomes).

In other words, exposures should provide patients with the opportunity to correct dysfunctional thoughts, reallocate attentional and memory resources more appropriately, and eliminate overt and subtle avoidance behaviors. Before an exposure exercise, the therapist should assess the kinds of catastrophic outcomes the patient predicts. After the exposure, the patient and therapist should determine together whether these outcomes actually occurred. In addition, when setting up exposure exercises, it is important that patient and therapist agree on clear behavioral goals. For example, in a simulated exposure to a casual conversation with a stranger, behavioral goals may be (a) to introduce oneself to the other person, (b) to maintain eye contact during the conversation, and (c) to say goodbye when the conversation is over. Patients realize that they usually meet their objective performance goals despite their subjective feelings of anxiety. This reinforces the notion that feelings of anxiety do not represent appropriate performance measures. In addition, specific goals provide an appropriate context for challenging dysfunctional thoughts about one's social performance. Patients learn that their feared catastrophic outcomes do not occur. Successful exposures also result in positive memories and adaptive expectations for engagement in future social situations. In sum, exposures are meant to represent "corrective" experiences that provide a newly attained sense of safety and more-rational cognitive strategies for patients.

The Role of Social Skills Training

In social skills training, patients are taught to use adaptive and normative behaviors in social contexts. Such training incorporates education about positive social interactions and modeling of target social behaviors by the therapist, followed by role-play rehearsals by the patient. For example, patient and therapist may role-play how to introduce oneself in a social situation. After the role-play, the therapist may provide the patient with corrective information about his or her performance. The corrective feedback could address questions such as the patient's ability to maintain eye contact, speak in an audible voice, or observe social convention (eg, shaking hands upon meeting). Patients are instructed to implement the practiced social skills in relevant situations. As is evident even in this brief description, social skills training naturally includes an important exposure component, and this feature may help explain varying estimates of the utility of these procedures (cf., Gould et al, 1997; Taylor, 1996). Moreover, there is some research to suggest that the majority of SAD patients have social skills, but may be prevented from applying them due to anxiety and avoidance, and that social skills training is effective only for the minority of patients with SAD who exhibit actual deficits (Heimberg & Barlow, 1991; Öst et al, 1981).

Treatment Outcome

A wide variety of studies suggest that short-term CBT (in the range of 15 sessions) provides significant benefit to patients with SAD (see Feske & Chambless, 1995; Gould et al, 1997; Heimberg, 2002; Taylor, 1996). Indeed, there is evidence that treatment gains continue to increase over follow-up intervals, suggesting that alternative strategies learned during short-term treatment can be further consolidated and applied by patients over time, resulting in additional benefit (eg, Heimberg et al, 1993).

Relative to other treatment options, it is clear that patients with SAD accrue significant benefit from either cognitive-behavioral or pharmacological interventions. Gould et al (1997) computed effect sizes for all controlled outcome studies of CBT and pharmacological treatment for SAD referenced between 1966 and 1995 (24 studies, 1079 subjects, 17 treatment comparisons). Effect sizes were computed such that positive values represent an advantage of active treatment over placebo on dependent measures at the end of treatment. The mean effect size for all studies using CBT as active treatment (N=27) was 0.74, with the highest effect sizes occurring for cognitive restructuring plus exposure (0.80) and exposure alone (0.89). The mean effect size for all pharmacotherapy studies (N=13) was 0.62, with two studies of selective serotonin reuptake inhibitors (SSRIs) (1.89) and two studies of benzodiazepines (0.72) providing the highest effect sizes. The small number of these studies, however, severely limited confidence in these results. Five studies of monoamine oxidase inhibitors (MAOIs) yielded an average effect size of 0.64. Differences in overall effect sizes for pharmacotherapy and CBT did not reach statistical significance, and the authors concluded that available evidence suggested roughly equivalent efficacy for these treatment modalities. Furthermore, drop-out rates for CBT (10%) and pharmacotherapy (14%) were not significantly different, indicating that both treatments were similarly tolerable.

Although meta-analytic data suggest that CBT and pharmacotherapy share statistically indistinguishable efficacy, few individual treatment studies have examined their relative benefit. Otto and colleagues (Otto et al, 2000) assessed the relative efficacy of 12 weeks of Heimberg's CBGT (Heimberg et al, 1995; Heimberg et al, 1993) versus 12 weeks of pharmacotherapy with clonazepam, a high-potency benzodiazepine commonly used as pharmacotherapy for SAD. These treatments were chosen for comparison in the study because clonazepam treatment produced the highest single-study effect size (6.95) in Gould et al's (1997) meta-analysis. In addition, Gould et al found an overall effect size of 0.72 for benzodiazepines, which is comparable to the effect size of CBT versus controls (0.74). The results of Otto et al's study supported the conclusion of Gould et al's meta-analysis: patients in both treatment conditions improved significantly, and no between-groups differences were apparent in the intent-to-treat analysis. However, among patients completing the study, patients receiving clonazepam had significantly better outcome at week 12 than patients receiving CBGT. This outcome may be explained partially by a higher level of attrition among the more severe patients in the clonazepam treatment group than in the CBGT group.

A multi-center comparison of Heimberg's CBGT and phenelzine (Heimberg et al, 1998; Liebowitz et al, 1999) provides additional evidence for the comparable efficacy of CBT and pharmacotherapy. CBGT and phenelzine resulted in similar response rates, and were each more effective than pill placebo and educational/supportive group therapy. Some evidence indicated that phenelzine was associated with a faster onset and greater magnitude of treatment gains than CBGT (phenelzine was significantly more effective than CBGT on almost half of the outcome measures).

To date, reliable predictors of differential treatment response have not been identified. For example, Otto et al's (2000) comparison of clonazepam and CBGT found that pre-treatment severity was a fairly reliable predictor of treatment outcome in both conditions. Sex, comorbidity with other anxiety or mood disorders, fear of anxiety symptoms, and dysfunctional attitudes failed to predict treatment outcome above and beyond severity measures. Thus, the authors concluded that pre-treatment measures of symptom severity do not provide guidance for the selection of one treatment over another.

The long-term maintenance of treatment gains represents a particular strength of CBT and especially CBGT. Patients are typically able to extend treatment gains over follow-up periods (Taylor, 1996). This finding is consistent with the notion that acute treatment helps patients eliminate patterns that perpetuate the disorder. With practice, patients then extend newly acquired and more adaptive patterns. This long-term maintenance of treatment gains renders CBT interventions particularly cost-effective. Gould et al's meta-analysis (1997) estimated the costs of pharmacotherapy and CBT for SAD. CBT emerged as a low-cost alternative to medication when long-term costs were taken into consideration. It is important to note that this cost analysis needs to be empirically validated in future research. However, similar estimates have been validated for the relative costs of medication and CBT in the treatment of panic disorder (Otto et al, 2000b).

Combined Treatment

Given the independent efficacy of cognitive-behavioral and pharmacologic treatments, it is natural to hope that the combination of these strategies will provide an especially powerful treatment. However, across the anxiety disorders available data indicate that combination treatment tends to offer only subtle advantages over CBT alone (Foa et al, 2002), and research to date appears to indicate that this trend may extend to SAD as well. In one study, 387 patients with SAD were randomized to one of four treatments representing the factorial combination of sertraline or placebo with exposure or no-exposure conditions (Blomhoff et al, 2001). In an unusual design feature, exposure treatment was provided by primary care physicians who had undergone training in exposure therapy. Also, rather than utilizing the prolonged session format adopted by Heimberg (Heimberg et al, 1990), treatment was provided in nine 20-minute sessions conducted over 16 weeks. In this design, combination treatment did not show an advantage over sertraline alone. However, this result may be explained by the brief-session format, and other research suggests that CBT may be particularly hard to transfer effectively to primary care physicians (King et al, 2002).

A full research report is still pending on a particularly important examination of combined treatment of SAD. A collaborative study at the University of Pennsylvania and Duke University succeeded in randomizing 309 patients with primary and generalized SAD to one of five conditions: placebo, fluoxetine, CBT, CBT plus placebo, or CBT plus fluoxetine (Foa et al, 2002). Early results do not appear to support the utility of combined treatment (Foa, 2002), but firm conclusions await the publication of this trial.

There are also concerns, derived from studies of panic disorder, that combined treatment strategies may reduce the longer-term efficacy of CBT, at least under conditions when CBT is not reinstated during future periods of medication discontinuation (see Otto, 2002). If this phenomenon were replicated in SAD, this would be of particular concern given evidence for continued gains with CBT for SAD over long-term follow-up intervals (Heimberg et al, 1993). However, at this point, there is insufficient evidence to draw conclusions about the ultimate efficacy of combined treatment for SAD.

Conclusion

The treatment literature consistently supports CBT and pharmacological interventions as efficacious treatment modalities for SAD. Based on available data, CBT and pharmacotherapy have comparable efficacy acutely, with a slight advantage for pharmacotherapy. CBT, however, provides more robust long-term maintenance of treatment gains and appears to be more cost-effective ultimately than pharmacotherapy. Additional research on strategies for the treatment of individuals with SAD who do not respond to initial intervention, and on the relative acute and longitudinal outcome for combined treatment is needed.

References

Amir N, Foa EB, Coles ME. Negative interpretation bias in social phobia. *Behaviour Research & Therapy*. 1998;36:945-957.

Asmundson GJG, Stein MB. Selective attention for social threat in patients with generalized social phobia: Evaluation using dot-probe paradigm. *Journal of Anxiety Disorders*. 1994;8:107-117.

Ball SG, Otto MW, Pollack MH, Uccello R, Rosenbaum JF. Differentiating social phobia and panic disorder: A test of core beliefs. *Cognitive Therapy and Research*. 1995;19:473-482.

Blomhoff S, Haug TT, Hellstrom K, Holme I, Humble M, Madsbu HP. et al. Randomised controlled general practice trial of sertraline, exposure therapy and combined treatment in generalised social phobia. *British Journal of Psychiatry*. 2001;179:23-30.

Clark DM, McManus F. Information processing in social phobia. *Biological Psychiatry*. 2002;51:92-100.

Clark DM, Wells A. A cognitive model of social phobia. In RG Heimberg, MR Liebowitz, DA Hope, FR Schneier (Eds.), *Social Phobia: Diagnosis, assessment, and treatment* (pp. 69-93). 1995; New York: Guilford Press.

Feske U, Chambless DL. Cognitive behavioral versus exposure only treatment for social phobia: A meta-analysis. *Behavior Therapy*. 1995;26:695-720.

Foa EB, Gilboa-Schechtman E, Amir N, Freshman M. Memory bias in generalized social phobia: Remembering negative emotional expressions. *Journal of Anxiety Disorders*. 2000;14:501-519.

Foa EB. Context in the clinic: How well do CBT and medications work in combination. Paper presented at the Anxiety Disorders Association of America Scientific Symposium, Austin, TX, 2002.

Foa EB, Franklin ME, Moser J. Context in the clinic: How well do CBT and medications work in combination? *Biological Psychiatry*. 2002;52:987-997

Gilboa-Schechtman E, Foa EB, Amir N. Attentional biases for facial expressions in social phobia: The face-in-the-crowd paradigm. *Cognition and Emotion*. 1999;13:305-318.

Gould RA, Buckminster S, Pollack MH, Otto MW, Yap L. Cognitive-behavioral and pharmacological treatment for social phobia: A meta-analysis. *Clinical Psychology: Science and Practice*. 1997;4:291-306.

Heimberg RG. Cognitive-behavioral therapy for social anxiety disorder: Current status and future directions. *Biological Psychiatry*. 2002;51:101-108.

Heimberg RG, Barlow DH. New developments in cognitive-behavioral therapy for social phobia. *Journal of Clinical Psychiatry*. 1991;52:21-30.

Heimberg RG, Dodge CS, Hope DA, Kennedy CR, Zollo LJ, Becker RJ. Cognitive behavioral group treatment for social phobia: Comparison with a credible placebo control. *Cognitive Therapy and Research*. 1990;14:1-23.

Heimberg RG, Juster HR. Cognitive-behavioral treatments: Literature review. In: RG Heimberg, MR Liebowitz, DA Hope, FR Schneier (Eds.), *Social phobia: Diagnosis, Assessment, and Treatment* (pp. 261-309). 1995; New York: Guilford Press.

Heimberg RG, Juster HR, Hope DA, Mattia JI. Cognitive behavioral group treatment for social phobia: Description, case presentation and empirical support. In: MB Stein (Ed.), *Social phobia: Clinical and research perspectives* (pp. 293-321). 1995b; Washington, DC: American Psychiatric Press.

Heimberg RG, Liebowitz MR, Hope DA. Cognitive behavioral group therapy vs phenelzine therapy for social phobia: 12-week outcome. *Archives of General Psychiatry*. 1998;55:1133-1141.

Heimberg RG, Salzman DG, Holt CS, Blendell KA. Cognitive-behavioral group treatment for social phobia: Effectiveness at five-year follow-up. *Cognitive Therapy and Research*. 1993;17:325-339.

King M, Davidson O, Taylor F, Haines A, Sharp D, Turner, R. Effectiveness of teaching general practitioners skills in brief cognitive behaviour therapy to treat patients with depression: Randomised controlled trial. *British Medical Journal*. 2002;324:947-950.

Liebowitz MR, Heimberg RG, Schneier FR, Hope DA, Davies S, Holt CS, et al. Cognitive-behavioral group therapy versus phenelzine in social phobia: Long-term outcome. *Depression and Anxiety*. 1999;10:89-98.

Mannuzza JS, Fyer AJ, Liebowitz MR, Klein DF. Delineating the boundaries of social phobia: Its relationship to panic disorder and agoraphobia. *Journal of Anxiety Disorders*. 1990; 4:41-59.

McManus F, Clark DM, Hackmann A. Specificity of cognitive biases in social phobia and their role in recovery. *Behavioral and Cognitive Psychotherapy*. 2000;28:201-209.

Mellings TMB, Alden LE. Cognitive processes in social anxiety: The effects of self-focus, rumination and anticipatory processing. *Behavior Research and Therapy*. 2000;38:243-257.

Öst L-G, Jerremalm A, Johansson J. Individual response patterns and the effects of different behavioral methods in the treatment of social phobia. *Behavioral Research and Therapy*. 1981;19:1-16.

Otto MW. Cognitive-behavioral therapy for social anxiety disorder: Model, methods, and outcome. *Journal of Clinical Psychiatry*, 1999;60(suppl. 9): 14-19.

Otto MW. Learning and "unlearning" fears: Preparedness, neural pathways, and patients. *Biological Psychiatry*. 2002;52:917-920.

Otto MW, Pollack MH, Gould RA, Worthington JJ III, McArdle ET, Rosenbaum JF. Heimberg RG. A comparison of the efficacy of clonazepam and cognitive-behavioral group therapy for the treatment of social phobia. *Journal of Anxiety Disorders*. 2000;14:345-358.

Otto MW, Pollack MH, Maki KM. Empirically supported treatments for panic disorder: Costs, benefits, and stepped care. *Journal of Consulting and Clinical Psychology*. 2000b;68:556-563.

Radomsky AS, Otto MW. Cognitive-behavioral therapy for social anxiety disorder. *Psychiatric Clinics of North America*. 2001;24:805-815.

Rapee RM, Heimberg RG. A cognitive-behavioral model of anxiety in social phobia. *Behaviour Research and Therapy*. 1997;35:741-756.

Roth DA, Heimberg RG. Cognitive-behavioral models of social anxiety disorder. *Psychiatric Clinics of North America.* 2001;24:753-771.

Stopa L, Clark DM. Social phobia and interpretation of social events. *Behaviour Research and Therapy.* 2000;38:273-283.

Taylor S. Meta-Analysis of cognitive-behavioral treatments for social phobia. *Journal of Behavior Therapy and Experimental Psychiatry.* 1996;27:1-9.

Veljaca K, Rapee RM. Detection of negative and positive audience behaviours by socially anxious subjects. *Behaviour Research and Therapy.* 1998;36:311-321.

Wells A, Clark DM, Salkovskis P, et al. Social phobia: The role of in-situation safety behaviors in maintaining anxiety and negative beliefs. *Behavior Therapy.* 1995;26:153-161.

Wells A, Papageorgiou C. Social phobia: Effects of external attention on anxiety, negative beliefs and perspective taking. *Behavior Therapy.* 1998; 29:357-370.